Crime
AND Criminal
Responsibility

Crime
^AND^Criminal
Responsibility

David A. Jones

University of Pittsburgh

Nelson-Hall Law Enforcement Series
George W. O'Connor, *Consulting Editor*
Superintendent of Public Safety, Troy, New York

Nelson-Hall / Chicago

Library of Congress Cataloging in Publication Data
Jones, David Arthur, 1946-
  Crime and criminal responsibility.

  Includes bibliographical references and index.
  1. Criminal law—United States. I. Title.
KF9219.J66   345'.73   77-25906
ISBN 0-911012-84-2

10 9 8 7 6 5 4 3 2 1

to my parents

Contents

Preface

Crime and Criminal Responsibility is intended to be a nontraditional book on the criminal law, for better or worse. While it may be useful for law students or even for attorneys, it is designed for the public at large and particularly for members of the public whose duty entails the enforcement of the criminal laws. The book does not presume that the reader possesses any prior knowledge of criminal law.

The average citizen who has not had legal training has come to view criminal law erroneously as being cut and dry, easy to understand without possibility of mistake. For this reason, the public is quick to criticize the police and the courts when a crime has been committed for which no person is deemed to bear criminal responsibility. Hopefully, this book may acquaint the reader with the complexity and the variety of concepts, elements, and principles which are contained within Anglo-American criminal law. The

xiii

reader should begin to realize why many criminal laws are difficult to understand.

This book is designed exclusively as an educational tool, however. It is not based upon the laws of any particular jurisdiction. It attempts to bind together the common threads of our body of criminal law which has evolved over a period of nearly one thousand years. The reader will not become competent, automatically, to give legal advice even to himself. If the reader is accused of having committed a crime, he should be represented immediately and continuously by an attorney who is licensed to practice law in the appropriate jurisdiction. This book is not arranged to function as a manual on how to defend oneself.

I am grateful for the assistance supplied to me by the staff of Nelson-Hall. Robert J. Dundon, who was Special Projects Editor when the initial manuscript for this book was prepared, provided me with an abundance of advice and patience. Barbara Moore, who edited the final manuscript for publication did an outstanding job, which I appreciate. Chapters 16 to 18 of this book are based upon research and recommendations produced by a variety of Congressional Committees and the Brown Commission, as these groups studied proposals for revising the Federal Criminal Code.

Undoubtedly, this book will contain some errors—and it may contain many—for which I alone am responsible. If the book is reasonably accurate and comprehensible, on the other hand, I must acknowledge my preparation under two persons: Professor Francis Howard Anderson, under whom I studied criminal law and procedure, family law, and military law, and Professor Fred Cohen, under whom I studied law as a means of social control, and penal code revision.

Introduction

Whenever the word *crime* is mentioned, many people think about behavior that they believe is bad, that they disapprove of, and that they also may fear. Some people tend to associate the word *crime* with people they dislike. The word *crime* is frequently used to describe deeds and activities that seem wrong or repulsive to a particular person or group of people. For this reason, the word often serves as a convenient *label* for any or all activities that are distasteful to the person who uses this word. To use the word *crime* in this context, however, is to use the word inaccurately.

Police and other law enforcement officials are less concerned with the word *crime* than they are with *specific crimes*. To most law enforcement personnel, specific crimes include particular behavior that is defined in their state penal code as being illegal. By reading any state penal code, one learns that a large number of specific crimes can be committed. By reading the *Uniform Crime Reports,* published by the Federal Bureau of Investigation (FBI), one learns that many specific crimes are in fact committed each day throughout the United States.

The *Uniform Crime Reports* lists twenty-six categories of specific crimes. Many of these categories will be discussed in this book. Specific crimes can be classified in many ways. The *Uniform Crime Reports* lists 26 specific crimes in decreasing order according to the *degree of harm* that each one causes in relationship to the others. In this book, specific crimes will be grouped by characteristics and discussed according to the *type of harm* that each crime causes.

For example, specific crimes such as assault, battery, rape, manslaughter, and murder will be discussed in Part 2 of this book as *offenses against the person.* These crimes cause harm to the victim's body. Such specific crimes as larceny, embezzlement, forgery, burglary, and arson will be discussed in Part 3 as *offenses against property.* These crimes cause harm to the victim's property rights instead of to his body. Several crimes, such as robbery and blackmail, are *offenses against person and property.* Another group of specific crimes, including adultery, disorderly conduct, prostitution, and gambling, will be discussed in Part 4 as *offenses against the public welfare.* These offenses, sometimes called "public order crimes," do not necessarily cause harm to any individual victim. They are also called "victimless crimes." No crime can be entirely "victimless," however, because every such crime is considered to cause harm or risk of harm to the public. Two additional kinds of crime against the public welfare are offenses involving national defense and those involving government processes.

The first four chapters of this book, which comprise Part 1, will not focus on any specific crimes. Even before a person can begin to understand the *differences* between various specific crimes, he must develop an understanding of the *similarities* among all crimes generally. Therefore, Chapter 1 explains what is meant by the word *crime* when that word is used accurately; Chapter 2 discusses the development of criminal laws and the general classes and degrees of crime; Chapter 3 explains criminal responsibility; and Chapter 4 explains defenses by which a person can free himself of criminal responsibility.

part 1

The Nature
of Crime

The Elements of Crime

Crime is *voluntary conduct that violates a public law and for which punishment may be imposed in the name of a state.* Whether or not a crime is committed always depends on the presence of four basic elements: (1) *Voluntary conduct* that (2) violates a *public law* and (3) for which *punishment may be imposed* (4) in the *name of a state.*

No crime can be committed unless all four of these basic elements are present at the same moment. Conduct that does not violate any public law cannot constitute a crime, even if it is voluntary. Nor can voluntary conduct that does violate a public law constitute a crime, unless punishment may be imposed for the conduct in the name of a state. Similarly, the mere fact that punishment may be imposed in the name of a state whenever a certain public law is violated does not in itself mean that a crime is committed, unless that public law is actually violated by a person's voluntary conduct.

3

The meaning of *voluntary conduct, public law, punishment,* and *in the name of a state* will be discussed in the remainder of this chapter. Each of these four basic elements of crime deserves careful attention. If even one of them is absent in any given situation, no crime is committed.

Voluntary Conduct

A crime is *voluntary conduct that violates a public law* and *for which punishment may be imposed in the name of a state.* No crime can be committed without some kind of conduct, and no crime can be committed without voluntary conduct. Conduct itself consists of two elements—a physical element and a mental one. Conduct results from a person's physical *action* and mental *intention.* Hence, conduct does not occur without human effort.

Physical action refers to movements of a person's body, while mental intention refers to thoughts that occur in a person's mind. Mental intention is also a kind of action, but it is nonphysical. For this reason, the word *action* is used to describe the physical element of conduct, whereas the word *intention* describes the mental element of conduct.

Physical Action

Physical action consists of either a person's *act* or a person's failure to perform a required act. Law enforcement officers may speak of a person's *commission* of an act. A person's failure to perform an act that his duty requires of him is called an *omission.* Conduct cannot exist without a person's commission or omission of an act.

To commit an act, a person must make some movement with his body. This bodily movement does not have to be great, forceful, or violent to be an act. On the contrary, a bodily movement may be very slight and hardly noticeable at all and still be an act. An act may be committed by a person even though no other person is present to witness it.

A person does not commit an act every time movement occurs inside or outside his body, however. An act is committed only when a person moves his body *of his own free will.* Hence, an act is a person's *voluntary* bodily movement. An act in legal terms is not committed every time a person's heart beats, each time he blinks his eyes, or whenever he swallows, coughs, or sneezes. Normally, these bodily movements are not voluntary. A person may commit an act, however, by voluntarily blinking his eyes as a signal to another person. One may commit an act by clearing his throat or making a facial scowl as a voluntary gesture. Of course, an act is committed every time a person walks, talks, moves his arms, raises his fists, or touches an object with his hands or fingers.

Example 1.1: Baxter winks at Adams, who yells to Jesse, who nods at Lefty, who punches Fred in the mouth with his fist.

Baxter's wink, Adams' yell, Jesse's nod, and Lefty's punch are all examples of acts. Each of these gestures is a person's voluntary bodily movement.

A person commits an act every time he makes a voluntary movement with his body. Not every act constitutes a crime, of course. People walk, talk, and make other voluntary bodily movements every day, usually without committing a crime. It is important to realize that no act constitutes a crime unless it violates a public law and unless punishment may be imposed for it in the name of a state.

A person who fails to perform an act that his duty requires him to perform has made an omission. One's omission of a required act constitutes conduct, just as if one had committed an act. Different people have different duties. For example, a person who is employed to do a job is normally required to complete his work before he receives his daily, weekly, or monthly pay. A person who fails to complete his work has made an omission of that work. In many instances a person's omission to do his job results in loss of pay and perhaps also loss of the job. Of course, a person's omission to go to work does not usually constitute a crime, unless the person is a public servant. This is because a person's failure to go to work does not generally violate a public law, and no punishment may be imposed in the name of a state (although punishment may be imposed by the employer).

Just as every act does not constitute a crime, neither does every omission constitute a crime. However, some omissions do violate public law and punishment may be imposed for them in the name of a state. For example, the mother of a child normally has a duty to feed the child. When a mother neglects to feed her child, this neglect becomes an omission of her duty. In most states, a mother's omission to feed her child violates a public law, and punishment for her conduct may be imposed in the name of a state. In most states, therefore, a mother's omission to feed her child is a crime.

Example 1.2: Tommy owns a dog named Sinbad. In the town where Tommy lives, a law requires every dog owner to obtain a new license for his dog each year. When Sinbad's license expired at the end of last year, Tommy failed to obtain a new dog license.

Tommy's failure to obtain a new license for his dog is an omission. The law imposes a duty on Tommy to renew his dog's license every year. This omission constitutes a crime only if the public law that it violates, or another public law, permits a person to be punished in the name of the state on account of this omission.

Conduct does not exist in the absence of an act or omission. Act and omission are the physical elements of conduct. *Thoughts* and *dreams* that run through a person's mind are not forms of conduct, because they are neither acts nor omissions. Thoughts and dreams do not depend on the presence or absence of a person's voluntary bodily movement. Because they are not forms of conduct, thoughts and dreams cannot constitute crimes by themselves.

Thoughts and dreams may, however, inspire a person to commit or omit an act and to engage in conduct that constitutes a crime. It is important to understand that a person cannot commit a crime by merely thinking or dreaming about a crime. Neither thinking nor dreaming is the same thing as acting or omitting to act. A crime cannot be committed without some form of conduct, and thoughts and dreams are not forms of conduct.

Example 1.3: After watching a movie about activities of the underworld, Billy falls asleep and dreams about participating in a bank robbery.

Although a bank robbery is an act that constitutes a crime in every state of the United States, Billy cannot commit a crime with his dreams alone. A person's dreams are not acts and are not omissions. Therefore, dreams are not forms of conduct. No crime can be committed without conduct.

Example 1.4: Frequently, John thinks about having an affair with Maureen, although he is married to Pat. Where John lives, any man who is married and has an affair with a woman other than his wife commits the crime of adultery.

John does *not* commit the crime of adultery by *thinking* about having an affair with Maureen. To commit a crime, a person must engage in some form of conduct, by committing or omitting an act. John's thoughts alone constitute neither an act nor an omission. His thoughts are not forms of conduct. Should John actually have an affair with Maureen while he remains married to Pat, he will then engage in conduct, and that conduct may constitute a crime.

Mental Intention

As we have seen, acts and omissions are always forms of conduct, because they are physical actions. Not every form of conduct constitutes a crime, of course, so not every act or omission constitutes a crime. To constitute a crime, conduct must violate a public law and must be punishable in the name of a state. As a rule, only voluntary conduct for which punishment may be imposed in the name of the state can violate a public law. As a rule, then, only voluntary conduct can constitute a crime. This is a general rule and is subject to a few exceptions that will be noted later.

Voluntary conduct is called *criminal conduct* if it violates a public law and is punishable in the name of a state. A person who intends to engage in criminal conduct for a wrongful purpose is presumed to have a *criminal intent*. The purpose of a person's conduct depends on his reason or reasons for committing or omitting the conduct in question. The purpose of a person's conduct is *wrongful* when the person means to cause harm by his conduct. Wrongful conduct may cause harm to a state itself, or to another person's body, or to another person's property. Because a person who possesses a criminal intent means to cause some kind of harm, a criminal intent is often referred to in legal terms as an "evil state of mind."

A person may engage in criminal conduct for a purpose that is not wrongful, however. People sometimes innocently commit or omit acts that result in conduct that violates a public law. For example, a person may engage in criminal conduct in order to *prevent* rather than to cause harm. In most situations, a person commits a crime only when he engages in criminal conduct *at the same moment* as he possesses a criminal intent.

Example 1.5: Sloan follows Brown into an alley and knocks Brown over the head to steal Brown's wallet.

Sloan hits Brown over the head for a *wrongful* purpose, because Sloan's intent is to cause harm. In this situation, Sloan's intent is to cause harm both to Brown's body and to his property. Sloan possesses a *criminal intent* at the moment he knocks Brown over the head.

Example 1.6: Officer Smith, an on-duty policeman, observes Sloan hitting Brown over the head. To prevent further harm to Brown and to prevent Sloan from escaping, Officer Smith knocks Sloan over the head with a billy club.

Officer Smith hits Sloan over the head for a *rightful* purpose rather than for a wrongful purpose. In this situation, Smith's intent is to prevent harm and to uphold the law. Smith does *not* possess a *criminal intent* at the moment he knocks Sloan over the head. This is true although Officer Smith commits the same act against Sloan that Sloan committed against Brown.

Intent is quite different from free will. Hence, a person may voluntarily commit or omit an act and still not possess a criminal intent. In Example 1.6, for example, Officer Smith's act of knocking Sloan over the head was a voluntary movement of Smith's body. Yet Smith did not possess a criminal intent because he meant to prevent rather than to cause harm.

An intent alone, without either an act or an omission, is not a form of conduct. This is true even when a person's intent is a criminal intent. One cannot commit a crime by possessing a criminal intent alone. Intent is nothing more than a person's thought or plan. Intent does not constitute conduct by itself, because intent is not a voluntary bodily movement. A person can intend to commit a crime without ever physically committing that crime by an act or omission. A criminal intent, without conduct in the form of either an act or omission, cannot cause any harm.

Example 1.7: Chadwick constantly plans to kill his wife, whom he hates. He has considered either shooting her or poisoning her, but he has never bought either a gun or any poison. Chadwick has never physically endangered his wife's life by act or by omission.

Chadwick's plans form a criminal intent, because they would cause harm to his wife if put into physical action. Chadwick has never transformed his criminal intent into physical action of any kind, however. An intent alone, without physical action in the form of an act or omission, is not conduct. As conduct is an essential element of any crime, no crime can be committed in the absence of conduct. Therefore, Chadwick's intent to kill his wife is not a crime in itself.

Although a criminal intent does not in itself constitute a crime, criminal conduct that is committed *unintentionally* may constitute a crime under some circumstances. These peculiar circumstances comprise what is known as strict criminal liability, or, more simply, as strict liability.

The following situations are examples of voluntary conduct that can violate a public law and for which punishment may be imposed in the name of a state, whether a person engages in this conduct *intentionally or unintentionally*. These strict liability situations include (1) illegal sales of intoxicating liquor, (2) sales of impure or adulterated food or drugs, (3) sales of misbranded articles, (4) violations of antinarcotic acts, (5) criminal nuisances, (6) violations of traffic regulations, (7) violations of motor vehicle laws, and (8) violations of general police regulations for the safety, health, and well-being of the community.

In the case of *Morisette* v. *United States* (1952),[1] the Supreme Court of the United States agreed that as a rule there can be no crime without a criminal intent. The Supreme Court recognized the foregoing eight exceptions to this general rule, however. Each exception has to do with conduct that could cause harm to a large segment of the public. Except for these eight exceptions, and possibly a few others, voluntary conduct can violate a public law and be punishable in the name of a state only when the conduct is accompanied by a criminal intent on the part of the offender.

Example 1.8: Malcolm intentionally fails to put the required coins in a parking meter where he parks his car. When a policeman writes out a traffic citation against Malcolm for a meter violation, Malcolm gets so upset that he drives away and drives his car through a red light, for which he is given another citation. Malcolm's red light violation was not committed intentionally.

A motorist who commits or omits an act that results in a traffic violation automatically violates a public law and is punishable. This is true whether the act or omission was *intentional or unintentional.*

Public Law

A crime is voluntary conduct that violates a *public law* and for which punishment may be imposed in the name of a state. Whenever a crime is committed, some public law is violated. No crime can be committed unless a public law is violated.

Public laws may be created only by political units such as nations and states (and subdivisions such as municipalities), as part of each nation's or state's sovereign power to govern activities within its geographic territory. The word *state* is used to mean the country, state, city, or other unit of government that has created the laws in question. Every state has many public laws that *require* persons within the state to perform certain acts and *prohibit* them from performing other acts. The public laws of a particular state are applicable only within the territorial limits of that state, and nowhere else. The federal laws of the United States of America apply within the territorial limits of *all* states and territories of the United States.

All independent nations of the world are states and possess the sovereign power to create and enforce public laws within their territorial limits. Each of the states of the United States is a sovereign state and has the power to create and enforce public laws within its boundaries. The United States is a federation of states and has the power to create and enforce public laws within its national boundaries. Under the federal Constitution, the public laws of the United States must be enforced by every state. Whenever the public law of an individual state conflicts with the federal Constitution or with any public law of the United States, the state law is not valid and the federal law must be obeyed.

In the United States, public laws are created in a number of ways. Laws may be enacted as *state statutes* by vote of a state legislature, or as *municipal ordinances* by vote of a city council or town selectmen. *Federal statutes* are enacted by Congress. Federal, state, and local public laws may be created by *judicial decisions* of courts of law. Both federal and state courts may enforce federal laws. Federal courts have the right to enforce state laws, but they rarely exercise that right.

In some states of the United States, public laws can be created only by legislative statute or by judicial decision. In many states, however, public laws that are older than the state itself may still be in force. This is because many states still recognize the public laws of England that were in force before the federal Constitution or that state's constitution was adopted. These early public laws of England form what is known as the English *common law.*

The English common law developed over hundreds of years. It originated from the unwritten customs of the Anglo-Saxon people, or from judicial decisions that affirmed and enforced those customs. The common law has been abolished by statute in some states, including California, Georgia, Indiana, Kansas, Michigan, Minnesota, Missouri, New York, Ohio, Oregon, and Texas. Nevertheless, the common law remains a vital part of the public laws of most states in America. Even in those few states where the common law has been abolished by statute, many of the principles that were established at common law remain in full force and effect.

Under the Constitution of the United States, conduct cannot constitute a crime unless it violates a public law that is in effect at the moment the conduct occurs. Some other nations permit new public laws to be enacted to make crimes of conduct that was not prohibited by any public law at the time the conduct occurred. A public law that makes a crime of conduct that was innocent and not prohibited by any public law when it occurred is called an *ex post facto* law. As the Latin words imply, an *ex post facto* law is enacted after the fact, meaning after the conduct took place.

Both the federal Constitution and decisions of the U.S. Supreme Court prohibit the United States from enacting any *ex post facto* law. Similarly, the state constitutions of all states of the United States contain clauses that prohibit enactment of any *ex post facto* law. In this country, then, no conduct can constitute a crime unless at the time of the conduct a public law is actually in force to prohibit that conduct. Hence, conduct can never be a crime in the United States unless it occurs *after* creation of a public law that makes it a crime.

Some countries have frequently created public laws that have made crimes of conduct that took place before any public law existed to regulate that conduct. Nazi Germany and the Soviet Union are the most notable examples of nations that have created *ex post facto* laws. In a country where *ex post facto* laws can be created, everyone must live in fear that his past conduct may be declared a crime in the future, even though it did not violate any public law when it took place. Of course, even the United States may create new public laws and thereby make new crimes possible. In the

United States, however, a new public law cannot make a crime of conduct that took place before the public law came into existence.

> *Example 1.9:* In a certain state, a new public law is created to become effective after midnight of December 31, 1977. This new public law provides that any person who intentionally kills a blue heron in this state on or after January 1, 1978, commits a crime.
>
> Ted intentionally kills a blue heron in this state on December 29, 1977. Dick intentionally kills a blue heron in this state on January 2, 1978.
>
> Dick violates the new public law by intentionally killing a blue heron in this state on January 2, 1978, which is *after* midnight of December 31, 1977, when the new law went into effect. Ted's identical conduct on December 29, 1977, did not violate the new public law, because his conduct took place *before* midnight of December 31, 1977, when the new law went into effect.
>
> The new law is not an *ex post facto* law because it does not make a crime of conduct that occurred before midnight of December 31, 1977, when the new law became effective.
>
> *Example 1.10:* In a foreign country, a new public law is created to become effective after midnight of December 31, 1977. This new public law provides that any person who ever in his life cut down a black walnut tree has committed a crime. Prior to creation of this new public law, this country had no public law that regulated the cutting down of black walnut trees.
>
> Boris cut down a black walnut tree in 1964 and again in 1971. Under this *ex post facto* law, Boris can be prosecuted as a criminal for having cut down the trees in 1964 and 1971, even though his conduct was totally innocent at the time it took place because no public law prohibited cutting down a black walnut tree.

Public laws are created by a state to regulate the conduct of people who are present in the state's territorial borders. Every person who is physically inside the boundaries of a state at any time has the duty to obey each and every one of that state's public laws. Any person who violates one of a state's public laws while he is present in the state commits a crime.

Only a state or a subdivision of a state such as a municipality (town, city, or county) can create a public law. No private person has the authority to make a crime of conduct that does not violate any public law. In addition, conduct may constitute a crime in one state and not constitute a crime in another state if only the first state has a public law prohibiting the conduct.

Example 1.11: A fraternal order passes a resolution that any member who fails to pay annual dues of ten dollars commits a crime. Failure to pay annual dues to this fraternal order does not violate any public law in the state where Jim lives. Jim is a member of this fraternal order but fails to pay annual dues this year.

Only a state has the authority to create a public law. Only conduct that violates a public law and for which punishment may be imposed in the name of a state can constitute a crime.

The state where Jim lives does not have any public law that requires members of fraternal orders to pay annual dues. Therefore, Jim's failure to pay annual dues to the fraternal order is not a crime. Of course, Jim may be expelled from membership in the fraternal order for violating one of the order's private rules.

It is important to remember that conduct that does not violate any public law in effect at the time the conduct takes place can not constitute a crime in the United States. Violation of a club's rules, regulations, resolutions, or "laws" is not necessarily the same as violation of a public law.

Punishment

A crime is voluntary conduct that violates a public law and for which *punishment may be imposed* in the name of a state. Conduct cannot constitute a crime, even though it violates a public law, unless punishment for that conduct may be imposed in the name of the state whose public law is violated. In other words, conduct that violates a public law is a crime only if a state has the right to punish that conduct. A state has the right to punish conduct that violates a public law only if one of that state's public laws authorizes punishment for that particular conduct.

Every public law of any state may be violated, but a crime is not committed when certain of these public laws are violated. Punishment in the name of the state may not be imposed on account of conduct that violates some public laws. Examples of such laws will be given later. Public laws that may be violated by conduct for which a state may impose punishment are called *criminal laws* or *penal laws* interchangeably.

All criminal laws are public laws, but not every public law is a criminal law. Criminal laws make up only a small portion of the public laws of most states, and conduct that violates one or more criminal laws is a crime. Conduct that violates a public law that is not a criminal law is not a crime.

Here are some examples of public laws that are not criminal laws. Most states have public laws regulating business transactions, payment of debts, sale and purchase of property, marriage and divorce, and election and removal of public officeholders. These are public laws that a person may violate without committing a crime. A state may not impose punishment on a person whose conduct violates one of these public laws, because punishment is not authorized.

For example, a public law in many states requires that every person who makes his last will and testament must sign that document in the presence of at least two persons who are not beneficiaries under that will. A person who signs his last will and testament in the presence of fewer than two witnesses does not commit a crime. Indeed, he may be dead before this omission is discovered. His last will and testament will be invalid, however. The consequence of conduct that violates this public law is invalidity of the document rather than punishment in the name of a state, because the state is not authorized to punish this conduct.

Punishment in the name of a state may be imposed only on account of conduct that violates a criminal or penal law. This is true because only a criminal law or a penal law authorizes the state to impose punishment. Furthermore, a criminal law or a penal law must be very specific concerning what kind of punishment and how much punishment may be imposed on account of particular conduct.

Punishment may be imposed in the name of a state only against an actual person or an actual group of people. Punishment may not be imposed against unidentified persons. Corporations and other organizations that are chartered or licensed by a state may be punished in the name of a state for violating one of the state's public laws. They can be punished in the name of any state whose laws they violate, not just in the name of the state that chartered or licensed them. Animals, plants, and nonliving things may not be punished, although they may be destroyed by an order of a state. (Punishment, of course, is not necessarily the same thing as destruction, although destruction sometimes results from punishment.) Punishment in the name of a state is always imposed intentionally by human beings other than the person or persons being punished. Punishment may never be imposed accidentally, or it ceases to be punishment and becomes injury.

Traditionally, several types of punishment have been imposed by states. These punishments include: (1) *death* (loss of a person's life), (2) *imprisonment* (loss of a person's liberty), (3) *banishment* (removal of a person from a particular state or community), (4) *fine* (forfeiture of a person's property), and (5) *civil disability* (forfeiture of a person's franchise to vote or to hold public office).

Punishment serves several functions. All punishment that is imposed in the name of a state is public vengeance, called *retribution.* The purpose of retribution is to give a state the opportunity to inflict pain and suffering on persons who have violated its criminal or penal laws. Punishment frequently serves other functions besides retribution, however. Certain punishments, such as death and imprisonment, cause *restraint* of persons who have violated criminal laws and prevent them from committing additional crimes. Death permanently restrains a person from committing another crime. Imprisonment restrains the prisoner from committing most crimes, at least until he is released from prison. (To be sure, some crimes may be committed even within prison walls.) Punishment also may be imposed in order to set an example for the public and discourage others from committing crimes. Hence, punishment may be imposed as deterrence—to persuade persons who have not committed crimes not to do so in the future. Punishment has a deterrent effect when it makes members of the public afraid of the pain and suffering that might result should they commit a crime. Thus, punishment is imposed to accomplish specific objectives, such as retribution, restraint, and deterrence.

In the Name of a State

A crime is voluntary conduct that violates a public law and for which punishment may be imposed *in the name of a state.* Conduct that violates a criminal or penal law is punished in the name of a state if it is punished at all. A crime may never be punished in the name of a private individual or even in the name of a private organization. This is true even though an individual person or a private organization may have been the victim of the crime.

A state is the sovereign political power that permanently governs a specific geographic territory. As such, it not only has the right to regulate the conduct of all persons present within its geographic boundaries, but it also has the duty to protect those persons from harm. In fulfilling that duty, a state may impose punishment in its name against a person whose conduct violates one of that state's criminal or penal laws.

When a person violates a state's criminal law or penal law, he is considered to cause harm or risk of harm to every person located within that state. He usually also causes harm to his immediate victim. A state imposes punishment against such a person because that person's conduct has caused harm or risk of harm to the public of that state. A state does not punish a person merely because that person has caused injury to an individual victim.

Every time a person engages in punishable conduct that violates a public law, that person commits a crime. A person is not punished every time a crime is committed, however. Frequently, conduct that violates a state's criminal law is never punished. Some crimes are never discovered. Others are discovered but are never reported to the police. Of those crimes that are committed, discovered, and reported to the police, only a small fraction are ever "solved" by the arrest of a suspect. Conduct that violates a state's criminal law cannot be punished unless a person is *convicted* of committing a crime by performing that conduct. Even after a person has been convicted of committing a crime, a judge often has discretion to determine whether or not punishment will in fact be imposed.

When a state accuses a person of having participated in conduct that violates one of its criminal or penal laws, the state *charges* that person with having committed a crime. The procedure that a state uses to charge a person will be discussed in Chapter 4. When a state accuses a person of having committed a crime, the formal accusation or charge must be brought in the name of the state itself or in the name of the state's symbol of sovereign power.

Some states of the United States charge a person in the name of the "people" of that state. This practice stems from the tradition in this country that a state's sovereign power is derived from its people. States in the United Kingdom charge a person with having committed a crime in the name of the British monarch or in the name of the British crown. The British monarch and his crown symbolize the sovereign power of states that are members of the United Kingdom. The following phrases are examples of the wording of criminal charges: *The United States of America* v. *John Smith, The State of New Hampshire* v. *John Smith, The Commonwealth of Massachusetts* v. *John Smith,* or *The People of the State of New York* v. *John Smith.* In the United Kingdom, criminal charges may read: *Rex* v. *John Smith* or *Regina* v. *John Smith.* The words *rex, regina,* and *versus* (v.) are all Latin words. *Rex* means "the king"; *regina* means "the queen"; and *versus* means "against." Crimes committed in the United Kingdom during the reign of Queen Elizabeth II are prosecuted in the name of "The Queen" (e.g., Regina v. John Smith).

When the United States of America accuses and charges an individual with having committed a crime, this means that the accused individual is charged with having committed that crime on behalf of each and every one of the American people. When each and every one of the American people, or each and every one of the people of any state, or even the queen of England accuses an individual of having committed a crime, the seriousness of the accusation becomes apparent. Indeed, to bear false witness against a person in order to cause a state to charge that person with having committed a crime usually constitutes a crime in itself.

CHAPTER 2

Criminal Laws

Every state has a vast number of public laws regulating the behavior and activities of persons who are within that state's boundaries, but only a small portion of any state's public laws are criminal laws. As Chapter 1 explained, the easiest way to recognize whether a particular law is a criminal law is to observe the *penalty* that is prescribed for violation of that law. The criminal laws of every state are enforced by *punishment imposed in the name of the state.*

Public laws that are not criminal laws may also be enforced by forms of punishment, but not in the name of the state. For example, a corporation that is not chartered by a particular state must usually obtain a license and qualify to do business in that state. A corporation that is neither chartered nor licensed in a particular state usually violates one of that state's public laws if it does business there. Such a corporation seldom violates a state's criminal law merely by doing business in that state without a license, however. Therefore, it cannot ordinarily be punished by the state. Instead, a corporation that engages in such conduct may receive other punishment. It may not be permitted to go to court to enforce contracts to which it is a party. Therefore, consumers who purchase its products may not be legally required to pay the purchase price.

As another example, married persons who reside in a particular state may be prohibited by a public law from obtaining a divorce decree from any other state. A husband or wife who resides in one state but obtains a divorce decree in another probably does not violate any criminal law of the state in which he or she resides. This does not mean that the person who obtains the divorce decree will not be punished, however. He or she will be punished to the extent that the state in which he or she resides will not recognize the foreign state's divorce decree. The couple will not be legally divorced in the state where they reside. They will not be punished in the name of the state, however, as long as they did not violate a criminal law.

In addition to being punished in the name of the state, a person who violates a state's criminal law may be punished in the name of any victim he harms. As Chapter 1 explained, a state cannot punish a person in the name of an individual victim. Instead, the victim himself may seek to punish a person who harms him, by means of a civil court action for money damages. For example, a person who drives his automobile into another person's automobile while he is drunk commits a crime, causes harm to the owner of the automobile he hits, and may cause harm to anyone who is inside it. By driving an automobile while he is drunk, a person commits a crime in nearly every state. By crashing his automobile into someone else's automobile, a person causes property damage to its owner, and he may cause personal injury to anyone who is inside. For driving an automobile while he is drunk, this person may be punished by the state for violating a criminal law. For causing property damage or personal injury to an individual victim, a person may be sued by the victim for money damages by means of a civil court action.

Thus, a person who injures another person's body or property while committing a crime is personally liable to his victim for payment of damages. A person who commits a crime is not relieved of liability to his victim merely because he is punished by the state. Punishment in the name of a state remains separate from damages that may be assessed against a person for causing injury to an individual victim of his crime, and the state may impose punishment whether or not the offender causes damage to an individual victim. Similarly, punishment imposed by the state is independent of the victim's decision to sue the offender for damages or to forgive the offender.

The Origin of Criminal Laws

Criminal laws developed over a long period of time. Because human beings are social animals, they tend to organize their lives around group activities with other humans. In order to assure that a group of human beings will live together as peacefully as possible, each member of the group must organize his personal habits so that they will not conflict with those of other group members.

In order to organize their habits for mutual benefit, individual members of a group of people must develop understandings with each other. These common understandings must include mutual respect for each other's lives, bodily integrity, property, and social rights and privileges. Formal agreements relating to these common understandings are called *rules* and *regulations*. Rules and regulations must define the kinds of individual behavior that the entire group will not tolerate from any individual member.

After rules and regulations concerning human behavior have been accepted by members of a group of people for years or centuries, these rules and regulations turn into *customs*. When a group of people permanently organizes under the leadership of a single government and occupies a fixed geographic territory, the group becomes a state. The rules and regulations that govern the behavior of persons within a state are called *public laws*. As mentioned, every state has public laws that require persons within its borders to do certain things and prohibit them from doing certain other things.

Although they make up only a small portion of the total body of public laws of any state, criminal laws are among the first laws to be created in any new state. Therefore, criminal laws are among the oldest public laws. Perhaps for this reason, the criminal laws of many states bear a striking similarity to the criminal laws of other states—much more so than do other public laws. This is particularly true of the criminal laws that developed in England under the common law.

The Heritage of English Common Law

The principles of the English common law have been adopted around the world by nearly every nation of Anglo-Saxon heritage. Once owned by England, the thirteen original American colonies directly inherited principles of common law. These principles spread from the original American states to the newer states as the United States expanded. Many American states were exposed to principles of law from other countries as well. Louisiana, for example, was originally exposed to French law, because France once owned Louisiana. Parts of Texas, New Mexico, Arizona, and California were once governed by Spain. Alaska was once governed by Russia, at least nominally. Hawaii was once an independent nation. Nevertheless, the principles of the English common law still prevail throughout the United States to a greater extent than do principles of any other historic body of law.

The English common law divided crimes into three categories: (1) *treasons,* (2) *felonies,* and (3) *misdemeanors.* The criminal laws of most states that follow principles of common law continue to divide crimes into at least two categories—felonies and misdemeanors. When crimes are divided only into felonies and misdemeanors, treasons become felonies.

There are several distinctions among treasons, felonies, and misdemeanors. Treasons are more serious crimes than either ordinary felonies or misdemeanors, because treasons cause the greatest harm or risk of harm to a state. Treasons usually threaten the very existence of a state. Felonies are more serious than misdemeanors, because they cause more serious harm or risk of harm to individual victims and to the public.

Because they are the most serious crimes, treasons are generally punished more severely than are ordinary felonies or misdemeanors. For the same reason, felonies are ordinarily punished more severely than are misdemeanors. Each of these three categories of common law crimes will be examined separately.

Treasons

At common law, treason was divided into high treason and petit treason. *High treason* involved conduct that consisted of plotting to kill or overthrow the king, giving aid or comfort to his enemies, forging or counterfeiting his seal, or killing one of his important officials. High treason was also committed when any of the king's subjects called him blasphemous (demeaning or irreverant) names.

Petit (pronounced "petty") treason was committed at common law when a wife plotted to or did kill her husband, a child plotted to or did kill his father, a vassal plotted to or did kill his lord, or a servant plotted to or did kill his master. A wife, child, vassal, or servant could also commit petit treason by calling the husband, father, lord, or master names that injured the latter's reputation.

Persons who called the king blasphemous names could be burned at the stake, but in fact in England they never were. Persons who committed an act of high treason were frequently put to death by hanging or by decapitation. In either event, the head of an executed traitor was removed from its body and affixed to a post on the side of London Bridge. There it was placed in disgrace for the public to view and desecrate.

The punishment at common law for acts of petit treason was normally less severe than was the punishment for high treason. Death by hanging was sometimes but rarely inflicted, and then only if the plot to kill succeeded. When petit treason did not result in murder, punishment was seldom more serious than a reprimand or a fine.

Petit treason is no longer a separate crime, either in England or in the United States. The murder of the offender's husband or father is treated as a felony, as is the murder of anyone else. In modern criminal law, acts that used to be called high treason are generally referred to as treason.

The crime of treason will be discussed in detail in Chapter 19.

Today, the crime is generally punished similarly to other felonies, by death or by imprisonment in a state prison or state penitentiary, usually for a period of time exceeding one year.

Felonies

The distinction between felonies and misdemeanors is very important, although it may be somewhat difficult to understand. Early in the formation of the common law, crimes were distinguished according to *why* they were wrong. The reasons for which crimes were originally considered wrong or evil formed the basis for the distinction between felonies and misdemeanors.

In early common law, all crimes were considered wrong for one of two reasons: (1) because they were thought to be wrong or evil in themselves *(mala in se),* or (2) simply because they were prohibited by a public law *(mala prohibita).* Only the following nine crimes were considered wrong or evil in themselves *(mala in se):* murder, manslaughter, rape, sodomy, robbery, larceny, arson, burglary, and mayhem. These nine crimes became common-law felonies, while other crimes became misdemeanors. Each of the nine specific crimes that became common-law felonies will be discussed in detail later in this book, as will a number of common-law misdemeanors.

Although the criminal laws of many states today recognize more than nine crimes as felonies, the basic distinction between felonies and misdemeanors remains the same as it was at common law. Felonies are crimes that cause greater harm or risk of harm to the public than do misdemeanors. Understandably, then, felonies have always been considered to be more serious than misdemeanors and have always been punished more severely.

At common law, the crown usually punished a person who was convicted of a felony by seizing all or a portion of his property in the name of the king. Sometimes the crown imposed death as an additional punishment. When the circumstances of the conduct warranted leniency, the crown frequently spared an offender his life, but banished him from the kingdom, either permanently or for a number of years. Many convicted felons were banished from England and transported to Norfolk Island, off the coast of Australia. The average term of banishment for a person who committed his first felony was usually about seven years. The sentence was often nearly doubled for each successive conviction.

Today, many states punish a person who has been convicted of a felony by confining him in a state prison or penitentiary for a period of time ranging from one year to life. In many states, a person who has been convicted of a felony may lose his right to vote and to hold public office, either permanently or during the course of his punishment.

The criminal laws of many states still prescribe death as a punishment that may be imposed against a person who has been convicted of certain felonies—murder, for example. Some states also prescribe death as punishment for the crimes of rape and burglary. Under the federal kidnapping statute (the Lindbergh Law), a person who has been convicted of kidnapping a victim who was not released unharmed may be punished by death.

Beginning in June 1972 the U.S. Supreme Court announced a series of decisions in which they held that the death penalty violates the Constitution when a state's criminal laws permit death to be haphazardly inflicted as punishment. Apparently, the Court believed that punishment is imposed haphazardly when it is imposed against *some, but not most,* persons who have been convicted of the same specific crime. The Eighth Amendment to the Constitution prohibits the infliction of cruel and unusual punishments. These Supreme Court decisions regarding the death penalty do not in any way indicate that capital punishment violates the Constitution because it is *cruel;* rather, they seem to hold that the death penalty violates the Constitution when it is imposed capriciously as an *unusual* punishment for a specific crime.

Misdemeanors

At common law, all crimes that were not treasons or felonies were misdemeanors. Unlike the nine common-law felonies, misdemeanors were not considered to be wrong or evil in themselves *(mala in se)*. They were thought to be wrong or evil only because they were prohibited by law *(mala prohibita)*. For this reason, conduct that constituted a misdemeanor at one historical period did not necessarily constitute a misdemeanor at other historical periods. On the contrary, the nine common-law felonies were labeled as felonies throughout the history of the common law.

Today, the criminal laws of most states classify as misdemeanors various crimes that are thought to be less serious than felonies. In most states, however, crimes that are not felonies may not be misdemeanors, either. Minor crimes such as traffic infractions, jay-walking and illegal parking are sometimes called *violations* rather than misdemeanors.

At common law, the property of a person who was convicted of a misdemeanor was not seized, nor could such a person be put to death. Rather, such conduct was punished by a fine or by a short term in the *gaol,* as the English jail was and still is called. Persons who were convicted of a misdemeanor were often publicly whipped or wedged into the pillory.

Under the criminal laws of many states today, persons who have been convicted of a misdemeanor may be imprisoned in a county jail for a period that does not exceed one year. They may also be fined, either in addition to or instead of being sentenced to jail. Conviction of a misdemeanor does not generally result in loss of a person's franchise to vote or to hold public office.

Classes and Degrees of Crimes

Today, both felonies and misdemeanors are subdivided into a number of grades in many states. Felonies may be divided into as many as five grades, while misdemeanors are often divided into two or three. Grades of felonies or misdemeanors are sometimes called *classes* and indicate the severity of the felony or misdemeanor in relationship to other crimes.

For example, murder and kidnapping are considered to be "class *A*" felonies in a number of states. Treason may also be graded as a class *A* felony. When a state's criminal or penal laws prescribe capital punishment for certain crimes, these crimes ordinarily include class *A* felonies.

Manslaughter is often graded as a class *B* felony, along with armed robbery, violent rape and sodomy, and arson. Imprisonment for fifteen to thirty years is frequently imposed as punishment for a person who has been convicted of a class *B* felony.

Burglary is often graded as a class *C* felony, along with robbery that is committed while the offender is unarmed, and larceny that involves theft of valuable property. Imprisonment for five to fifteen years may be imposed as punishment for a person who has been convicted of a class *C* felony.

Bribery, assault, battery, and perjury are examples of a wide variety of crimes that are sometimes graded as either class *D* or class *E* felonies. Imprisonment for one to five years may be imposed as punishment for a person who has been convicted of such a felony.

Crimes involving the unauthorized use of a motor vehicle, presentation of a false insurance claim, illegal gambling, and impersonation of a police officer are examples of hundreds of crimes that are graded as class *A* misdemeanors in many states. Imprisonment for up to one year and a fine of hundreds of dollars may be imposed as punishment.

A person using a telephone who unlawfully refuses to yield a party line to another party for an emergency telephone call may commit a class *B* misdemeanor. A person who permits his premises to be used for prostitution or to create a nuisance also sometimes commits a class *B* misdemeanor. Imprisonment for up to six months as well as a small fine may be imposed as punishment.

Different crimes fall into different grades of felonies and misdemeanors in different states. The foregoing examples simply illustrate the major classes of felonies and misdemeanors that are prescribed in the criminal or penal laws of many states. Some states do not grade crimes into classes. Furthermore, some states grade certain crimes more seriously than do other states. For example, burglary may be a class *B* felony in one state and only a class *C* or a class *D* felony in a neighboring state.

In addition to grading felonies and misdemeanors by classes, many states grade felonies and misdemeanors by *degrees*. For example, murder may be divided into *first-degree* murder and *second-degree* murder. Rape, robbery, and burglary may be divided into as many as three degrees, as may a number of other crimes. Thus, for example, robbery may be divided into first-degree robbery, second-degree robbery, and third-degree robbery.

First-degree murder is considered more serious than second-degree murder. For this reason, the death penalty is sometimes prescribed as punishment for a person who has been convicted of first-degree murder. Life imprisonment may be prescribed as punishment for a person who has been convicted of second-degree murder. Still, both first-degree and second-degree murder may be graded as class *A* felonies.

On the other hand, different degrees of the same crime may be graded as different classes of felony or misdemeanor. For example, first-degree robbery or burglary may be graded as a class *B* felony, while second-degree robbery or burglary may be graded as a class *C* felony, and third-degree robbery or burglary may be graded as only a class *D* felony.

Grades of crimes cannot be summarized by class or by degree for all states together. A person who is interested in learning the precise class of felony or misdemeanor that a particular degree of a specific crime falls into should consult his state penal code. The district attorney, public defender, or an attorney in a community might help interpret the code.

For the purposes of this book, it is sufficient to explain that many crimes are graded according to *severity* in many states. A crime is normally considered more serious if it was committed violently than if it was committed without violence. Similarly, a crime that causes harm to a person's body is usually considered more serious than a crime that causes harm only to a person's property. The degree to which a victim's body is permanently injured on account of a crime may determine the seriousness of that crime. Likewise, the value of property that is stolen may bear heavily on the severity of crimes involving theft.

The criminal, or penal, laws of every state reflect the viewpoint of the majority of people within that state. People seldom disagree that serious crimes such as murder, robbery, rape, and burglary should be prohibited by criminal laws. People frequently disagree as to whether such crimes as prostitution, gambling, and drunkenness should be prohibited by criminal laws. The goal of this book is not to strengthen or weaken these agreements or disagreements. In the following chapters, the elements of many different crimes will be outlined, discussed, and explained. Every citizen should have an understanding of *what* conduct constitutes a specific crime, *why* that conduct violates a criminal law, and *how* a person may be punished when his conduct violates a specific criminal law.

CHAPTER 3

Criminal Responsibility

Under the American system of justice, all persons are presumed innocent until proven guilty of bearing criminal responsibility for a particular offense. The word *offense* is used here to mean any felony, misdemeanor, or other infraction of the criminal law. To establish a person's criminal responsibility, the state must prove beyond a reasonable doubt that a particular individual engaged in unlawful *conduct*. In addition, the state must prove beyond a reasonable doubt that the same individual had a sufficient criminal *intent* at precisely the same moment he participated in the illegal conduct. Thus, criminal responsibility consists of a combination of two elements: (1) criminal conduct and (2) criminal intent.

Criminal conduct, also known technically as *actus reus,* involves all physical elements of a crime, and without the occurrence of these elements, no offense may be committed. For instance, the crime of murder cannot take place unless one person causes another to die. However, the physical elements of an offense may take place without resulting in criminal responsibility on the part of the perpetrator—that is, the person who performs the act. A person may cause another to die, for example, without bearing criminal responsibility for murder and possibly without bearing any criminal responsibility at all. To be criminally responsible for offensive conduct, a person must be shown to have *intended* the consequences of the conduct. In this way, for example, a person who causes unlawful conduct to occur by accident is distinguished from another who causes similar conduct to occur by design, or intentionally. Criminal intent is known in legal terminology as *mens rea*, which means "state of mind." One's state of mind at the time he causes unlawful conduct to take place may determine whether criminal responsibility for the conduct exists at all, and if it does exist, to what extent. Thus, state of mind may aggravate (increase) or mitigate (decrease) the degree of criminal responsibility to be borne by a person whose physical conduct has resulted in the occurrence of a crime.

Criminal Conduct

Criminal conduct has been discussed in Chapters 1 and 2, so it need not be defined again in detail. To review briefly, criminal conduct may result from the commission of an act forbidden by law or from the omission of an act or other obligation required by law. Conduct may be repulsive and may even cause harm to persons or property without being illegal; and conduct may even be illegal without constituting a crime if no statutory provision is made for punishment in the name of the state. Without a criminal act or omission, however, no crime may be committed, and no person may become criminally responsible for an offense. It is never a crime to harbor a criminal intent unless one begins some physical effort to carry out the intent. Thus, the balance of this chapter does not apply if no criminal conduct has taken place.

Criminal Intent

A criminal intent is a person's mental determination to violate a criminal law for a wrongful purpose. As mentioned earlier, criminal intent has been termed an "evil state of mind" because it involves an individual's decision to behave in a fashion that he knows or should know to be wrong. Different persons' judgment may vary with the situation at hand, however. What one person may believe to be right another may believe to be wrong, and in the end the presence or absence of a person's criminal intent on any specific occasion must be determined by the judge or jury before whom the person stands trial. Since many persons have been put on trial to determine their criminal intent, in addition to determining whether they engaged in the unlawful conduct of which they were accused, certain legal standards have developed.

Criminal intent may be either general or specific. A *general* criminal intent is nothing more than a person's mental determination to participate generally in illegal conduct for a wrongful purpose. One possesses a general criminal intent when he wants to cause harm to the body or property of another person, to the public at large, or to the state. It is not necessary for him to have planned to violate any specific criminal law or to harm any specific victim in any particular way in order to possess a general criminal intent. A mere desire to cause harm is a general criminal intent, even though the person who desires to cause the harm does not have in mind any firm plans or means to carry out the desire.

A criminal intent will lead to criminal responsibility only if a person has a criminal intent at the moment when he engages in criminal conduct. This does not mean that the person had no such criminal intent prior to the time when he engaged in the criminal conduct. He may have formed an intent first and then performed the conduct, or he may have formed the intent while participating in the conduct. In either of these two situations, one may bear criminal responsibility for criminal conduct in which he engages. On the contrary, one may not bear criminal responsibility if he possessed no criminal intent at the time he participated in criminal conduct, regardless of whether he possessed a criminal intent prior to or after engaging in the conduct itself.

Ordinarily, the law presumes that a person has a general criminal intent whenever he participates voluntarily in criminal conduct of any kind. This is because the law presumes that a person of sound mind knows and realizes the natural and probable consequences of his behavior and that harm to a person or to property is the foreseeable consequence of illegal behavior. This presumption is not conclusive, however, and may be refuted by evidence that negates criminal intent. In the case of criminal intent, as in that of criminal conduct, voluntary behavior is distinguished from behavior that occurs through accident, inadvertence, or compulsion. In most situations, the state must prove the existence of criminal intent, as well as the existence of criminal conduct, and if the defendant raises defenses that cast doubt on his state of mind during the occurrence of a crime, the state must dispell such doubts. Some defenses, known as *affirmative defenses,* must be raised and proven by the defendant. Specific defenses will be discussed in Chapter 4.

Several degrees of criminal intent are distinguished by law in many jurisdictions. Usually, the higher the degree of criminal intent, the greater the criminal responsibility if the intent is proven to exist. Degrees of criminal intent are known technically as degrees of *culpability* or blame. Some persons who engage in criminal conduct while possessing a criminal intent may be more culpable or blameworthy than others because of the seriousness of the crime, the extent of the offender's malice, or other aggravating or mitigating circumstances. Degrees of culpability are commonly associated with such terms as *intentionally, knowingly, recklessly,* and *negligently.*

The highest degree of culpability exists when a person engages in conduct *intentionally.* One engages in criminal conduct intentionally when the behavior is purposeful—that is, when the perpetrator specifically plans to participate in a prohibited act or failure to perform a required act or obligation. One who kills another person on purpose bears a high degree of criminal responsibility as a rule because of his intentional conduct. Such a person bears a higher degree of culpability or blame than one who kills a sick friend to end his agony or who kills a despised enemy out of passion and rage.

A high but slightly lower degree of culpability exists when a person engages in conduct *knowingly* but not intentionally. One engages in conduct knowingly when he understands what he is doing or at least has a firm belief and no substantial doubt as to what he is doing, regardless of his purpose or motive. For example, a person might intentionally set fire to a garage next to a house for the purpose of destroying only the garage but with knowledge that the adjacent house might be burned too.

A lesser degree of culpability exists when a person engages in conduct *recklessly*. Conduct is reckless when it is clearly unjustifiable in view of the likelihood of foreseeable harm that is or should be perceived but that in fact is disregarded. Reckless conduct involves a gross deviation from acceptable standards of behavior, but it does not have to involve an intentional or even knowing state of mind.

There is a difference between "recklessness" and "gross negligence," although the two degrees of culpability are more similar than distinct. Gross negligence has been defined as constituting a wanton or reckless disregard for human life. However, while the person who does foresee the likelihood of harm but who chooses to ignore the risk is clearly reckless, the person who should have but in fact did not foresee that likelihood may only be grossly negligent.

The lowest degree of culpability exists when a person acts *negligently*. One is negligent when he fails to exercise the care that a reasonably careful and prudent person would be expected to exercise under identical circumstances. Ordinary or simple negligence involves an honest error of judgment in performing a lawful act. Ordinary negligence does not constitute either criminal conduct or a criminal intent. *Criminal* negligence may occur when a person makes (1) a dishonest error of judgment in performing a lawful act or (2) an honest error of judgment in performing an unlawful act. Criminal negligence of the first kind frequently occurs during the operation of a motor vehicle, such as when a driver decides to leave the scene of an accident without stopping to assist victims or to make a police report. Had he stopped, ordinary rather than criminal negligence would have been his highest culpability. The second kind of criminal negligence is typified by the driver of an automobile whose ability to function has been impaired by alcohol or other drugs, and therefore whose honest error in judgment (such as miscalculation of the distance between his and another vehicle) may result in criminal negligence.

Several other degrees of culpability have been known in the traditional criminal law, but many of these have been deleted in most recent criminal code revisions. A common but archaic term is *felonious*. "Felonious conduct" has often been used as a synonym for "intentional criminal conduct," but the word *intentional* is more specific. The word *willfully* has been used as a synonym for *know-*

ingly, and *wantonly* has been used for *recklessly.* Recently the Brown Commission, which was empaneled to study proposed revisions in the Federal Criminal Code, found seventy-eight different terms describing culpability in existing federal laws. Many of these terms are elusive and impractical, and the resulting confusion tends to cloud important distinctions among states of mind of persons accused of criminal conduct.

A general criminal intent is not always sufficient to make a person bear criminal responsibility for unlawful behavior. Sometimes a *specific* criminal intent must be proven. A specific criminal intent may take many shapes and forms, usually related to the purpose of the criminal behavior. For example, a specific intent to steal is required to make one criminally responsible for many theft offenses. A specific intent to kill is required to make one criminally responsible for crimes such as murder and assault with intent to commit murder. A specific intent to commit a felony is required to make one criminally responsible for burglary. It is not possible to outline every conceivable specific intent. Instead, specific criminal intents will be discussed throughout this book along with the other elements of the offenses for which a specific criminal intent is required.

A person bears *criminal responsibility* if he is blameworthy enough to deserve being punished for unlawful behavior. A person bears criminal responsibility only for conduct for which he has been proven to deserve blame. For this reason, some people who are factually guilty of illegal conduct do not bear criminal responsibility. For example, some people are presumed by law to be unable to possess a criminal intent because of their youth or mental incapacity. Others who may participate in unlawful conduct may not be blamed because the conduct is justified by law or by emergency. A person who possesses a *general* criminal intent when he participates in conduct that constitutes a crime only when accompanied by a *specific* criminal intent may not be blamed for that conduct. (In this situation, however, the individual may be blamed for a lesser offense that requires only a general and not a specific criminal intent.) Criminal responsibility is not a rigid concept; it is flexible and affected by different factors for different crimes. These factors will be noted individually when the major specific offenses are defined and discussed in later chapters.

Imputed Criminal Intent

Criminal intent for particular conduct may be *imputed* to an individual even though he possessed a lower degree of criminal intent at the time when he began participation in unlawful conduct. Thus, for example, a person who participates in a bank robbery intending to steal money without hurting anyone may bear criminal responsibility for murder if in fact someone dies during the holdup. This may be true whether or not the offender himself causes the death of the victim. One offender may bear criminal responsibility for the conduct of an associate or cohort during a criminal episode in which both participate. On the contrary, criminal intent cannot be imputed to a person who did not possess any criminal intent at all, whether or not he participated in unlawful conduct. So, if two persons decide to hold up a bank and dupe a third person into driving a getaway car without telling the latter that a crime is to be committed, the latter would not bear criminal responsibility at all—for his own conduct or for that of the persons who deceived him—at least until the moment when he discovered the true purpose of the activity.

Imputed criminal intent is covered in three legal principles: (1) the felony-murder rule, (2) the misdemeanor-manslaughter rule, and (3) the doctrine of vicarious criminal responsibility.

The Felony-Murder Rule

In most states, the common-law felony-murder rule remains in full force and effect. This rule provides that whenever a person participates in a felony for which physical harm or death of any victim may be foreseen, then if any perpetrator of the crime causes the death of any victim, all perpetrators are considered to have intended the murder and will bear criminal responsibility for murder, in addition to criminal responsibility for the intended crime.

The purpose of the felony-murder rule is simple; it is designed to deter persons from committing violent crimes. The offender who risks harming or killing a victim by committing a violent crime cannot argue afterward that he did not intend to harm or kill anyone. To be criminally responsible under the felony-murder rule, a conspirator to a crime need not have been present during actual commission of the offense. Thus, the mastermind of a bank robbery may be criminally responsible for murder committed during the robbery by one of his co-conspirators, even if he (the mastermind) was hundreds of miles from the scene of the crime at the time of the robbery. A person who participates in the planning of a crime but who repudiates the plan and ceases to participate before actual commission of the crime may avoid criminal responsibility under the felony-murder rule. In a number of jurisdictions, such an ex-conspirator may then have a duty to report to the police that the crime may occur or to attempt in some other way to prevent the crime from taking place.

Under the felony-murder rule, traditionally, a participant in a crime may become criminally responsible only for harm caused directly by himself or by an accomplice. Thus, if a policeman shot at escaping robbers and by mistake killed an innocent bystander (or even one of the robbers), the robbers would not bear criminal responsibility for this killing under the felony-murder rule. Of course, robbers *would* be criminally responsible in the opposite situation—if one or more of them killed a bystander while trying to elude police. A weapon does not have to be used. An offender may become criminally responsible for murder under the felony-murder rule by hitting a bystander with his auto during a police chase during immediate flight from a holdup.

The Misdemeanor-Manslaughter Rule

As with the felony-murder rule, the misdemeanor-manslaughter rule remains in full force in many states. It is a counterpart to the felony-murder rule in nearly every respect. Under this legal doctrine, whenever a person participates in conduct constituting a misdemeanor for which physical harm or death of any victim may be foreseen, then if any perpetrator of the crime causes the death of any victim, all perpetrators are considered to have intended the death and will bear criminal responsibility for manslaughter (but not murder) in addition to responsibility for the contemplated crime.

Since manslaughter is a lesser included offense of murder, a person who causes another's death while perpetrating a felony may bear criminal responsibility for manslaughter or for murder (but not for both for the same offense), depending on the inclination of the jury. The reverse is not true, however. A person who causes another's death while perpetrating only a misdemeanor and not a felony cannot be considered to have intended to commit murder, but only to have intended to commit manslaughter.

Vicarious Criminal Responsibility

The doctrine of vicarious criminal responsibility has emerged in several states, particularly California, to fill the gap that existed traditionally under the felony-murder and misdemeanor-manslaughter rules. Under either of those rules, a criminal offender would not bear criminal responsibility for harm caused by anyone other than himself or a co-participant in a crime. Thus, a situation in which a policeman shoots an innocent bystander by mistake would not be covered by those rules. This situation is covered under the doctrine of vicarious criminal responsibility, which makes the perpetrator of a crime responsible for *any* harm directly resulting from the crime.

Under this doctrine, the person who causes another's death does not have to be a policeman. For instance, the owner of a liquor store that is being held up may shoot at one of the robbers but hit and kill an innocent customer in the store. Or a private citizen might chase after armed assailants on foot or in an automobile and during the chase kill himself or a bystander. These and similar circumstances may make an offender bear criminal responsibility vicariously—in other words, bear responsibility for an act performed by someone else. The offender is considered responsible for all harm caused to anyone during the progress of a violent crime and during its immediate aftermath. In addition, unlike felony-murder and misdemeanor-manslaughter, modern vicarious criminal responsibility statutes do not limit this imputed liability to situations in which death occurs. An offender may bear vicarious criminal responsibility if a policeman or a victim of crime or another person wounds but does not kill a third person. In this situation, of course, the vicarious responsibility would be for aggravated assault rather than for murder, unless the victim should die.

Under the doctrine of vicarious criminal responsibility (but not under either the felony-murder or misdemeanor-manslaughter rule), a participant in a violent crime may bear criminal responsibility for harm caused to a co-participant. He may be liable, for instance, if a policeman shoots a co-participant, whether or not the cohort is slain. One is not criminally responsible for harm caused by another to himself, however. It must be stressed that many states do not follow the doctrine of vicarious criminal responsibility.

Strict Liability

At common law, there could be no criminal responsibility at all without a coexistence of criminal conduct and criminal intent. However, criminal offenses exist today that are different from those known to the common law. Some of these recently defined offenses would be difficult to prove if on each occasion the offender's "evil state of mind" had to be shown. Moreover, some of these offenses are viewed as being potentially so serious that the offender should have to bear criminal responsibility even in the absence of such a state of mind.

Confusion existed for a number of years over the constitutionality of "strict liability" statutes. The U.S. Supreme Court resolved this confusion in 1952 in the case of *Morissette* v. *United States.*[1] In that case, the Supreme Court held unanimously that "strict liability" is constitutional for certain offenses, particularly for those that were unknown to the common law. In this way, the Court avoided a confrontation with traditional principles of law and spoke in the context of new principles that might be appropriate in a new age. The *Morissette* case may be one of the most important decisions ever handed down by the Supreme Court.

Despite the importance of *Morissette,* the case is not well known and some explanation of its scope and meaning is necessary for a complete understanding of criminal responsibility in general and of strict liability in particular. The Supreme Court spoke of "public welfare offenses" as being the likely targets of strict liability and defined the offenses that the justices believed should fall within this category of crimes. After the *Morissette* decision, some but not all of these public welfare offenses became known as "regulatory offenses."

Almost all the offenses for which the principle of criminal intent has been abandoned are crimes that, if they had existed at common law, would have been viewed as *mala prohibita* rather than as *mala in se.* As explained in Chapter 2, crimes that are *mala prohibita* are those that are believed to be crimes because they are prohibited by law, not because the acts are wrong in themselves. In addition, offenses considered *mala prohibita* are ordinarily punished with light rather than severe penalties—often by fine rather than by imprisonment. Certainly one purpose that seems to have been on the minds of Supreme Court justices in *Morissette* and of legislators when statutes of this sort were enacted is that of deterrence. The offenses for which strict liability may be imposed are those that are preventable as a rule through due care and attentiveness. What is more important, these offenses are likely to result in harm to the public generally (as opposed to one victim alone) if they occur.

While it is difficult to define the boundaries within which "strict liability" or "regulatory" offenses fall, several different types of such offenses can easily be identified. As listed in Chapter 1, these include (1) illegal sales of intoxicating liquor, (2) sales of impure or adulterated food or drugs, (3) sales of misbranded articles, (4) violations of antinarcotic acts, (5) criminal nuisances, (6) violations of traffic regulations, (7) violations of motor vehicle laws, and (8) violations of general police regulations for the safety, health, and well-being of the community.

For example, health and safety laws include a wide variety of state statutes and local ordinances, some of which overlap. In most communities, for instance, one or more laws prohibit the dumping of garbage anywhere except at designated locations and under specified conditions. Other laws restrict the places where tobacco smoking is permitted. Others prescribe the kinds of materials that must be used in order to ensure the safe construction of buildings. Still other rules require the construction and maintenance of fire escapes on apartment or office buildings, elevator inspections in public buildings, proper ventilation of lavatories. These laws protect the public generally rather than protecting just a few citizens. Disregarding these regulations intentionally or unintentionally may subject the violator to a penalty.

Motor vehicle laws, too, are designed to protect the public at large. Whether one commits a "moving violation" or simply fails to put the required change in a parking meter, his intent at the time is unimportant under the *Morissette* decision and in current legal thought. Similarly, a person who fails to obey leash laws and permits his dog or other animal to trespass on land he does not own may incur a penalty at law regardless of his state of mind at the time. Leash laws are examples of numerous antinuisance regulations. To prevent the public from being annoyed, loud noises may be prohibited in residential neighborhoods or in quiet zones near hospitals. Zoning ordinances may restrict the style of building that may be erected in a given area of a community in order to protect property values.

Strict liability statutes may provide the most severe penalties when dangerous commodities are mislabeled or sold in violation of the law. For several years, toddlers clothing had to be fireproofed and labeled as such to be sold. Food stores may be required to state the date after which perishable foods should not be purchased. Prescription drugs in particular must be labeled properly by the pharmacist and, needless to say, a pharmacist is held strictly liable for dispensing those drugs and only those drugs that have been authorized by a physician. Beer and hard alcohol may not be sold legally to persons under the age of majority (whether this is eighteen or twenty-one).

Strict liability is not as rigid a concept as it may appear to be. Circumstances surrounding the offensive event will as a rule be considered in determining the presence or absence of criminal responsibility and in assessing the appropriate punishment to be imposed. For example, the storekeeper who is duped by a minor who presents false identification of his age may be less culpable than another storekeeper who sells alcohol to a minor knowing the true age of the purchaser. The purpose of strict liability statutes is to urge persons handling dangerous or potentially dangerous items to be especially careful. Whether the item is an automobile, a lethal drug, a cigarette, or some other commodity that may be harmful if abused, care is necessary to avoid harm to others. In the limited situations to which strict liability principles apply, simply causing harm may be sufficient to create criminal responsibility, even in the absence of malice, willfulness, recklessness, or negligence on the part of the person who has caused the harm.

CHAPTER 4

Defenses to Criminal Responsibility

Defenses are legal excuses for criminal acts or omissions for which a person would bear criminal responsibility if no defense were shown. It is never necessary for anyone to set forth a defense, however, unless he has been formally accused of a crime, and even if accused, he is presumed innocent until proven guilty. A person becomes formally accused of a crime only when he is given written notice of the accusation in accordance with state or federal law. This written notice accusing a person of committing a crime is known as a criminal *charge*.

In many states, a person cannot be charged with a felony except through a grand jury *indictment*. An indictment is a written document, signed under oath by citizens selected to sit on the grand jury, expressing their belief that there is *probable cause* to believe the person so accused may have committed the crime that is charged. In other states, a person may be charged with committing

41

a crime through a document signed under oath by a district attorney, a police officer, or a complaining witness. This document may be known as an accusatory instrument, complaint or information.

Once a person is formally charged with a crime, he must be taken before a judge or some other judicial officer as soon as possible and given the opportunity either to admit or to deny the charge against him. This procedure is called an *arraignment*. At his arraignment, a person who is charged may admit criminal responsibility for the offense by pleading *guilty*. Or, by pleading *not guilty*, a person denies criminal responsibility for the offense and maintains his innocence. A person who remains silent and refuses to plead either guilty or not guilty is considered by law to plead not guilty.

Obviously, a person who pleads guilty to a criminal charge cannot raise a defense for his conduct, since he admits full criminal responsibility for the offense with which he is charged. On the other hand, a person who pleads *not* guilty to a criminal charge is under no obligation to raise a defense, either, unless he so chooses. Whether or not he raises a defense, a person who pleads not guilty to a criminal charge is entitled to a *trial*. Every person who is charged with a serious offense is entitled to a trial by jury under the laws of every state. A person may waive (give up) his right to a jury trial and choose to be tried before a judge sitting without a jury, however.

At his trial, a person who is charged with a crime becomes a *defendant*, since he is defending his innocence against the accusation that he committed a crime. A defendant does not have to prove his innocence at the trial. Instead, the state has the burden of proving the defendant guilty of criminal responsibility beyond a reasonable doubt.

A defendant who did not commit any element of the offense for which he is charged may not need to raise any defense at all, since the state will be unable to prove him guilty. Similarly, a defendant who committed some but not all of the elements required to constitute a particular criminal offense may not need to raise a defense, either. The state must prove the defendant guilty of each and every element of the offense for which he is charged. Only in this way can the defendant be *convicted* of, or determined to bear criminal responsibility for, the crime he denied committing. If the state does not prove the defendant guilty, he is *acquitted,* or cleared of the charge.

By raising one or more *defenses* at the time of his trial, a defendant may avoid being determined criminally responsible for an offense, even though he did commit the act or the omission that constitutes the crime. As defined earlier, defenses are legal excuses for criminal acts or omissions for which a person would bear criminal responsibility if no defense were shown.

A person who is on trial may raise one or many defenses. The major defenses, which will be discussed in this chapter, can be grouped into three categories: (1) defenses based on the absence of the defendant's *criminal capacity,* (2) defenses based on the absence of the defendant's *criminal culpability,* and (3) defenses based on *legal exemptions.*

Absence of Criminal Capacity

A person who has been charged with committing a crime may raise one or more defenses based on the absence of criminal capacity in order to show that he was unable to possess a criminal intent at the moment he committed an act or an omission that constitutes a crime. The word *capacity* is used in criminal law to describe the *mental ability* of a person to formulate (put together or make up) a criminal intent.

As earlier chapters explained, a person cannot bear any kind of criminal responsibility for most crimes unless he possesses a criminal intent at the moment he commits the criminal act or omission. Therefore, a person who lacks full criminal capacity when he commits a criminal act or omission cannot be criminally responsible for his conduct. This remains true even if the person regains full criminal capacity after the crime.

Criminal capacity is measured differently from state to state. It may be measured according to whether the person (1) knows the difference between right and wrong, (2) understands the nature and consequences of his actions, or (3) realizes what kinds of conduct are prohibited by the criminal laws.

By raising a defense based on the absence of criminal capacity, a person who is accused of a crime admits implicitly (by implication) that he committed the act or omission necessary to constitute the crime. He simply denies that he possessed the mental ability to formulate a criminal intent at the time the crime took place.

Infancy, insanity, and *involuntary intoxication* are complete defenses to criminal responsibility for any offense. One who is an infant, or who is insane, or who is involuntarily intoxicated cannot formulate either a general or a specific criminal intent (see Chapter 3). Voluntary intoxication is a defense to criminal responsibility only for offenses that require a specific criminal intent. It is no defense to responsibility for offenses that require only a general criminal intent. Thus, a person who has voluntarily become intoxicated cannot formulate a specific criminal intent, but his general criminal intent is implied from his voluntary act of becoming intoxicated.

Infancy

The defense of infancy is based on a child's inability to formulate a criminal intent of any kind. If successfully demonstrated, infancy is a complete defense to criminal responsibility for any offense. This means that no child can bear criminal responsibility for conduct that he commits during his infancy. The age of infancy varies slightly from state to state under certain conditions.

Infants under Age Seven. In all states, an infant of either sex who is not yet seven years old is considered to lack the mental capacity to possess a criminal intent under any conditions. It does not matter whether a child this young may be more physically "mature" than other children of the same age. Children under seven years of age are presumed not to have reached the age of reason. Therefore, they are not regarded as being rational human beings who should be responsible for their behavior.

Although a child who is under seven years old cannot bear criminal responsibility for his misconduct, he may be made a ward of the court and placed in a juvenile detention facility for his own benefit and protection. When a court sends a child to a juvenile facility, its objective is to place the child under constant supervision rather than to punish the child.

Children between Ages Seven and Fourteen. In most states, a child of either sex who has not reached fourteen years of age is considered to lack the mental capacity to possess a criminal intent under any conditions. Therefore, even children between the ages of seven and fourteen cannot be criminally responsible for their misconduct in these states.

In some states, however, a person over seven years of age is considered old enough to formulate a criminal intent under certain limited conditions. A child within this age range may be considered old enough to possess full mental capacity if the child can be shown to be more "mature" than the average child of the same age. "Maturity" may be determined by the child's ability to distinguish right from wrong or to understand the results of his conduct.

Since the creation of juvenile delinquency statutes in most states, few children under fourteen years of age have been made criminally responsible for their behavior. In medieval England, children of this age were less fortunate—history has recorded the hanging of an eight-year-old boy and the burning of a thirteen-year-old girl.

Children over Age Fourteen. Most states presume that a child who is fourteen years of age or older should know the difference between right and wrong and should understand the nature and consequences of his actions. Therefore, in most states a child of this age is considered to possess the full capacity to formulate a criminal intent. In these states, a child over age fourteen will have difficulty in successfully raising infancy as a defense to criminal responsibility. Some states do permit a child who is fourteen or fifteen years old to raise this defense, however, when he can be shown to be "immature" in comparison with other children of the same age.

There is a difference between being an infant and being a minor. A person does not usually acquire all the rights of an adult until he becomes eighteen years old. Thus, one may not be permitted to drink or to vote until his eighteenth birthday. Still, a person older than age fourteen but younger than age eighteen may be a minor without being an infant. A minor who is not an infant may still bear criminal responsibility for his criminal acts or omissions.

As a rule, however, a child between the ages of fourteen and eighteen will be charged with and tried for juvenile delinquency rather than a criminal offense if he is accused of committing an act or omission constituting a crime.

Insanity

The defense of insanity is based on a person's mental inability to formulate a criminal intent. If successfully shown, insanity is a complete defense to criminal responsibility for any offense. In this respect, insanity as a defense is similar to infancy as a defense. The defense of infancy depends on the child's age at the time the crime he is accused of committing took place. The defense of insanity has nothing to do with one's age. It depends on one's mental ability as measured by tests that vary from state to state. In no state is a person criminally responsible for conduct he committed while he was insane. This is true even if the person recovers sanity after committing a criminal act or omission.

Insanity is much different from mental illness. One who is insane certainly is also mentally ill, but many people who are mentally ill are not insane. The definition of mental illness varies considerably from state to state. To be mentally ill, a person must generally be in need of psychiatric treatment and supervision because he cannot care for himself adequately and therefore may be a danger either to himself or to others. Mental illness by itself is never a defense to criminal responsibility.

It is more difficult to show that a person is insane than to show that he is mentally ill. All persons are presumed by law to be sane, and all adult persons are presumed by law to possess a sufficient degree of reason to be responsible for their behavior. Any person who is charged with a crime may raise insanity as a defense to criminal responsibility for his conduct. This defense will be successful only when supported by sufficient evidence, and several legal tests are used for determining insanity as a defense. Each of the major tests deserves attention.

The M'Naghten Rule. One of the most far-reaching rules for determining insanity as a defense to criminal responsibility was laid down by England's House of Lords in M'Naghten's Case (1843) (10 Cl. & F 200, & Eng. Rep. 718) In this decision, which became known as the M'Naghten rule, England's court of last resort decided that:

> . . . to establish a defense on the ground of insanity it must be clearly proved, that, at the time of the committing of the act, the party accused was labouring under such a defect of reason from disease of the mind,

as not to know the nature and quality of the act he was doing; or, if he did know it, that he did not know he was doing what was wrong.

Under the M'Naghten rule, a defendant must show that, at the time of his criminal conduct, he lacked "a sufficient degree of reason to know that he was doing an act that was wrong."

The M'Naghten rule has been accepted and adopted in every state as a valid test for determining insanity. Some of these states recognize the M'Naghten rule as the *only* valid test for determining insanity. In states where M'Naghten is the only recognized test for insanity, the defense of insanity will not be successful unless the defendant can show either (1) that he did not know what he was doing when he committed the crime, or (2) that he did not know that what he was doing was wrong at the time he committed the crime.

The Irresistible Impulse Test. In every state, a person who does not know the difference between right and wrong is considered insane. In some states, a person may be considered insane even though he does know the difference between right and wrong. Some of these states follow what is known as the "irresistible impulse test" for determining insanity as a defense to criminal responsibility.

Under the irresistible impulse test, a person is considered to have been insane at the time he committed a criminal act or omission if he felt compelled to accomplish the act or omission because of an impulse that he was powerless to control. An impulse is a temporary loss of a person's self-control or ability to reason. It has been described as an "inner-springing force" that cannot be overcome by the individual despite his attempts to subdue it. To support the defense of insanity under the irresistible impulse test, the defendant must have been unable, rather than merely unwilling, to control his conduct at the time of his criminal act or omission.

An example of an irresistible impulse is an epileptic seizure, during which a person cannot control the movements of his body. A criminal act or omission is seldom committed during an epileptic seizure, however. States that use this test for insanity recognize that an irresistible impulse akin to an epileptic seizure may be caused by intense anger, hatred, jealousy, or passion. Ordinary spells of such emotions will not support the defense of insanity under the irresistible impulse test, however. The defendant must be totally unable to control these feelings and his resulting behavior.

The irresistible impulse test has been criticized as being misleading, because it suggests that a crime must be committed under a sudden, explosive fit to be committed impulsively. Psychiatrists have argued that a person's behavior may be calculated and planned, rather than sudden and explosive, but still be impulsive. Conduct that is committed as the result of excessive brooding and melancholy is not considered to be impulsive under the irresistible impulse test.

The Durham Rule. A more liberal test for determining legal insanity as a defense to criminal responsibility was announced by the U.S. Court of Appeals for the District of Columbia Circuit in the case of *Durham v. United States* 214 F.2d 862 (D.C. Cir. 1954). This test, known as the Durham rule, has been adopted in only one state, Maine. Even the U.S. Court of Appeals for the District of Columbia has abandoned the Durham rule in the case of *United States v. Brawner,* 471 F.2d 969 (D.C. Cir. 1972).

Under the Durham rule, a person may successfully raise the defense of insanity if his criminal act or omission can be shown to have been the "product" of either mental disease or mental defect. Hence, under this test, it is important to understand the meaning of mental disease, mental defect, and the word *product.*

Any abnormal condition of the mind that substantially affects mental or emotional processes and that substantially impairs behavioral control may constitute a mental condition. A mental condition may be either a disease or a defect. A mental *disease* under the Durham rule is a condition that is considered capable of either improving or deteriorating. A mental *defect* is a condition that is not considered capable of improving or deteriorating. A mental disease or defect may have been inherited or caused by injury. A mental defect may have been caused in the same way or by some physical or mental disease.

The federal court that created the Durham rule was dissatisfied with both the M'Naghten rule and the irresistible impulse test. This court believed that a person might know the difference between right and wrong and might be able to control his impulses, yet still might be insane. The chief advantage of the Durham rule is that it does not require a jury to rely on specific mental properties, such as "impulse" or "ability" to distinguish right from wrong. Instead, this test permits a jury to consider a defendant's *total* emotional state at the time of his criminal act or omission.

Psychiatrists feel that the Durham rule permits them to be honest and straightforward in their testimony. They do not feel compelled to "juggle" the facts in order to establish the insanity of a person whom they are convinced did not act on impulse and could distinguish right from wrong. This test takes into account brooding, reflecting, and melancholy as indicators of insanity.

Despite these obvious advantages, the Durham rule does have one serious deficiency. Under this test, a jury must decide whether the defendant's conduct was the "product" of mental disease or defect. However, the court that created the Durham rule did not define the meaning of *product* sufficiently. Each jury must define this word to its own satisfaction. This means that many juries will infer different meanings, and one jury may find a defendant "sane" while another jury finds another defendant "insane," even though both defendants had the same mental condition at the moment they committed the same crime. Lack of uniformity, therefore, makes this test unfairly applied from case to case.

The Model Penal Code Test. In 1953, the year before the Durham rule was announced, the American Law Institute (ALI) began an exhaustive study of criminal conduct. Part of this study was concerned with legal insanity as a defense to criminal responsibility. After nine years of research, ALI published the results of its study in the form of a Model Penal Code (Proposed Official Draft 1962). Section 4.01 of the Model Penal Code provides that:

> A person is not responsible for criminal conduct if at the time of such conduct as a result of mental disease or defect he lacks substantial capacity either to appreciate the wrongfulness of his conduct or to conform his conduct to the requirements of law.

The Model Penal Code test for determining insanity differs markedly from the previous tests. Other tests divide the human mind into at least three artificial compartments—the intellect, the will, and the emotions—and then concentrate on only one compartment. Hence, the M'Naghten rule concentrates on the intellect (ability to distinguish right from wrong). The irresistible impulse test concentrates on the will (powerlessness to control an impulse).

The Durham rule concentrates on emotions (brooding, reflecting, melancholy). On the contrary, the Model Penal Code test views the human mind as a unified entity and recognizes that mental disease or defect may impair its functioning in more than one way.

The Model Penal Code test for insanity recognizes that persons may be insane in various degrees. By using the phrase "substantial capacity," this test recognizes that not every incapacity is sufficient to justify avoidance of criminal responsibility. But total incapacity is not necessary, either. Thus, "substantial incapacity" is sufficient.

The Model Penal Code test is concerned with whether the defendant understands the moral, social, and legal reasons why his conduct is wrong, rather than whether he distinguishes right from wrong in the abstract. This test asks whether the defendant can understand or "appreciate the wrongfulness of his conduct," rather than measuring his knowledge of the nature of his act. This test looks at a defendant's ability "to conform his conduct to the requirements of law," rather than his "irresistible impulses."

Although the Model Penal Code test is not as rigid as either the M'Naghten rule or the irresistible impulse test, neither is it as vague as the Durham rule. The jury is not given the impossible task of measuring the precise cause of insanity. It is sufficient under the Model Penal Code test that the defendant's conduct occurred as a "result," rather than as the "product," of mental disease or defect. The plain language used in this test establishes a standard that can be more uniformly understood and followed by every jury. Hence, the Model Penal Code test decreases the likelihood that two persons who possess the same mental condition while committing the same crime will receive different verdicts by different juries.

The Model Penal Code test for determining insanity has been rejected in several states, and it has not yet been adopted word for word in any state. Several states, including Illinois and New York, have adopted modified versions of the Model Penal Code test through court decisions. Other states that are revising their criminal laws are debating adoption of a modified version of this test for insanity.

Intoxication

A person who is charged with committing a crime may raise the defense of intoxication to establish the absence of criminal capacity. A person becomes intoxicated when he has consumed a sufficient quantity of alcohol, a narcotic, or any other drug or substance to cause him to lose control over his will. Intoxication may cause a person to lose control over his body, his mind, or both. Intoxication affects a person's perception, certainty of thought, clarity of ideas, and muscular coordination. A person who is intoxicated lacks the ability to make a sound judgment, because his powers of reasoning and decision-making are impaired. For this reason, one who is intoxicated may not be capable of formulating a criminal intent under certain conditions.

When considering intoxication as a defense to criminal responsibility, it is important to distinguish between the defense of involuntary intoxication and that of voluntary intoxication. *Involuntary* intoxication is a complete defense to criminal responsibility for any offense that requires a criminal intent. This is true because the acts or omissions of an involuntarily intoxicated person are not the result of his choice; they are not voluntary. *Voluntary* intoxication is a defense to criminal responsibility only for an offense that requires a specific criminal intent. It is not a defense to criminal responsibility for an offense that requires only a general criminal intent, because the person who voluntarily becomes intoxicated does so through his own free choice.

Involuntary Intoxication. Involuntary intoxication is a complete defense to criminal responsibility for any offense that requires a criminal intent. It is usually a defense even to an offense that imposes strict liability (see Chapter 3), if the offense requires knowledgeable conduct, since one who is intoxicated does not really know what he is doing.

The condition of an involuntarily intoxicated person does not result from any misconduct on his part. One may become involuntarily intoxicated in several ways. An intoxicating substance may be forced down his throat or into his body in some other way by physical violence and without his consent. Or an intoxicating substance may be administered to him by deceit—if the nature of the substance is disguised, for example, and the person is tricked into consuming it. Or a person may consume an intoxicating substance by mistake, not realizing its identity or not realizing its potential effects. This unintentional consumption may be viewed as producing involuntary intoxication.

Recently, some courts have considered whether a chronic alcoholic or a dependent drug addict becomes intoxicated voluntarily or involuntarily. It can be argued that such a person becomes intoxicated through compulsion rather than by free choice. The U.S. Court of Appeals for the District of Columbia Circuit has held that chronic alcoholism may constitute a defense to criminal responsibility for an offense such as public intoxication.[1] This was the court that created the Durham rule for determining insanity. Other federal courts have reached the opposite conclusion. No court has recognized intoxication as being involuntary unless the intoxicating substance is consumed by force, by fraud, or by mistake.

Voluntary Intoxication. Voluntary intoxication is a defense to criminal responsibility for most offenses that require a *specific* criminal intent, such as an intent to steal, defraud, rob, rape, or kill. It may not be a defense to responsibility for an offense for which *recklessness* is considered to constitute criminal intent. Voluntary intoxication is never a defense to criminal responsibility for an offense that requires only a general criminal intent, since a general criminal intent requires only that the offender's act or omission be voluntary. A person who becomes intoxicated other than by force, fraud, or mistake is considered to become intoxicated through his own free choice.

When a person is actually intoxicated, he is not considered, under law, to be mentally capable of formulating a criminal plan or scheme. An intoxicated person does not retain sufficient mental coordination to bear in mind a particular objective, since he loses his will power. It does not matter whether one becomes intoxicated voluntarily or involuntarily if the crime he commits requires concentration on a particular objective. Thus, even voluntary intoxication is a defense to criminal responsibility for offenses that require a specific plan or design.

Difficulty may arise when a person formulates a specific criminal intent while he is sober, then drinks to reinforce his nerve. Some courts have held that one who has already formulated a specific criminal intent before he becomes intoxicated may still possess this intent after he becomes intoxicated. Thus, an intoxicated person may be considered mentally capable of *carrying out* a criminal plan, design, or scheme that he has formulated before becoming intoxicated. Such court decisions seem to contradict the principle that criminal intent must be possessed by the offender at the very moment of his act or omission in order to make him criminally responsible.

On the other hand, one should not be permitted to escape criminal responsibility by voluntarily consuming a large quantity of an intoxicating substance as he is about to carry out a criminal plan. Someone who does this, however, would ordinarily carry out his plan before feeling the effects of intoxication. It can be argued that a person who is actually intoxicated, rather than pretending to be intoxicated, is not mentally capable either of *formulating* a criminal plan or of *carrying out* a criminal plan that he formulated before becoming intoxicated, except by coincidence.

Absence of Criminal Culpability

A person who has been charged with committing a crime may raise one or more defenses based on the absence of criminal *culpability,* trying to show that he should not be *blamed* for an act or an omission that constitutes a crime. Blame is an essential element of criminal responsibility. A person can be blamed for his conduct only when it is wrongful. Conduct is wrongful when a person who commits a criminal act or omission means to do what he knows is bad rather than what he reasonably believes to be good or at least necessary under existing circumstances.

The circumstances surrounding an act or an omission will often determine whether the conduct is blameworthy. Certain conduct is usually regarded as being wrongful and bad in itself. Examples are murder, manslaughter, rape, sodomy, robbery, kidnapping, and burglary. Yet even conduct that is usually bad may be right—or the only thing possible to do—under certain conditions. As a rule, the conditions that make a person blameless for a criminal act or omission are very limited. These conditions seldom occur, but when they do, a person may commit a criminal act or omission without bearing criminal responsibility.

By raising a defense based on the absence of criminal culpability, a person who is accused of committing a crime admits by implication that he committed the act or omission necessary to constitute the crime. He simply denies that his conduct was wrongful and asks that he not be blamed for it. A person's intent at the moment he acts or fails to act determines whether he may be blamed for the conduct. One's intent may be influenced by natural or human events, however.

Each of the defenses based on the absence of criminal culpability, if properly shown, is a defense to criminal responsibility for most offenses. Some of the defenses do not justify or excuse the killing of another human being, however.

A person who is charged with committing a crime may set forth one or more defenses based on the absence of culpability, either instead of or in addition to raising a defense based on the absence of criminal capacity. One does not generally raise a defense relating to his culpability, however, unless he cannot successfully raise a defense relating to his capacity. Therefore, one who does raise a defense relating to the absence of criminal culpability is usually a sane adult who was not intoxicated at the time his act or omission took place.

Defenses that Justify Conduct

A person may raise one or more defenses based on the absence of criminal culpability in order to justify his conduct. One's conduct is justified when he has a *legal privilege* that permits him to act or fail to act. Thus, a justification is a legal reason, rather than just a moral excuse, for the fact that a person is not to be blamed for his conduct.

Public Duty. The "public duty" defense usually arises in connection with some form of law enforcement. Any person is legally privileged to use force, for example, either to prevent the commission of a crime that is about to occur, or to prevent the completion of a crime that is being committed. This defense is valid only when the person using the force reasonably believes that a crime is about to be committed or is being committed. Moreover, this defense is valid only to the extent that the degree of force used is reasonable under the circumstances. One is never privileged to use excessive force. Force is excessive when it is greater than the amount required to terminate the criminal act or omission.

As the degree of force must be reasonable, one is not justified in using *deadly* force except to prevent the commission of a felony that is dangerous to human life. One uses deadly force when he kills another person, but one does not have to kill another to use deadly force. Deadly force is used whenever a person makes use of a deadly weapon or other instrument that has the capability of killing a person. One is not privileged to use deadly force to prevent all felonies, since not all felonies are dangerous to human life. Only felonies involving serious violence, such as murder, voluntary manslaughter, forcible rape, forcible sodomy, kidnapping, mayhem, and arson are ordinarily considered dangerous to human life. Seldom is a person privileged to use deadly force to prevent the commission or completion of a felony that is not dangerous to human life. One is never justified in using deadly force to prevent the commission or completion of a misdemeanor.

A police officer, or any person acting on the direction of a police officer, is justified in using reasonable force either to *make a lawful arrest* or to *prevent the escape* of a person who has been lawfully arrested. The arrest of a person is lawful only when the person who makes the arrest has legal authority to do so.

The authority to make an arrest is regulated by statute in nearly every state. As a general rule, a police officer is authorized to make an arrest (1) pursuant to an arrest warrant, or (2) without a warrant when he has reasonable grounds to believe the person he arrests is committing, has just committed, or is about to commit a felony, or (3) without a warrant for any offense committed in his presence. Normally, a private citizen who does not act on the direction of a police officer may lawfully arrest another person only for committing an offense in his presence.

In most states, a police officer or anyone acting on the directions of an officer may use deadly force under certain conditions to subdue a person who resists arrest, but only when the arrest is lawful to begin with. Deadly force is justified only when the person making the arrest reasonably believes that deadly force is necessary to prevent serious bodily harm from being inflicted on himself or someone else by the person being arrested.

In many states, a police officer or anyone acting on the direction of an officer may use deadly force under certain conditions to subdue a person who is fleeing from a lawful arrest. Deadly force usually may be used only to subdue a person fleeing from arrest for a felony and not to subdue one who flees from arrest for a misdemeanor.

Any person who acts on the direction of a police officer has the same authority as the officer himself to make an arrest or to prevent the escape of a person who has been arrested. In most states, a private citizen is required by law to respond to any lawful request by a police officer for assistance. Since the person whose help the officer requests may not delay to inquire about the officer's authority, his good faith assistance may be justified even though the officer exceeds his own authority.

A public official who acts pursuant to a lawful court order is also privileged to use such force as may be required to carry out the court order. Thus, a police officer or a correctional officer may use force to keep a prisoner in custody pursuant to law or to prevent a prisoner from escaping. Similarly, an executioner who kills a condemned prisoner pursuant to a lawful death sentence is privileged to do so. A public official who acts pursuant to a valid court order is justified in using reasonable force to carry out the order, even if the court order turns out to be invalid or an underlying statute turns out to be unconstitutional. The official may not be justified in carrying out a court order that he has reason to believe is defective or otherwise invalid, however.

A soldier, sailor, or other member of the armed forces or of the National Guard during an emergency has a duty to obey and to carry out all lawful orders that are given to him. Normally, a serviceman is justified in carrying out the orders given to him by a superior officer, unless an order is clearly unlawful. An order is clearly unlawful when it would violate the Geneva Convention rules or the traditional rules and usages of war. A soldier is not privileged to carry out a clearly unlawful order. If he does and thereby commits a criminal act or omission, he cannot set forth his public duty as a defense to criminal responsibility, since his conduct is not justified.

Self-Defense. A person who is physically attacked or otherwise threatened with immediate bodily harm by another person may use reasonable force to defend himself from danger. The degree of force one is privileged to use depends on the degree of danger that threatens him. Thus, a person must use only nondeadly force, unless he is threatened with immediate death or with immediate serious bodily harm. Then he is privileged to use deadly force in self-defense. As a rule, one is justified in using deadly force only when threatened with a deadly weapon.

One is never justified in using force to defend himself unless he honestly believes he is in danger of *immediate* bodily harm. Unless the harm is immediately threatened, one has an obligation to prevent the harm from occurring without violence. When, for example, a person is threatened with bodily harm that will take place in the distant future, he should seek police protection.

The defense of self-defense does not generally apply to a person who provoked another into threatening him with immediate bodily harm. However, even the aggressor in a fight may withdraw from the encounter by notifying his opponent of his withdrawal. After that, the person who was initially the aggressor may use reasonable force to defend himself from his opponent's retaliation. In addition, one who starts a fight using only his fists or a nondeadly weapon may use reasonable force to defend himself from an attack in which his opponent picks up a deadly weapon. This action by the initial aggressor is justifiable, since his opponent is not justified in using deadly force to repel nondeadly force.

Whenever a person is threatened with nondeadly force, he must withdraw or retreat as far as possible before he is privileged to use force in self-defense. This means that a person who is attacked or threatened with bodily harm is not justified in using force against the aggressor if he can safely run away. A police officer, however, is not under an obligation to retreat when he is attacked or threatened with force while making a lawful arrest.

In many states, even a private citizen is not required to retreat before using force to defend himself from a *deadly* attack. This general rule remains true even when the person defending himself fails to retreat before using deadly force to repel a deadly attack. Although a person who starts a fight using nondeadly force is privileged to defend himself from his opponent's use of deadly force, a person who was once the aggressor must retreat as far as possible before using deadly force against his opponent.

Difficulty often arises with respect to a person's right to defend himself from an unlawful arrest. Of course, no person has any right to use force to prevent a lawful arrest. In most states, a person is privileged to use reasonable but nondeadly force to prevent himself from being unlawfully arrested, provided the arrest is in fact unlawful. In most states, on the other hand, one is not privileged to use deadly force to prevent himself from being arrested, as long as he has reason to believe the person making the arrest intends to take him into custody without doing him any bodily harm. In states that follow the Model Penal Code, a person is not justified in using force of any kind to resist an unlawful arrest when he knows the person making the arrest is a police officer. Indeed, one who is unlawfully arrested may resort to several legal remedies in recourse, and should not need to use violence.

Defense of Another Person. As a rule, a person is privileged to use force in the defense of another person when he reasonably believes that force is necessary to prevent immediate bodily harm to the other person. As in self-defense, the degree of force used must be reasonable under the circumstances, depending on the degree of harm that appears to be threatened. Use of deadly force is reasonable only when the person being rescued appears to the defender to be in danger of immediate death or immediate serious bodily harm.

To be justifed in using any force in the defense of another person, one must honestly believe that this other person is in immediate danger of bodily harm. The appearance of immediate danger to the rescuer is essential. Even if the danger turns out not to have been as imminent as the rescuer believed it to be, the rescuer is still justified in the use of reasonable force, provided he honestly perceived the danger as being immediate.

Some states have limited the privilege to use force in defense of another person. In these states, by statute, one may be justified in using force to defend another person only when the other person is a close relative or someone else for whose safety the rescuer is responsible.

Difficulty arises when the person who appears to be in danger of immediate bodily harm is actually being arrested pursuant to law. Traditionally, many courts have held that one who uses force to defend another person has no greater right to use force than the person being rescued possesses himself. Under this view, a person would not be justified in using force to prevent another from being lawfully arrested, even when the rescuer honestly but erroneously believes the person whom he tries to rescue to be in immediate danger of unlawful bodily harm. In states where criminal laws have been revised recently, this traditional view has been changed by statute. The modern view, therefore, is that a person is privileged to use reasonable force to defend another person from what appears to him to be an unlawful danger of immediate bodily harm.

Defense of Property. A person is privileged to use reasonable force to protect property that he owns or for which he is responsible. The defense of one's property may be accompanied by reasonable force only when force is necessary, however. As a general rule, no force is reasonable if a person can protect his property by requesting or demanding verbally that the person who threatens to harm his property not do so.

Deadly force is justified in defense of one's property only under very limited conditions. In general, deadly force is not reasonable unless the interference with one's property is accompanied by a threat of deadly force. When one's property is threatened by an invasion of the dwelling or house that he occupies, however, use of deadly force may be justified even though the invading person does not actually threaten deadly force. One may use deadly force against someone who unlawfully enters his dwelling, since a person whose dwelling is invaded may reasonably believe that the intruder might cause serious bodily harm to anyone inside the dwelling should he be discovered and identified.

Not every entry to another person's dwelling is unlawful. Someone might enter another's house to evict the occupant, for example, and this entry might be lawful if the intruder has a right to evict the occupant. The Model Penal Code takes the position that, in this situation, deadly force may be used when "the person against whom the force is used is attempting to dispossess him [the occupant] of his dwelling otherwise than under a claim of right to its possession." Thus, a tenant would not be justified in using deadly force to prevent his landlord from evicting him, but he might be justified in using deadly force to prevent someone who has no legitimate right to the premises from evicting him.

Although a person may be privileged to use deadly force in order to resist intrusion to his dwelling, he would not be justified in using deadly force to reenter premises from which he has been dispossessed, except in "hot pursuit." Thus, one might be privileged to use deadly force to reenter his house immediately after he has been thrown out of it, but not after considerable time has elapsed.

A person is not privileged to use deadly force merely to prevent his property from being stolen, except when the property lies within his dwelling, and even then use of deadly force to protect property is prohibited in many states under recent court decisions. For this reason, one is not justified in erecting a spring-gun or other mechanical device in his store or barn, for example, to kill someone who might enter the building. In most states, one would be justified in using a mechanical device to create force only to the extent that he would be privileged to use force in person if he were present. The Model Penal Code rejects this view and maintains that a person is never justified in setting a *deadly* mantrap. The danger of such a device is obvious. It may kill or seriously injure an innocent person who does not threaten to use deadly force or any force at all.

Traditionally, a person was not privileged to recapture property that was stolen by using force against the thief. Indeed, a person whose property has been stolen may obtain the return of his property through legal proceedings, if he knows who the thief is and where the property is located. The Model Penal Code recommends, however, that a person should be privileged to recover by reasonable but nondeadly force any tangible and movable property that he believes has been stolen from him.

A person is not privileged to recapture or even to defend property that he neither owns nor is responsible for, however. The use of even the slightest amount of force is unjustified, therefore, when one begins to recapture or defend property belonging to someone else without any authority from its owner. One who has been hired to guard property, such as a security guard, is justified in defending his employer's property as if it were his own.

Consent. Many acts or omissions constitute a crime only when done without the consent (agreement) of the victim—the individual who is harmed. When an element of a criminal act requires that it be done without the consent of the victim, then a person who commits the act with the victim's consent does not bear criminal responsibility. He is privileged, since the victim has agreed to the act by expressing consent.

A person who owns property can usually give his consent to let anything happen to the property. Thus, he can agree to permit someone else to take the property away from him, damage it, or destroy it. Only under a few limited circumstances, however, can a person validly consent to letting his body be harmed. While the victim's consent is usually a defense to criminal responsibility for an offense involving harm to property, it is seldom a defense for an offense involving harm to the victim's body.

Normally, a person has the legal right to consent to being touched, but he has no legal right to consent to being permanently harmed. Similarly, one has no legal right to consent to being killed. A female person who has reached the "age of consent" has a legal right to consent to sexual intercourse, but one who has not reached the minimum age of consent has not. No person has the right to consent to purchasing unlabeled or adulterated food or drugs. When the victim of an act or an omission that constitutes a crime gives his or her "consent" without having a legal right to do so, the "consent" is not valid. An invalid consent is never a defense to criminal responsibility.

Custodial Authority. Ancient authority recognized the right of a husband to discipline his wife physically in order to command her obedience to him. Later in the common law, however, this right disappeared, and it does not exist today in any state. Spouse beating is treated as a family law matter rather than as a crime in some states, however.

In every state, either parent of a minor child is privileged to discipline the child physically in order to correct the child's misbehavior. This privilege is normally extended to a legal guardian, a schoolteacher, and other persons who have temporary or permanent custody of a child, *in loco parentis*. In some states, by statute, the right of a schoolteacher to use corporal punishment may be limited, or such punishment may be prohibited.

Whenever a child is disciplined, the punishment must be moderate and the child cannot be abused. Neither a parent nor any other custodian of a child is justified in using excessive physical force to discipline a child. Force is considered to be excessive when it results in death or serious bodily injury to the child.

At common law, the father's right to discipline his child was extended to an employer. Today, an employer has no such privilege unless it is expressly given to him by a child's parent. Certain persons other than parents and guardians of children may be privileged to use physical force on another person to promote the victim's welfare. The guardian or any person in charge of supervising a mentally incompetent person may use reasonable force to safeguard the patient, to prevent the patient's misconduct, or to maintain discipline in an institution.

By statute in many states, a person who is in charge of a public conveyance (a means of transportation) or of any place where the public is assembled may use such force as is necessary to maintain order. Thus, the captain of a ship, the pilot of an airplane, the conductor on a train, or a bus driver may be privileged to use physical force on an unruly passenger to remove the passenger from the conveyance. This privilege extends to anyone acting on the direction of such a person in authority.

Defenses that Excuse Conduct

Other defenses based on the absence of criminal culpability are those that excuse rather than justify conduct. Under certain conditions, one's conduct may be excused when he acts or fails to act under a compelling force of coercion, duress, or necessity, or when he acts or fails to act by mistake. A person may be excused from blame for his criminal conduct when he abandons a criminal plan by withdrawing from the criminal conduct before it is completed. Conduct may be excused from blame even though it is not justified and even though the person has no legal privilege to act the way he does.

Coercion or Duress. A person who commits an act or an omission under either coercion or duress acts under a compelling force caused by another human being. One who acts or fails to act under coercion or duress does not do so of his own free choice. Therefore, his conduct is not voluntary. A person who acts under *coercion* is forced bodily to do what he does through the physical violence of another person. One who acts under *duress* is threatened with physical violence unless he does what another person commands him to do.

Either coercion or duress may be a complete defense to criminal responsibility for any offense except one that results in the death of an innocent human being. Neither coercion or duress is a defense to any criminal homicide, although a person who kills someone else under coercion or duress may be *less* criminally responsible than if he committed the same act without coercion or duress. Thus, either of these defenses may reduce a charge of murder to one of manslaughter, for example (see Chapter 8).

In order to raise coercion or duress as a defense to criminal responsibility, however, the defendant must reasonably believe his act or omission to be necessary to avoid imminent death or imminent serious bodily injury. That is, he must reasonably believe that death or serious bodily injury, not slight or moderate injury, will result *immediately,* not in the distant future.

Coercion or duress may excuse a person's criminal conduct even though the harm that is threatened will not be directed toward his own body. One may act or fail to act in order to avoid imminent death or imminent serious bodily injury to someone other than himself, provided serious harm is capable of being inflicted on this other person in the immediate future. Some states will permit this defense only if the other threatened person is a close relative of the defendant.

At common law, a married woman who committed any criminal act except murder or treason in the presence of her husband was presumed to be acting under his coercion. No state recognizes this presumption today, and few states will permit a married woman to escape criminal responsibility under this defense unless her husband threatened her or someone close to her with imminent death or imminent serious bodily harm.

A minor child who committed a criminal act in the presence of one or both of his parents was *not* presumed to be acting under coercion or duress at common law. Nevertheless, such a child may successfully raise this defense in some states, especially when it can be shown that the parent who was present threatened to beat the child unless he committed the crime. A defense of coercion or duress seldom has to be raised on behalf of a child since the creation of juvenile delinquency statutes. This defense never has to be raised, of course, when the defense of infancy may apply.

Necessity. A person who commits an act or an omission out of necessity acts under a compelling force caused by the physical forces of *nature.* One who acts or fails to act out of necessity does not do so through his own free choice even though he may consciously decide to do what he does. Necessity may excuse a person from criminal responsibility under certain limited conditions.

Necessity excuses criminal responsibility only when the person who acts or fails to act reasonably believes that any harm he causes will prevent or avoid greater harm. Harm to human life is considered to be greater than harm to property. Thus, a person who reasonably believes he must damage or destroy property to save his own life or another person's life may act out of necessity. Under rare circumstances, a person who causes one person's death in order to save two other people's lives may be considered to have acted out of necessity.

The defense of necessity excuses criminal responsibility only when the defendant has been confronted with a choice between two evils with no way out. It does not apply when the defendant has a third alternative that is less harmful than the criminal act or omission. For this reason, courts have held that a hungry person who is not actually starving does not act out of necessity by stealing food from a store, because he could receive public assistance. As a general rule, there is no defense based solely on "economic necessity."

Two classic examples of this defense were raised in connection with shipwrecks on the high seas. In an English shipwreck case that was decided in 1884,[2] three sailors and a cabin boy were adrift at sea for twenty days more than a thousand miles from land. Having no food, the seamen killed the cabin boy, ate his body and drank his blood, and were rescued four days later. The court recognized that the boy was in the weakest condition of all and that one or more of the three seamen probably would not have survived if they had not used his body for nourishment, yet the men were convicted of murder. The death sentence was imposed, but it was commuted to six months' imprisonment.

In an American shipwreck case that was decided in 1842[3] (before the English case), nine seamen and thirty-two passengers were adrift in an overcrowded lifeboat that was close to sinking in a storm. To lighten the lifeboat, some of the crew threw fourteen male passengers overboard to their deaths, but the seamen and the remaining passengers survived. The trial court instructed the jury that some crew members were necessary to navigate the boat, but that those crew members who were unnecessary should have been sacrificed before any passengers. Furthermore, the court noted that the passengers to be thrown overboard should be selected by lot. The ranking crew member was convicted of manslaughter and sentenced to six months' solitary confinement at hard labor.

Ignorance or Mistake of Fact. A person is ignorant of or mistakes a fact when he does not know or realize that a given fact exists at a particular moment, or when he reasonably believes a fact to be different from what it actually is. A fact is difficult to define specifically. It usually includes any actual event that occurs or that has occurred at some time in the past.

Ignorance or mistake of fact may be a defense to criminal responsibility, but only for an offense that requires some kind of criminal intent. Thus, one who commits an act or an omission for which he is strictly or absolutely liable by statute cannot raise this defense to excuse his criminal responsibility.

This defense may be raised successfully only if the fact in question is *pertinent* to the criminal intent required for the offense he is accused of committing. Even if the fact is pertinent to this required criminal intent, the defendant's ignorance or mistake must have been *reasonable*—that is, it must be such that an ordinary, reasonable man would have made the same mistake under similar circumstances.

Ignorance or Mistake of Law. Ignorance or mistake of *law* is much different from ignorance or mistake of *fact*. Generally, every person is expected and presumed to know what conduct is lawful and what is unlawful. As a rule, therefore, ignorance or mistake of law does not constitute a defense to criminal responsibility for any offense.

Under certain extremely limited conditions, however, a person may be able to raise ignorance or mistake of law as a valid defense. One could do this if he has relied on an *official statement* that erroneously interpreted the law he is accused of violating. One could do this if he is charged with violating a criminal law that is so new that he did not receive fair notice of its elements before violating it.

Not every statement that interprets a law is an official statement. Indeed, one who relies on the advice of his attorney cannot point to that advice as a defense if it turns out to have been erroneous. A statement made by a public official during a news conference seldom will be considered official. Reliance on a proclamation or other "public notice," made and published by a high government official, may excuse one who relies on its accuracy even though the statement turns out to be inaccurate.

The public is entitled to *fair notice* of any changes in the language or the scope of a state's criminal laws. For this reason, each state must warn the public by publishing each newly enacted law as soon as possible after it is approved by the legislature and the governor. Until a new criminal law is published in an official state publication, one who violates it may generally raise ignorance or mistake of law as a defense to criminal responsibility. Most new criminal laws are published for several months prior to taking effect.

Entrapment. Entrapment occurs when a person is enticed or induced by a law enforcement official to commit a criminal act that otherwise he would not have committed, for the purpose of prosecution. When it can be proven, entrapment constitutes a defense to criminal responsibility for any offense.

Entrapment has been held by the U.S. Supreme Court to exist "when the criminal design originates with the officials of the government and they implant in the mind of an innocent person the disposition to commit the alleged offense and induce its commission in order that they may prosecute."[4] Entrapment exists only when a person is lured into committing a crime by a law enforcement officer or someone acting on behalf of a law enforcement officer. Furthermore, it exists only when the offender is lured for the purpose of prosecuting him. This defense does not apply when a private citizen persuades a person to commit a crime; nor does it exist even when a policeman persuades one to commit a crime if the policeman's objective is anything other than to prosecute the offender.

The entire criminal idea must originate with the law enforcement official in order for entrapment to occur. Thus, the whole crime must be thought up, planned, and worked out by the official, who must encourage the offender to commit the criminal act or omission. The official does not have to be a commissioned police officer. Any person who works on behalf of a public law enforcement agency—federal, state, or local—may cause an entrapment, even if the person is only a paid informer. It is not entrapment for a law enforcement official to cooperate fully with someone who plans to commit a crime, however, if the offender thought up the plan originally.

In many states, the defendant who raises entrapment as a defense has the burden of proving that it took place. For this reason, entrapment is known in these states as an "affirmative" defense, in contrast to most other defenses, which the prosecution has the burden of disproving once they are raised by the defendant. The U.S. Supreme Court has determined that a conviction based on evidence obtained by entrapment is a violation of due process of law.[5]

Renunciation. As a rule, a person becomes criminally responsible for an offense at the moment both his conduct and his intent fulfill all the elements required for the particular offense. Thus, in the absence of a statute providing the opposite, a person who *begins* to commit a crime while possessing the criminal intent required for that crime bears criminal responsibility for the offense. This remains true even if the offender does not succeed in *completing* the crime.

Some states have created the statutory defense known as *renunciation* to eliminate criminal responsibility for a person who voluntarily abandons or withdraws from a criminal act before it is completed. Similarly, a person who voluntarily decides to do his duty while he still has the chance may not bear criminal responsibility for an omission, even though he began to omit a duty required of him. The offender's change in mind must be voluntary in order for the defense of renunciation to be raised successfully. Hence, one is not relieved of criminal responsibility under this defense by surrendering to a police officer who interrupts the criminal act or omission. The offender must make a complete and absolute withdrawal by totally abandoning a criminal act or by preventing a criminal omission through discharging his duty.

Legal Exemptions

A person who has been charged with committing a crime may raise one or more defenses to show that he is *exempt by law* from bearing criminal responsibility for a criminal act or omission. A person who is exempt from criminal responsibility for certain conduct cannot be convicted of or punished for any criminal offense resulting from that conduct. It does not matter whether a person who is exempt by law possessed the mental capacity required for ordinary criminal responsibility, nor whether he possesses the culpability for his conduct. These defenses are classified as legal exemptions or concessions and are permitted for the good of the public welfare rather than on account of the defendant's own merit.

Former Jeopardy

The common law firmly recognized "that a man shall not be brought into danger of his life or limb for one and the same offense more than once."[6] Furthermore, such *double jeopardy* is prohibited under the federal Constitution as well as by state constitution, statute, or common law in every state. Jeopardy is the danger any person faces of losing life or freedom when he is made to defend himself at trial against the accusation that he committed a crime.

Once a person has been on trial to determine whether he is guilty of committing a crime, he cannot as a rule be put on trial again for the same offense. The defense of former jeopardy may be raised by a defendant who has gone to trial on a previous occasion for the same offense that he is now charged with committing. This defense is not designed to protect guilty defendants; rather, it is intended to prevent a state from continuously putting the same person on trial for the same offense until he is finally convicted. Thus, this defense protects every citizen from a possible abuse of the state's judicial power.

In most states, jeopardy attaches in any criminal trial at the moment the trial actually begins. A trial before a jury begins when the jury is sworn in and the first witness is called to offer testimony. Once jeopardy has attached even for a short period of time, the trial must continue until the defendant is either acquitted or convicted, unless the trial is stopped on the defendant's own motion (if he asks the judge to declare a mistrial, for example). If the jury is unable to agree on a verdict after deliberating for a reasonable time, the judge may declare a mistrial and this will not bar the defendant from being tried again for the same offense before a new jury. Similarly, a defendant who appeals a conviction to a higher court and succeeds in obtaining a new trial at his own request cannot successfully raise the defense of former jeopardy to prevent himself from being tried again for the same offense.

In most states, a person who is convicted or acquitted of an offense, such as manslaughter, cannot be prosecuted for a more serious offense, such as murder, for the same criminal act or omission. In many states, a person who is convicted or acquitted of a serious offense, such as murder, cannot be prosecuted for a less serious offense, such as manslaughter, for the same criminal act or omission.

Former jeopardy is a bar to subsequent prosecution only when the *same person* is charged with committing the *same offense* in the *same jurisdiction*. A person sometimes may be prosecuted in more than one jurisdiction for the same offense, and prosecution in the first jurisdiction may not always be a bar to prosecution in the second. For example, a person who commits an offense that violates the laws of the United States as well as of the state where it is committed may be prosecuted for both the federal offense and the state offense, in either order, and neither prosecution will bar the other. A person may not be prosecuted by both a municipal (city or town) government and a state for violating a municipal ordinance, since any municipality is only a subdivision of the state in which it is located. Therefore, one who has been convicted of violating a city ordinance may not be reprosecuted for violating a state statute covering the same criminal act or omission. In other words, for purposes of double jeopardy, a municipality and the state in which the city or town is located are considered to be a single jurisdiction.

Statutes of Limitations

At common law, a prosecution could be initiated against any person for any crime at any time, no matter how long ago the criminal act or omission took place. Most states have enacted statutes that limit the amount of time following a crime within which a person may be prosecuted for that crime. These are known as statutes of limitations.

Prosecution begins when a person is charged with committing a crime, either by grand jury indictment or by some other written accusation made pursuant to law. A person who has been charged with committing a crime may raise a defense by showing that the statute of limitations for the offense he is accused of committing makes him exempt from prosecution.

No statute enacted in any state sets a limitation on the time within which a prosecution for murder may be begun, but a time limit for prosecution for most other offenses is fixed. Serious felonies usually have longer statutes of limitations than do less serious felonies or misdemeanors. Thus, a person may be charged with committing a serious felony up to ten years after the act or omission occurred in many states. Crimes that are regulated by long statutes of limitations may include manslaughter, forcible rape, forcible sodomy, kidnapping, robbery, arson, and burglary. Most other felonies are considered less serious and therefore are regulated by shorter statutes of limitations. In many states, a person may be charged with committing homicide from criminal negligence, statutory rape, battery, and most theft offenses during a period ending only five years after the act or omission occurred. Misdemeanors are commonly regulated by a two-year statute of limitations.

Normally, the statute of limitations that pertains to any offense begins to run as soon as the crime is committed and continues without interruption until it expires. A statute of limitations may be interrupted in some states, however, during any time when the defendant who raises this defense was absent from the state. Thus, for example, a person who is charged with committing a crime that carries a five-year statute of limitations would ordinarily be able to raise the statute of limitations successfully as a defense if prosecution is begun five years and one day after the crime was committed. In many states, however, this would not be true unless the defendant never left the state during the five-year period. If he left the state for a total of one year during the five-year period, the normal five-year statute of limitations would be extended to six years.

Sovereign Immunity

At common law, the English monarch was immune from all prosecution for any civil action or criminal offense. Although Charles I was beheaded, this act was committed quite unlawfully by the followers of Oliver Cromwell. Today, the issue of sovereign immunity seldom arises concerning the head of a state himself.

More often, it arises in connection with ambassadors, consuls, and other high-ranking diplomatic officials who represent the heads of foreign states.

Representatives at the Sixth International Conference of American States in Havana in 1928 outlined the specific immunities to which a high-ranking diplomat of a foreign country and his family and staff should be entitled. Under Article 19 of the resulting convention, "diplomatic officers are exempt from all civil or criminal jurisdiction of the state to which they are accredited." This exemption is extended to the immediate family members and to the staffs of diplomats under Article 23. In addition, Article 23 exempts diplomats and their families and staffs from the civil and criminal jurisdiction of all states they must cross to arrive at their post or to return to their own country. Section 252 of Title 22 of the United States Code provides immunity for diplomats, their families, and their staffs.

Thus, members of diplomatic missions are exempt from criminal prosecution not only in the country in which they are situated, but also in all states they pass through en route to their assignment. They may not, however, be entitled to sovereign immunity in countries they visit on vacation or on unofficial business. And they may not be afforded sovereign immunity in countries that do not subscribe to the articles of the Havana Convention. The United States does subscribe to these articles.

Similarly, officers and agents of the United States are immune from prosecution in a state court for any criminal offense arising out of their official duty. Such a criminal offense must be removed to and tried in a federal court, under section 1442(a) of Title 28 of the United States Code. This statute requires removal from state court to federal court of any criminal prosecution against "any officer of the United States or any agency thereof, or person acting under him, for any act under color of such office or on account of any right, title or authority claimed under any Act of Congress for the apprehension or punishment of criminals or the collection of revenue."

Part 2

Offenses Against the Person

CHAPTER 5

Criminal Injury Offenses

Assault and battery are the most basic criminal injury offenses. Criminal injury offenses involve harm or potential harm to a person's body. Assault and battery are not the only offenses that involve bodily harm, however. Mayhem as well as rape and other forcible sexual offenses (Chapter 7) result from bodily injury also. However, these offenses involve specific forms of bodily injury, whereas assault and battery involve bodily injury or potential bodily injury of any kind at all. In addition, murder, manslaughter, and other criminal homicides (Chapter 8) result from bodily injury, since a person must be physically hurt in order to be killed.

Assault and battery are viewed as being *lesser included offenses* to most other criminal injury offenses such as mayhem, rape, murder or manslaughter. This is true because a person who is raped or killed, for instance, is also assaulted and battered. Rape is a more specific form of assault and battery. Murder and manslaughter are more serious forms of assault and battery. Since assault and battery are lesser included offenses to mayhem, rape, murder and manslaughter, it will be important to remember when reading subsequent chapters in Part Two of this book that whenever mayhem, a rape or murder is committed, an assault and battery are committed as well.

Criminal injury offenses that are discussed in this chapter include assault, battery, and mayhem, together with consolidated injury offenses such as reckless endangerment, terrorizing, and terroristic threats.

Criminal Assault

The elements of criminal assault can be outlined as follows:
  A. The Criminal Act:
    1. a threat or an attempt
    2. to cause another person immediate bodily harm
    3. [having the present ability to inflict the harm]
  B. The Criminal Intent:
    4. a specific intent
      (*a*) to frighten or
      (*b*) to do general bodily harm or
      (*c*) to do specific bodily harm

A Threat or an Attempt

Either a *threat* or an *attempt* to cause another person immediate bodily harm is required to constitute the act of criminal assault. In every state, an attempt constitutes the crime of criminal assault, and in most states, a threat (without an actual attempt) also constitutes criminal assault. In each state, however, *either* a threat *or* an attempt alone is sufficient to constitute assault. No state requires both.

There is a difference between a threat and an attempt. A threat usually falls short of an actual attempt to commit an act. An attempt to commit an act sometimes follows a threat, but it may occur without any threat at all. For this reason, it is important to understand the meanings of *threat* and *attempt* as each applies to the definition of criminal assault.

Threat. A threat consists of any physical expression by one person for the purpose of scaring another person. Usually a threat consists of spoken words, but it can just as easily consist of a facial expression, clenched fists, a written note, or be conveyed by one of countless other methods of communication.

To constitute the act of criminal assault, a threat must succeed in causing the victim a reasonable apprehension of immediate bodily harm. That is, the victim must perceive or foresee that he may be harmed immediately. In other words, a threat cannot constitute a criminal assault unless the victim understands that the objective of the threat is to frighten him. In addition, the victim's apprehension of immediate bodily harm must be reasonable—that is, it must be such that an ordinary person would apprehend or perceive the same expression from the other person as a threat of immediate bodily harm.

There is a difference between an apprehension and fright, however. A threat will constitute criminal assault if the victim reasonably apprehends or perceives the possibility of bodily harm, whether or not he is frightened. A person may become the victim of a criminal assault even if he is too courageous to become scared or frightened.

Attempt. An attempt, as opposed to a threat, to cause another person immediate bodily harm may also constitute criminal assault. If the offender attempts and *succeeds* in causing the victim immediate bodily harm, then he commits the act of criminal battery, and the assault becomes part of the battery. If the offender attempts and *fails*, then he commits the act of criminal assault only.

While the objective of a threat is generally to scare the victim without actually hurting him, the objective of an attempted battery is frequently to cause immediate bodily harm. In this respect, the only difference between an assault and a battery may be the success or failure of the offender. An attempt to commit any crime requires that the offender come close to accomplishing his objective. Hence, the act of criminal assault stems from an attempted battery only when the offender very nearly inflicts immediate bodily harm on his victim.

Immediate Bodily Harm

Regardless of whether criminal assault is committed by a threat or by an attempt, the objective of the act must be either to create in the victim the *apprehension* of immediate bodily harm, or else actually to *inflict* immediate bodily harm. At this point, two questions frequently arise. What is meant by *bodily harm*? And what constitutes *immediate* bodily harm?

Bodily harm may consist of any unlawful or offensive *contact*, inflicted or threatened by one person against another person's body. Bodily harm includes *direct* physical contact between the offender's body, or an object in contact with his body, and the victim's body, such as when the offender stabs the victim with a knife, bruises the victim with a club or with fists, or makes forcible sexual contact with the victim. Bodily harm also includes *indirect* physical contact between the offender and the victim's body, such as when the offender shoots the victim, causing a bullet to penetrate the victim's body. Neither direct nor indirect physical contact needs to be violent, although both kinds often are. Indeed, the offender may commit criminal assault merely by threatening or attempting to kiss the victim or to place the victim in contact with poison or an obnoxious odor.

Only *immediate* bodily harm can be the basis for criminal assault. The offender must threaten or attempt to inflict immediate, rather than delayed, bodily harm on the victim. In the case of a threat, for example, it is not criminal assault for the offender to threaten the victim with bodily harm in the distant future (although this might constitute blackmail; see Chapter 14). The victim must reasonably apprehend the threat as meaning bodily harm within seconds or minutes, rather than within days or weeks. Similarly, in the case of attempt, the offender must be in the process of trying to inflict bodily harm on the victim momentarily, rather than plotting to harm the victim sometime later.

It is sufficient but not necessary that the offender threaten immediate bodily harm to the victim himself. However, the offender may threaten instead to inflict immediate bodily harm on the victim's wife, child, or parent or on another person who stands in a close personal relationship to the victim of the threat. In such a situation, this third person must either be physically present at the scene of the threat or else be in immediate danger of being harmed by an accomplice of the offender who makes the threat.

Normally the act of criminal assault consists of a threat or an attempt to cause immediate harm only to the victim's *body*. A threat or an attempt to injure a person's character or reputation will not generally constitute criminal assault. Some courts have held, however, that a threat or an attempt to separate a person from either his *clothes* or his *automobile* (even without physical bodily contact) also constitutes criminal assault.

Present Ability to Inflict the Harm

In most states, a threat or an attempt to cause another person immediate bodily harm constitutes the act of criminal assault, whether or not the offender has the actual or apparent present ability to inflict the harm. To commit criminal assault in some states, however, the offender must have at least the *apparent* if not the actual present ability to inflict the harm he threatens or attempts. And in some states, the offender must possess the *actual* present ability to inflict the harm.

Take, for example, a situation in which an offender points a paper bag at the victim and threatens to shoot him. In a state where *neither* actual nor apparent present ability to carry out the threat is necessary, the offender obviously commits the act of criminal assault. In a state where *either* actual or apparent present ability is required, the offender may not commit an act of criminal assault, since the victim has no more than the offender's "word" that a gun is inside the bag.

As another example, suppose an offender points a toy pistol at the victim and threatens to shoot. In a state where *apparent* (but not actual) present ability is required, the offender commits the act of criminal assault, since the victim presumably has no way of knowing whether the gun is or is not "real." In a state where *actual* present ability is required, however, the offender commits no act of criminal assault, since the toy gun is not "real" and therefore cannot actually inflict immediate bodily harm on the victim.

Specific Intent

No person may be convicted of criminal assault unless he can be shown to have possessed a specific criminal intent at the moment he threatened or attempted to cause another person immediate bodily harm. A general criminal intent is not sufficient to support a conviction for criminal assault. Therefore, it is crucially important to determine what *was* and what *was not* on the offender's *mind* at the moment he made the threat or the attempt.

By statute in many states, criminal assault may be divided into two categories: *simple criminal assault* and *aggravated criminal assault.* More often than not, the two are called "simple assault" and "aggravated assault." The difference between simple assault and aggravated assault rests with the *intent* of the offender at the moment he commits the criminal act.

Simple Assault. Any criminal assault is a simple assault unless it becomes an aggravated assault for a specific reason. Simple assault consists of a threat or an attempt to cause another person immediate bodily harm. To bear criminal responsibility for simple assault, an offender must be proven either to have intended to *frighten* his victim or to have intended to do *general bodily harm* to his victim at the moment of his criminal act. There is a difference between a specific intent to frighten and a specific intent to do general bodily harm.

Specific Intent To Frighten. If the offender threatens (rather than attempts) to cause the victim immediate bodily harm, the offender may be convicted of simple assault if it can be shown that his intent at the time of his act was to frighten the victim. This is true even if the offender did not ever intend to inflict any bodily harm. Of course, it can be argued that an intent to frighten another person is synonymous with an intent to cause bodily harm, since fright can often harm a person.

Specific Intent To Do General Bodily Harm. If the offender threatens *or* attempts to cause the victim immediate bodily harm, the offender may be convicted of simple assault if it can be shown that his intent at the time of his act was to do general bodily harm to the victim. It is not necessary to show that the offender contemplated any *specific* type of bodily harm; it is necessary to show that he contemplated *some* kind of bodily harm. Quite often it is apparent from the nature of the offender's criminal act that he intended to do some kind of harm to the victim's body. If the offender's intent to harm is apparent by the nature of his act, he will seldom be excused from criminal responsibility by later claiming (after the fact) that his secret (undisclosed) intent was to back away from his victim at the last possible moment, leaving the victim un-harmed.

Similarly, an offender who threatens to harm his victim *unless* the victim complies with the offender's demands will not be excused from criminal responsibility by claiming that his intent to do harm was conditional on the victim's behavior. The fact that the offender may well have intended not to inflict bodily harm on the victim unless the victim refused to comply has no bearing on the offender's criminal responsibility.

Aggravated Assault. A criminal assault changes from a simple assault to an aggravated assault on account of the nature of the offender's intent at the moment he made the threat or the attempt to harm his victim. Generally, an offender who intends to cause his victim special (rather than general) bodily harm commits aggravated assault.

An offender who threatens or attempts to cause another person a special kind of bodily harm—such as death or rape—usually commits aggravated assault. This is true, of course, unless the offender *succeeds* in touching his victim, in which case he commits aggravated battery, and unless he *succeeds* in killing or raping his victim, in which case he commits murder or rape respectively.

Assault with intent to commit murder, assault with intent to commit rape, and assault with intent to commit robbery are three examples of aggravated assault. Under the language of many statutes, assault with intent to commit murder, rape, or robbery constitutes one or more separate crimes under separate labels.

In many states, an offender who carries in his possession any kind of *dangerous weapon* (as defined by statute) at the time he makes a threat or an attempt to cause another person immediate bodily harm commits aggravated assault. The definition of "dangerous weapon" varies considerably from state to state and will be discussed in greater detail in the section on aggravated battery.

Criminal Battery

The elements of criminal battery can be outlined as follows:
  A. The Criminal act:
      1. offensive physical contact
      2. with another person's body

B. The Criminal Intent:
3. a general or specific criminal intent

Offensive Physical Contact. Some degree of offensive physical contact is required to constitute the act of criminal battery. The act may consist of any physical contact inflicted by one person against another person's body, so long as the contact is unlawful or offensive to the victim. Physical contact is *offensive* if it is unwanted by the victim, but sometimes the meaning of *physical contact* itself is unclear.

Physical contact may be direct or indirect. As mentioned earlier, *direct* physical contact occurs when the offender's body, or an object in contact with the offender's body, touches the body of the victim, as when the offender stabs the victim, hits the victim with a club or with his fists, or has forcible sexual contact with the victim. *Indirect* physical contact occurs when the offender causes an object that is not in contact with the offender's body to touch the victim's body, as when the offender shoots the victim or throws something that hits the victim.

Neither direct nor indirect physical contact needs to be violent, although both kinds often are. Direct physical contact may consist of nothing more than a kiss or a pat with the hand, but this is sufficient to constitute criminal battery if the contact is offensive to the victim. Indirect physical contact may consist of nothing more than the emission of a foul odor in the direction of the victim's nose, and this also is sufficient to constitute the act of criminal battery if it is offensive to the victim.

Unlike apprehension in the situation of assault by threat, physical contact does not have to be offensive to an ordinary person to constitute the act of battery. *Any* physical contact may properly be the basis for the act of criminal battery, as long as it is offensive to the individual victim himself. Thus, one runs a greater risk of committing battery if he touches a person who can't stand to be touched than if he touches the average person.

Another Person's Body

Normally, criminal battery is committed when the offender

either touches the victim's body or causes another object to touch the victim's body. This is not the only way in which criminal battery can occur, however. For example, if the offender strikes or whips the horse on which the victim is riding, causing the horse to throw its rider to the ground, this will generally constitute battery. A similar act of battery could occur if the offender wrongfully shoots out a tire of the victim's automobile, causing the vehicle to crash.

A court once upheld a criminal battery conviction based on the offender's act of persuading a child to touch the offender's sexual organ. A battery also may be committed if the offender infects the victim's body with a disease or a poison. Moreover, a battery may be committed by omission as well as by commission of an act if the offender has a duty to prevent the victim from offensive physical contact and fails to discharge his duty. For example, if a hospital attendant fails to warn a blind patient who is in his care that the patient is about to walk through a window, the attendant may commit criminal battery if the patient walks through the window and falls.

A person who offensively touches another person's body may commit criminal battery even if the victim is *not injured* as a result of the contact. Injury is not an element of criminal battery. Of course, if the victim *is* injured on account of offensive physical contact, that fact does not prevent the contact from constituting criminal battery. Nor is there any requirement that physical contact be directed against a special part of the victim's body in order to be offensive and constitute criminal battery. The purpose of criminal battery statutes is to protect persons from all varieties of offensive physical contact.

General or Specific Criminal Intent

As a rule, no specific criminal intent is required to support a conviction for criminal battery. Battery is a "cause-and-result" crime in which the offender's general criminal intent is usually apparent from his conduct. A conviction for criminal battery may ordinarily be obtained on proof that the offender *voluntarily* made an offensive physical contact with another person's body.

By statute in many states, however, criminal battery, like criminal assault, may be divided into two categories: *simple criminal battery* and *aggravated criminal battery,* usually called "simple battery" and "aggravated battery." As with assault, too, the difference between simple battery and aggravated battery rests with the *intent* of the offender at the moment he commits the criminal act.

Simple Battery. Any criminal battery is a simple battery unless it becomes an aggravated battery for a specific reason. Simple battery consists of any kind of offensive physical contact with another person's body. To bear criminal responsibility for simple battery, an offender must be proven to have *voluntarily* made an offensive physical contact with another person's body. To be convicted of simple battery, the offender need *not* generally be shown to have intended any special type of harm to result from the offensive contact.

Aggravated Battery. A criminal battery changes from a simple battery to an aggravated battery because of the nature of the offender's criminal intent when he made an offensive physical contact with the victim's body, or because the offender carried a dangerous weapon on his person when he made the offensive contact.

Generally, an offender who makes an offensive physical contact with another person's body with intent to cause a special type of bodily harm—such as death or rape—commits an aggravated battery. As in the case of assault, of course, if he succeeds in killing or raping his victim, the offender commits murder or rape. Battery with intent to commit murder, battery with intent to commit rape, and battery with intent to commit robbery are three examples of aggravated battery. In many statutes, battery with intent to commit murder, rape, or robbery constitutes one or more separate crimes under separate labels.

In many states, an offender who carries in his possession any kind of dangerous weapon (as defined by statute) at the time he makes an offensive physical contact with another person's body commits aggravated battery. Definitions of a *dangerous weapon* vary considerably from state to state and may or may not include "deadly weapons" and "lethal weapons." Any firearm, and especially any handgun, ordinarily falls into the category of a dangerous weapon. Moreover, any knife with a blade over four (or six or eight) inches long, a sword cane, a blackjack, brass knuckles, and any other instrument of violence may also be classified as a dangerous weapon. Under some circumstances, a motor vehicle such as an automobile, a boat, or an airplane may constitute a dangerous weapon if used recklessly to cause an offensive contact with another person's body. A chainsaw or an animal could be used for the same purpose and could also become a dangerous weapon.

Criminal Mayhem

The elements of Criminal Mayhem can be outlined as follows:
A. The Criminal Act:
  1. the permanent
  2. (*a*) dismemberment or
     (*b*) disablement or
     (*c*) disfigurement
  3. of another person's body
B. The Criminal Intent:
  4. a specific criminal intent

Permanent Injury

Permanent, rather than temporary, bodily harm is required to constitute the act of criminal mayhem. In this respect alone, mayhem is different from criminal battery, which requires only temporary bodily harm.

Sometimes it may be difficult to determine whether a particular bodily injury is permanent. Usually some portion of the victim's body must be so drastically injured that it becomes useless or its usefulness is greatly impaired. It is sufficient, but not necessary, that the victim be deprived of a portion of his body—that is, that part of the victim's body be taken off.

As a rule, ordinary bruises to the victim's body are presumed to be temporary rather than permanent in nature. For this reason, an ordinary bruise can seldom support a charge of criminal mayhem, although it may frequently support a charge of criminal battery. On the other hand, if for any reason the victim becomes unable to walk or unable to use an arm, hand, leg, or foot as a result of an attack, the injury may be presumed to be permanent in the absence of evidence showing that it is temporary.

Three different kinds of permanent injury can support a charge of criminal mayhem. *Either* permanent dismemberment *or* permanent disablement *or* permanent disfigurement of a vital bodily organ of the victim is sufficient to constitute criminal mayhem. Note that only one of these three types of injury is required, although any of these types of injury may occur in combination.

Dismemberment

The removal of the victim's arm, hand, finger, leg, foot, or toe constitutes a dismemberment within the scope of criminal mayhem. Similarly, the removal of the victim's eye, ear, nose, or *front* tooth constitutes a dismemberment. The removal of a molar or a wisdom tooth does *not* constitute dismemberment under most criminal mayhem statutes. The severance of either the penis or the testicles of a male person always constitutes dismemberment.

Under many criminal mayhem statutes today, the removal of one of a woman's sexual organs also constitutes mayhem, although this was not so at common law. Many statutes also state or imply that the removal of a person's lip or tongue will constitute a dismemberment sufficient to support a charge of criminal mayhem.

Within the meaning of most criminal mayhem statutes, a dismemberment occurs when an appropriate part of the victim's body is removed either by the offender himself or by surgery as a direct consequence of the offender's attack. Of course, the removal of a vital part of a person's body is always considered to be permanent and not temporary. Whether medical progress in the area of organ transplants will change the permanence of dismemberment cannot be foretold.

Disablement

The disablement, as well as the dismemberment, of many bodily organs can constitute criminal mayhem. While dismemberment is always permanent rather than temporary, the disablement of a person's body may be either permanent or temporary. Sometimes it may be very difficult to determine the extent to which the victim of an attack will recover from a disabling injury.

A victim may become disabled as a result of injury to his arm, hand, finger, leg, foot, or toe, even though the organ is not dismembered. A mere fracture of a limb seldom results in permanent disability, because with proper medical treatment the fracture can be set and the limb restored. However, if muscles, nerves, or joints of the victim's limb are injured, the injury may indeed be permanent. Paralysis of a limb is an example of a permanent injury.

There seems to be no authority concerning whether injury to a victim's front tooth is permanent if enough of the tooth remains intact to permit capping. Similarly, there is some doubt as to whether injury to a sexual organ causing sterility constitutes permanent disablement if the organ is not dismembered. If impotence results from injury to a sexual organ, the chances are greater that the organ would be considered permanently disabled.

Surprisingly, a court has held that cutting a victim's throat does not constitute the act of criminal mayhem. Apparently, the reasoning is that if the victim lives he can still breathe, and if the victim dies the crime is murder! What if the victim is administered a caustic substance that permanently tears away the lining of his throat? The answer to this question is not settled in the law.

Disfigurement

In addition to dismemberment and disablement, the disfigurement of a victim's body may also constitute criminal mayhem if the disfigurement is sufficiently permanent and grotesque.

Mild disfigurements, although they may be permanent, seldom constitute mayhem. For example, the slight disfigurement left by surgical stitches on the victim of a stabbing or bullet wound does not constitute mayhem. Similarly, the permanent recession of the victim's hairline due to a head wound would not generally constitute mayhem.

As a rule, only facial disfigurements are considered sufficiently grotesque to constitute mayhem—they could be caused by the slicing of a victim's lip, cheek, nose, or ear. Bludgeoning a victim's skull to the extent that a permanent scar is created may constitute mayhem. There seems to be no authority concerning whether plastic surgery, if it successfully alters an otherwise permanent scar, precludes a conviction for criminal mayhem.

Another Person's Body

At common law, according to Blackstone, mayhem was defined as "violently depriving another of the use of such of his members as may render him the less able in fighting, either to defend himself, or to annoy his adversary." Thus, at common law, mayhem included only dismemberments and disablements that rendered the victim less skillful as a soldier. Permanent injury to any limb was included, as was castration and destruction of a front tooth (presumably used to bite the enemy!). No disfigurement of any kind constituted mayhem at common law. Mayhem originated more as a crime against the right of the English king to the military services of his subjects than as one against the right of the subject to a sound and complete body.

By statute in most states, any portion of a person's body may properly be the subject of dismemberment. Any working part of the body may be the subject of disablement. Any normally visible part of the body may be the subject of disfigurement. Although a person's ear, nose, or lips may have no effect on his capability as a warrior, these and all other vital bodily organs are nevertheless protected from mutilation under modern laws.

Specific Criminal Intent

Neither the permanent dismemberment, nor the permanent disablement, nor the permanent disfigurement of another person's body can constitute the crime of mayhem unless the offender possessed a specific criminal intent at the moment he committed the criminal act. The nature of this specific criminal intent can vary from state to state. In some states, the offender must act "maliciously"; in others, he must act "willfully." In a few states, a specific intent to "maim," to "disfigure," or to "injure" is required by statute.

It is crucially important to understand, however, that mayhem is not a "cause-and-result" crime. While a victim's arm or leg can be destroyed accidentally, such an accidental destruction cannot constitute criminal mayhem. Unless the offender intends to cause serious bodily harm to the victim at the moment of his attack, mayhem cannot be committed under any statute. Under most statutes, moreover, the offender must contemplate the specific harm that results, in order to commit mayhem.

Consolidation of Criminal Injury Offenses

Some states have departed from the traditional distinctions among assault, battery, and mayhem. These states have either enacted or proposed statutes that would consolidate (1) assault with battery and mayhem or (2) battery with mayhem. For example, the New York Penal Law combines battery with mayhem and labels the consolidated offense "assault."

The New York Penal Law provides for three degrees of assault, as follows:

§ 120.00 *Assault in the third degree.*—A person is guilty of assault in the third degree when:

1. With intent to cause physical injury to another person, he causes such injury to such person or to a third person; or

2. With criminal negligence, he causes physical injury to another person by means of a deadly weapon or a dangerous instrument.

§ 120.05 *Assault in the second degree.*—A person is guilty of assault in the second degree when:

1. With intent to cause serious physical injury to another person, he causes such injury to such person or to a third person; or

2. With intent to cause physical injury to another person, he causes such injury to such person or to a third person by means of a deadly weapon or a dangerous instrument; or

3. With intent to prevent a peace officer from performing a lawful duty, he causes physical injury to such peace officer; or

4. He recklessly causes serious physical injury to another person by means of a deadly weapon or a dangerous instrument; or

5. For a purpose other than lawful medical or therapeutic treatment, he intentionally causes stupor, unconsciousness or other physical impairment or injury to another person by administering to him without his consent, a drug, substance or preparation capable of producing the same.

§ 120.10 *Assault in the first degree.*—A person is guilty of assault in the first degree when:

1. With intent to cause serious physical injury to another person, he causes such injury to such person or to a third person by means of a deadly weapon or a dangerous instrument; or

2. With intent to disfigure another person seriously and permanently, or to destroy, amputate or disable permanently a member or

organ of his body, he causes such injury to such person or to a third person; or

3. Under circumstances evincing a depraved indifference to human life, he recklessly engages in conduct which creates a grave risk of death to another person, and thereby causes serious physical injury to another person; or

4. In the course of and in furtherance of the commission or attempted commission of a felony or of immediate flight therefrom, he, or another participant if there be any, causes serious physical injury to a person other than one of the participants.

Under these New York statutes, the traditional offenses of battery and mayhem are combined. Note, however, that the traditional offense of assault is not covered under the New York statutes that bear its name. Instead, the traditional offense of assault is covered by several other statutes, labeled "menacing" and "reckless endangerment." The elements of these offenses are as follows:

§ 120.15 *Menacing.*—A person is guilty of menacing when he intentionally places or attempts to place another person in fear of imminent serious physical injury.

§ 120.20 *Reckless endangerment in the second degree.*—A person is guilty of reckless endangerment in the second degree when he recklessly engages in conduct which creates a substantial risk of serious physical injury to another person.

§ 120.25 *Reckless endangerment in the first degree.*—A person is guilty of reckless endangerment in the first degree when, under circumstances evincing a depraved indifference to human life, he recklessly engages in conduct which creates a grave risk of death to another person.

As a result of the California Penal Code Revision Project (1971), several statutes were proposed to consolidate battery and mayhem, following the New York example. The offense of "criminal injury" was created and defined as follows:

(a) A person is guilty of criminal injury when, with intent to inflict bodily injury upon another person, he inflicts bodily injury upon any person.

Under this revised statute, criminal injury is a misdemeanor unless:

(1) The injury is inflicted with a deadly weapon; or

(2) The person injured is a peace officer or fireman engaged in the performance of his duties and the defendant knows or reasonably should know that fact.

The offense of criminal injury becomes a felony when either of these two conditions is present.

The California Penal Code revised statute for criminal injury does not specify any degrees of the crime. Instead, a separate offense of *aggravated* criminal injury covers infliction of *serious* bodily injury, and is defined:

(a) A person is guilty of aggravated criminal injury when, with intent to inflict serious bodily injury upon another person, he inflicts serious bodily injury upon any person.

Under this statute, aggravated criminal injury is a felony in every instance. It becomes a more serious felony when the injury is inflicted with a deadly weapon or when the person injured "is a peace officer or fireman engaged in the performance of his duties and the defendant knows or reasonably should know that fact."

By creating the offenses of criminal injury and aggravated criminal injury, the California Penal Code revisers enlarged the scope of mayhem and aggravated battery. No longer would the area of the victim's body that is injured determine the criminal offense, as it traditionally has with mayhem. (Remember, mayhem generally covers only dismemberments, disablements, or disfigurements.) Instead, the seriousness of the victim's bodily injury would determine the criminal offense, regardless of what part of his body is hurt. Furthermore, use of a deadly weapon to cause bodily injury or serious bodily injury could increase the punishment for criminal injury or aggravated criminal injury.

As in the New York statutes, the traditional offense of assault would not be covered under the California revised statutes. The offense of "aggressive conduct" was substituted for the traditional offense of assault. This offense was to be defined as follows:

(a) A person is guilty of aggressive conduct when, with intent to intimidate or abuse another person, he touches or threatens to touch any person.

Note that this proposed offense would cover all abusive threats that have traditionally fallen within the scope of assault. In addition, however, aggressive conduct would include actual bodily contact that is offensive but that does not result in any significant amount of bodily injury. Hence, this offense would overlap the traditional offense of battery, which normally covers any bodily contact, whether or not it results in significant injury to the victim.

An unsuccessful effort to revise the Criminal Code of Massachusetts contained a proposal for creating the offense called "terrorizing." Under this proposal, terrorizing would be defined as follows:

> § 9. *Terrorizing.* A person is guilty of terrorizing, a class C felony, if he makes a threat involving a crime of violence or unlawful act dangerous to human life and the natural and probable consequence of such threat or threats, whether or not such consequence in fact occurs, is:
>
> (a) to place another person in fear of serious bodily injury;
>
> (b) to cause evacuation of a building, place of assembly, or facility of public transportation; or
>
> (c) otherwise to cause serious public inconvenience, disruption, or alarm.

The new criminal statutes recently adopted by Pennsylvania include the offense called "terroristic threats," which is substantially similar to the offense of terrorizing as proposed for Massachusetts.

Some states have either enacted or proposed special statutes that increase the seriousness of an assault committed by a prison inmate, and further increase the seriousness of an assault committed by an inmate sentenced to death or to life imprisonment. The Pennsylvania statutes are representative:

> § 2703. *Assault by prisoner.* A person who has been sentenced to imprisonment for any term of years in any penal or correctional institution, located within this Commonwealth, is guilty of a felony in the second degree if he, while undergoing imprisonment, intentionally or knowingly commits an assault upon another with a deadly weapon or instrument, or by any means or force likely to produce serious bodily injury.

> § 2704. *Assault by life prisoner.* Every person who has been sentenced to death or life imprisonment in any penal institution located in this Commonwealth, and whose sentence has not been commuted, who commits an aggravated assault with a deadly weapon or instrument upon another, or by any means of force likely to produce serious bodily injury, is guilty of a crime, the penalty for which shall be the same as for murder of the first degree.

CHAPTER 6

Criminal Coercion Offenses

Offenses involving criminal coercion occur when one person detains or transports another against his will, or when the offender forces the victim to do something he does not want to do or prevents the victim from doing something he has a right to do. Coercive offenses are serious forms of assault in most instances, and therefore assault is a lesser included offense to most crimes that involve criminal coercion. Coercive offenses may be serious forms of battery, also, but this is not always true. Battery may not be a lesser included offense to a crime such as false imprisonment, since the victim who is falsely imprisoned need not be physically touched. Battery may be a lesser included offense to kidnapping, because in order to be moved from one location to another a victim is likely to be touched by his offender.

Coercive offenses include false imprisonment, kidnapping, and criminal coercion.

False Imprisonment

The elements of false imprisonment can be outlined as follows:
A. The Criminal Act:
   1. the detention of another person
   2. against his will
B. The Criminal Intent:
   3. *(a)* a general criminal intent or
      (b) with a specific intent
         (1) to sell him into involuntary servitude or
         (2) to hold him to involuntary servitude

Detention of Another Person

The detention of another person against his will is required to constitute the act of false imprisonment. A detention may occur whenever one person interferes with or restrains another person's freedom by any means or at any place.

To constitute a detention, it is not necessary that the victim be restrained for any specific length of time. A moment may be sufficient, depending on the circumstances. Similarly, there is no requirement that the offender physically touch the victim in order to detain him. No force of any kind is necessary, although a detention may and often does occur as a result of forcible restraint. In the absence of force, however, there can be no detention unless the victim apprehends a threat of force. Unlike the case with assault, however, this apprehension need not be reasonable. If the victim senses that the offender is interfering with his (the victim's) right to leave a particular place at a particular time, a detention occurs.

Against His Will

More than a mere detention is required to constitute the act of false imprisonment, however. The detention must be accomplished against the victim's will. If the victim *consents* to the detention, the crime of false imprisonment is not committed.

Sometimes the presence or absence of a victim's consent is unclear. Certainly any verbal demand or any physical attempt on the part of the victim to be set free would signal the absence of consent, but this does not mean that either a demand or a physical attempt is mandatory for the detention to be against the victim's will. In many instances, the victim's own account of the detention—after the fact—may determine whether the detention was against his will.

A person who at one moment consents to be detained may revoke his consent any time he wishes. Normally, a person who has once consented to be detained must communicate his change of mind to the captor before the detention can turn into false imprisonment. Once a person notifies his captor—either by words or by an attempt to walk away—that he wishes to be set free, the captor must immediately set him free. Otherwise, the detention will at that moment constitute false imprisonment.

General Criminal Intent

One who detains another person against the other person's will normally bears criminal responsibility for false imprisonment if he voluntarily restrains the victim. Everyone is generally presumed to intend the natural and probable consequences of their acts. It does not usually matter whether the offender detained his victim for a specific reason—such as sexual abuse—or for no reason at all. In either instance, false imprisonment can occur.

A person cannot bear criminal responsibility for false imprisonment if he detains another person pursuant to law—that is, if he is performing a lawful act. In some states, for instance, statutes specifically say that a person cannot be criminally responsible for false imprisonment if he has reasonable grounds to make a "citizen's arrest" in order to thwart the commission of a crime or prevent the escape of a criminal. In some states, statutes specifically say that law enforcement officers cannot bear criminal responsibility even if they make an "illegal" arrest without sufficient reasonable grounds. In many of these states, administrators and staffs of prisons, jails, and mental hospitals cannot be criminally responsible for false imprisonment in the event that an inmate under their supervision is later determined to be "innocent" or "sane."

Specific Criminal Intent

It is a federal offense to detain another person against his will with intent to sell the victim into involuntary servitude or with intent to hold the victim to involuntary servitude.[1] Moreover, it is a separate federal crime to confine a person against his will on any vessel with intent to make the victim a slave,[2] or to hold any person in a condition of peonage.[3]

Involuntary servitude includes but is not limited to chattel slavery. Involuntary servitude may encompass any situation in which the detained victim will foreseeably become compelled to do labor or to perform any service against his will. In order for one to bear criminal responsibility under the federal statutes just cited, the specific intent outlined in the statute must be shown. An offender may not be convicted under one of these statutes just because he voluntarily detained another person against the latter's will. He must also have planned to sell the victim into or hold the victim to any condition of involuntary servitude.

Kidnapping

The elements of kidnapping can be outlined as follows:
    A. The Criminal Act:
        1. the transportation of another person
        2. against his will
    B. The Criminal Intent:
        3. *(a)* a general criminal intent or
              (b) a specific intent
                    (1) to hold him for ransom or reward or
                    (2) to use him as a shield or hostage or
                    (3) to threaten or inflict bodily harm on him or
                    (4) to use him in involuntary servitude or
                    (5) to use him to facilitate commission of a crime

Transportation of Another Person

The transportation of another person against his will is required to constitute the act of kidnapping under most state laws. Transportation is slightly different from detention, which alone is required to constitute the act of false imprisonment. It should be noted, however, that detention without transportation may constitute the act of kidnapping in a few states.

A person is transported against his will whenever he is compelled to move from one location to another while in detention. To be transported within the definition of kidnapping, the victim need not be moved any great distance. In theory, a few feet would be sufficient. In practice, however, a detention turns into a transportation only after the offender causes the victim to move from one geographic location to another. The required distance varies under different statutes. Some states require the offender to move the victim from one county to another. Under most statutes, however, a transportation occurs if the offender moves the victim from one building to a separate building, or if the offender compels the victim to ride in any vehicle during the period of detention.

Although it may seem obvious, it should be noted that the offender will not escape responsibility for the transportation merely because he later moves the victim back to the original place of detention. Indeed, this movement constitutes an additional transportation.

Against His Will

Like a detention in false imprisonment, a transportation must be accomplished against the victim's will in order to constitute kidnapping. If the victim *consents* to the transportation, the act of kidnapping is usually not committed. As in false imprisonment, too, a person who consents to being transported may withdraw that consent any time he wishes by communicating his withdrawal to the captor. Thereafter, if the transportation continues, it will go on against the victim's will.

It would be possible for a person to consent to a detention, but to object to a transportation. In this situation, the captor would not commit false imprisonment by detaining the victim, but would commit kidnapping by moving the victim from one location to another.

Although any adult person of sound mind is capable of consenting to a detention, a transportation, or both, not every human being is an adult person of sound mind. Thus, although a child or an insane person may "consent" to either a detention or a transportation, the law may not recognize such a person as being capable of giving his or her consent. A "consent" offered by a person whom the law considers incapable of giving consent is not valid. Thus, a person may commit the act of kidnapping by transporting a child under age sixteen, unless the child's parent or guardian consents to the transportation. In some states, a person may commit the act of kidnapping by transporting a person whom the captor knows is legally insane without the consent of the insane person's legal guardian.

General Criminal Intent

One who transports another person against the victim's will normally bears criminal responsibility for kidnapping if he voluntarily restrains and moves the victim. No specific criminal intent is required under most statutes to support a conviction for "simple" kidnapping. Simple kidnapping is frequently labeled "kidnapping."

A person cannot bear criminal responsibility for kidnapping if he transports another person pursuant to law. Thus, a law enforcement officer who has proper grounds to arrest a person suspected of having committed a crime cannot ordinarily be criminally responsible for kidnapping, even if he transports the suspect to the police station. On the other hand, a law enforcement officer who takes a "suspect" on an unlawful ride for an unlawful purpose may indeed become criminally liable for kidnapping.

Any kidnapping constitutes a federal offense if the victim is transported in interstate commerce—that is, if, during the course of the transportation, the victim is taken across any state line. The federal kidnapping statute, known as the Lindbergh Law,[4] provides that an offender may be punished by death if he does not release his victim unharmed and if the jury so recommends. The U.S. Supreme Court has held the death-penalty clause in the federal kidnapping statute unconstitutional, however.[5] The Court reasoned that, since the death penalty for kidnapping can be imposed only by a jury following trial and not by a judge sitting without a jury, this provision discourages an offender's rights to plead not guilty and demand a trial by jury as guaranteed under the Fifth and Sixth Amendments to the Constitution.

Specific Criminal Intent

While simple kidnapping does not generally require proof of

any specific intent on the part of the offender, proof of certain specific intents may "aggravate" the act of kidnapping. Some forms of aggravated kidnapping are punished more severely than simple kidnapping, under state or federal statutes or both.

One who transports another person against the latter's will may be criminally responsible for an aggravated kidnapping if, at the moment of the transportation, the offender possesses one or more of the following specific intents: (1) to hold the victim for ransom or reward, (2) to use the victim as a shield or hostage, (3) to threaten or inflict bodily harm on the victim, (4) to use the victim in involuntary servitude, or (5) to use the victim to facilitate commission of a crime.

Holding Victim for Ransom or Reward. Proof that an offender transported his victim against the victim's will, with intent to hold the victim for ransom or reward of any sort, will normally aggravate a simple kidnapping. Because kidnapping for ransom or reward is actually a crime against both person and property, it will be discussed in detail in Chapter 14.

To bear criminal responsibility for this form of aggravated kidnapping, a person need *not* take part in all three phases of the criminal plan: the transportation, the confinement, and the demand for a ransom or reward. A person may be criminally responsible for aggravated kidnapping if he participates voluntarily in any *one* of these three activities, provided that he has knowledge of the plan to demand a ransom or reward.

Using Victim As Shield or Hostage. Proof that an offender transported his victim against the victim's will, with intent to use the victim as a shield or a hostage will normally aggravate a simple kidnapping. One intends to use another person as a *shield* if he plans to use the victim in order to protect himself during the course of some activity. The planned activity usually is illegal, but does not have to be under most statutes. One intends to use another person as a *hostage* if he plans to use the victim for the purpose of preventing his (the offender's) capture or arrest.

It is a federal offense to commit the act of kidnapping during the course of robbing a national bank.[6] Under this statute, the federal offense is committed whether or not the victim is transported across any state line.

Threatening or Inflicting Bodily Harm. Under many state laws, one who transports another person against the latter's will with intent to threaten or to inflict bodily harm on the victim may be criminally responsible for an aggravated form of kidnapping. In some of these states, there must be proof that the offender actually intended to inflict bodily harm on the victim during the course of the kidnapping act. In most of these states, however, a kidnapping may become aggravated by proof that the offender intended merely to frighten the victim by threatening bodily harm. Seldom is the actual infliction of bodily harm required in order for a kidnapping to become aggravated, although it may be difficult to prove the offender's intent unless he threatens or inflicts harm.

Under most statutes, a kidnapping may become aggravated by the offender's threat or infliction of any type of bodily harm. The harm usually need not be serious or constitute a high risk to the victim's life. Of course, harm that results to the victim accidentally will not as a rule aggravate a kidnapping in the absence of proof that the offender actually intended some amount of bodily harm. The felony-murder rule (see Chapter 3) is an exception to this general statement, however.

Using Victim in Involuntary Servitude. It is a federal offense to transport any person with intent to use him in or sell him into involuntary servitude.[7] Also, it is a separate federal offense to bring any person into the United States who is held as a slave or in involuntary servitude.[8] Other federal statutes prohibit anyone from enticing, persuading, or inducing another person to go on board any vessel or to any other place with the intent that the victim be made a slave,[9] or to engage in the slave trade,[10] or to serve on a slave-trading vessel,[11] or to outfit a vessel for the slave trade.[12]

Involuntary servitude includes chattel slavery, but also encompasses any situation in which the kidnapped victim will foreseeably become compelled to do labor or to perform any service against his will. Note that it is a separate federal offense to kidnap another person with intent to hold him in or sell him into involuntary servitude. This offense is different from that which prohibits one from simply "holding" another person in a condition of involuntary servitude. The latter offense was discussed earlier in this chapter in conjunction with false imprisonment.

Using Victim to Facilitate Commission of a Crime. Under many state laws, one who transports another person against the latter's will with intent to use the victim to facilitate commission of any crime may be criminally responsible for an aggravated form of kidnapping. In many of these states, the kidnapping becomes aggravated only if the offender intends to use the victim to facilitate commission of a *felony*. As a rule, the felony or other crime need not ever be committed in order for the kidnapping to become aggravated, so long as the offender can be proven to have intended using the victim for this purpose at some point during the kidnapping act.

Intent to use the victim to facilitate commission of a crime may or may not be the same as an intent to use the victim as a shield. An offender generally uses his victim as a shield in order to protect himself from possible or actual harm. An offender may use his victim to facilitate commission of a crime in this way or in a number of other ways. For example, one may kidnap the president of a bank to obtain the combination to the bank's vault rather than to protect oneself.

Custodial Interference Offenses

Nearly every state has enacted one or more statutes making it a criminal offense to remove either a child or a committed person from the custody of his legal guardian. Similarly, many states have enacted additional statutes making it an offense for anyone to conceal a child from his legal guardian. These statutes will be discussed with reference to several major categories of offense.

Abduction

The offense of abduction is defined differently from state to state. Basically, it involves the act of compelling a female person to enter into marriage, concubinage, prostitution, or other instances of sexual intercourse. In most states, this offense is applicable only when the female victim is a minor, less than age eighteen in some states, or less than age sixteen or fourteen in others.

Abduction is not regarded as a crime of violence, so no degree of force is required. This fact makes abduction quite different from kidnapping. As a rule, the victim does not have to be taken any specific distance, but must simply be removed from the custody of her legal guardian. Usually one or both of a child's parents are his or her legal guardians. If not, then a relative or someone appointed by a court of law may be the legal guardian. The intent required for abduction is generally an immoral purpose of any kind. The immoral purpose need not be accomplished, nor does the female victim have to be separated from her legal guardian for any particular length of time.

Interference with Custody of a Child

In addition to, or instead of, the offense called "abduction," many states have enacted statutes making it a criminal offense to interfere unlawfully with a child's custody. Generally, one may commit this offense by taking or enticing a male or female minor child from the custody of his or her legal guardian, knowing that he has no right to do so. Because it applies to both sexes, it is different from abduction. Moreover, this offense may be committed even if the offender does not have any immoral purpose in mind, another difference from abduction.

In some states, this kind of interference with custody of a child can be committed only by a relative of the child victim, such as an estranged parent, a grandparent, uncle, aunt, brother, sister, or cousin. Otherwise, in these states, the offender may commit kidnapping. Ordinarily, the child's age also determines whether this offense may be committed. The child must be a minor, which means he must not have reached the legal age of adulthood in the state where he resides. Frequently, this age is sixteen or eighteen.

In some states, a more serious degree of this offense may be committed when, after removing the child from his legal guardian's supervision, the offender exposes the child to a risk that may either endanger the child's safety or impair his health. In some states, also, a person may not be criminally responsible for this offense if he believed his action was necessary to preserve the child from danger to his or her welfare in the hands of the legal guardian. This belief may not be sufficient to eliminate criminal responsibility if the offender knows that the child was awarded to the custody of the legal guardian by order of a court.

Interference with Custody of a Committed Person

Most states have enacted statutes making it a criminal offense to interfere unlawfully with custody of a committed person. This offense is similar to that of interfering with custody of a child. In many of these states, a person who has been committed to a mental hospital, a sanitarium, or a correctional facility (prison) is viewed as having no more legal rights than a child has. Hence, a committed person in these states cannot consent to be removed from the custody of his or her legal guardian. In many instances, the victim of this offense may be an adult rather than a child. Of course, the adult victim may be male or female. As a rule, the legal guardian of a committed person will be the superintendent of the institution where the person is committed. A committee of three people may also serve as the person's guardian.

As with the offense of interference with custody of a child, this offense does not require that the offender have in mind any immoral purpose. The offender must have some knowledge that the victim has been committed to another person's custody, however.

Harboring a Child

In some states, by statute, it is a criminal offense for anyone to harbor a child with intent to conceal the child's whereabouts from his legal guardian. One may harbor a child by giving the child shelter in one's home or in any other place outside the home of the child's guardian without the guardian's consent.

This offense is different from interference with custody of a child, since this offense does not require that the offender have anything to do with taking or enticing the child from the guardian's custody. A person may commit this offense by giving any aid to a child who has run away from his guardian's home, with intent to keep the child's whereabouts secret. This offense may be committed even though the child requests the offender not to notify the guardian. No immoral purpose is required for this offense. Normally, however, this offense may not be committed when one legal guardian (such as one of two parents) conceals a child from another legal guardian having joint custody of the child. This does not mean that the offense cannot be committed by a child's parent; a parent may commit this offense when he no longer has legal custody of his child, such as pursuant to a court order.

Substitution of Children

Some states have created statutes that specifically make it a criminal offense for any person intentionally to substitute one child for another. Obviously, this can only be done with very young children, since children over one year old usually have identifiable features. One may commit this offense if one is temporarily entrusted with a child and then returns a different child to the guardian of the first child, intending to deceive the guardian. Seldom is this offense committed by returning the wrong child to its natural parent or parents. It does occur with orphaned or abandoned children, however.

Other Coercive Offenses

Many states have enacted statutes to create the offense known as "coercion." The specific contents of this offense may vary slightly from state to state. The New York Penal Law probably contains one of the most comprehensive coercion statutes, which reads as follows:

§ 135.60 *Coercion in the second degree.*—A person is guilty of coercion in the second degree when he compels or induces a person to engage in conduct which the latter has a legal right to abstain from engaging in, or to abstain from engaging in conduct in which he has a legal right to engage, by means of instilling in him a fear that, if the demand is not complied with, the actor or another will:

1. Cause physical injury to a person; or

2. Cause damage to property; or

3. Engage in other conduct constituting a crime; or

4. Accuse some person of a crime or cause criminal charges to be instituted against him; or

5. Expose a secret or publicize an asserted fact, whether true or false, tending to subject some person to hatred, contempt, or ridicule; or

6. Cause a strike, boycott, or other collective labor group action injurious to some person's business; except that such a threat shall not be deemed coercive when the act or omission compelled is for the benefit of the group in whose interest the actor purports to act; or

7. Testify or provide information or withhold testimony or information with respect to another's legal claim or defense; or

8. Use or abuse his position as a public servant by performing some act within or related to his official duties, or by failing or refusing to perform an official duty, in some manner as to affect some person adversely; or

9. Perform any other act which would not in itself materially benefit the actor but which is calculated to harm another person materially with respect to his health, safety, business, calling, career, financial condition, reputation or personal relationships.

§ 135.65 *Coercion in the first degree.*—A person is guilty of coercion in the first degree when he commits the crime of coercion in the second degree, and when:

1. He commits such crime by instilling in the victim a fear that he will cause physical injury to a person or cause damage to property; or
2. He thereby compels or induces the victim to:
   (a) Commit or attempt to commit a felony; or
   (b) Cause or attempt to cause physical injury to a person; or
   (c) Violate his duty as a public servant.

Notice that one may commit the offense of coercion either by compelling another to do something that the other person has a right not to do, or by compelling another not to do something that the other person has a right to do. Thus, for example, one may commit coercion by forcing someone else to join an organization or by forcing him to resign from an organization, since a person normally has a right to belong or stop belonging to any organization he pleases. It is not coercion for a person to be compelled to join a union as a condition of keeping his job, however, since the employee has the choice of working elsewhere.

CHAPTER 7

Sexual Offenses

Sexual offenses are particular varieties of both assault and battery as a rule. The victim is touched at specific areas of his or her body. Therefore, assault and battery are lesser included offenses to many sexual crimes. Some sexual offenses such as rape are more serious than others because a greater amount of force is used by the offender against the victim. The severity of a sexual offense such as statutory rape may depend upon how young the victim is instead of the amount of force, if any, that is used. The severity of an offense such as sodomy may be in relation to the extent to which a state perceives the forbidden conduct to be "deviate." The modern trend has been for states to reduce the severity of "deviate" sexual conduct that is not accompanied by force.

Sexual offenses include forcible rape, statutory rape, sodomy, seduction, sexual misconduct, and sexual abuse.

Forcible Rape

Elements of forcible rape can be outlined as follows:
A. The Criminal Act:
 1. sexual intercourse
 2. by a male person with a female person
 3. with force
 4. without her consent
B. The Criminal Intent:
 5. a general criminal intent

Sexual Intercourse

The act of sexual intercourse is required to constitute the act of forcible rape. Sexual intercourse occurs whenever a male penetrates his penis into a female's vagina. Ordinarily, any amount of penetration, however slight, accomplishes sexual intercourse in the eyes of the law. No seminal emission is required, nor is it necessary that the hymen be broken if the victim is a virgin.

A minimum amount of penetration must be proven, however. Mere contact between the male's organ and a part of the female's body other than her vagina will not constitute rape, although it may constitute a criminal act other than rape.

Under some very recent statutes, the penetration of a male's penis into the anus or the mouth of either a female or another male is defined as "sexual intercourse." In the true sense of the word, only penetration into the vagina constitutes sexual intercourse. Penetration into the anus or the mouth constitutes "deviate" or "abnormal" sexual behavior. Traditionally, rape could occur only in cases of genital intercourse, and "deviate" or "abnormal" sexual intercourse constituted sodomy. Under some recent statutes, however, sodomy has been eliminated as a separate crime. Under these statutes, anal and oral penetration have sometimes been construed to constitute "sexual intercourse" for the purpose of rape.

Between Male and Female Persons

Only sexual intercourse between a male person and a female person can constitute common law rape. Thus, sexual intercourse between two animals cannot be rape, nor is it rape if a male person penetrates a female animal's vagina with his sexual organ. This latter act may constitute the crime of bestiality, which will be discussed in greater detail as a form of sodomy later in this chapter.

A "person" must be a living human being. Thus, it is not rape for a male person to penetrate the vagina of a deceased female person. Obviously, rape still occurs if the female dies during the penetration.

Force

Only sexual intercourse by a male person with a female person and accomplished by *force* constitutes *forcible* rape. Forcible rape is not the only type of rape, however. Another kind, known as statutory rape, will be discussed in the next section. Force is not an element of statutory rape.

The meaning of the word "force" as it applies to forcible rape has remained unclear throughout the development of law. Early in the common law, sexual intercourse was viewed as being accomplished by force only if the female victim "resisted to the uttermost" the entire act of copulation. If the female victim stopped resisting even for a moment during the intercourse, under this theory, the element of force was lacking, and the criminal act of forcible rape had not taken place.

Under modern theory in every state, the female victim need no longer resist "to the uttermost." Some resistance still is required, however. The degree of resistance required varies under different court interpretations, but in any event must be more than mere resistance for the sake of appearance.

Force is not always measured in terms of physical coercion, although physical coercion is generally sufficient to constitute force. A threat by the aggressor to inflict bodily injury either on the victim herself or on another person who stands in a close personal relationship to her may constitute force. In this sense, force may consist of an *intimidation* instead of, or in addition to, physical coercion.

The element of force may be automatically fulfilled if the aggressor resorts to various types of *fraud* in order to subdue his victim. Although fraud may have an effect on both force and consent, it will be discussed in relationship to consent.

Lack of Consent

If a female *consents* to having sexual intercourse with a particular male at any time during penetration, forcible rape is not committed under most statutes, whether or not the male uses force. If the female refuses to consent during penetration, but has a "change of heart" sometime afterward, some statutes will recognize this after-the-fact consent, but some will not.

A female may consent to having sexual intercourse with a particular male at one moment, but change her mind. If the female notifies the male prior to penetration that she withdraws her earlier consent, forcible rape may then be committed if the male penetrates her by force, unless she consents during penetration or has a "change of heart" afterward. Similarly, a female may engage in consensual sexual intercourse on one occasion, but refuse to consent to intercourse with the same male on a later occasion. Her previous consensual intercourse does not prevent her from withdrawing her consent on a later occasion.

Throughout history, the element of consent has caused nearly as much confusion as the element of force. The absence of consent is apparent under conditions where the female flatly refuses to submit voluntarily to intercourse and communicates her refusal to the male by words or actions. When a doubt exists, bruises and scrapes on the victim's body may provide evidence that she refused to consent. This is not always the case, however, because a female may consent to be bruised under many criminal battery statutes. Thus, bruises may show the presence of force without proving the absence of consent and without conclusively supporting the occurrence of forcible rape. A female may resist her male aggressor until penetration has been achieved, for example, but then submit to sexual intercourse without resisting.

A female may consent to having sexual intercourse expressly or by implication. A statement that she consents would constitute an express consent. But a female also may consent to sexual intercourse without actually saying she consents if her overall behavior would lead an ordinary man to believe that she consents. The female who consents during penetration but who feels shame or remorse following the deed cannot withdraw her consent later to turn consensual intercourse into rape.

Sexual intercourse with an unconscious woman is presumed to be without the woman's consent unless the evidence clearly shows that she gave her consent before losing consciousness. Likewise, sexual intercourse with a woman who is senseless because she is intoxicated is presumed to be without her consent unless the evidence shows that she gave her consent (and did not withdraw it) before becoming intoxicated.

As mentioned earlier, forcible rape may be committed if the woman's consent is obtained by certain types of *fraud*. The classic example is when the male aggressor pretends to be the victim's husband, either by "marrying" her in a fraudulent wedding ceremony or, if she is married, by masquerading as her husband. Most courts have held that forcible rape is not committed when a man pretends to marry a woman fraudulently and then proceeds to have sexual intercourse with her as his "wife." On the contrary, most courts have held that forcible rape may indeed occur when an intruder masquerades as another man who in fact is married to the victim. Courts have distinguished these two situations. By agreeing to marry her suitor, a woman expresses her willingness to have sexual intercourse with him, even though she may be deceived as to the validity of the marriage ceremony. If an intruder masquerades in the dark as the victim's real husband, however, the woman does not agree to have sexual intercourse with this particular man, unless she knows he is not her husband.

In either the "sham wedding" or the "masquerade" situation, of course, the woman consents to sexual intercourse if she perceives the fraud and does not protest the intercourse.

Fraud may also invalidate a "consent" in another way. Both physicians and "quacks" have been known to have sexual intercourse with their patients under the pretense of performing an examination or surgery. If the woman consents to vaginal penetration by a medical instrument, this does not amount to consent to sexual intercourse. However, if a physician or a quack persuades his patient to have sexual intercourse as a form of treatment or therapy, the woman's consent will usually preclude the act of forcible rape.

The victim's character and chastity do not have any effect on her capacity to refuse to consent to sexual intercourse. A woman may consent to have sexual intercourse with one man, but refuse to consent to having it with another man. Even a prostitute can enjoy the law's protection from sexual intercourse by force and without her consent. It may be important to note, however, that a prostitute who consents to sexual intercourse for a fee cannot withdraw her consent should the fee not be paid. In other words, one does not commit forcible rape by having sexual intercourse with a prostitute with her consent and then refusing to pay her. A consent cannot be contingent on the payment of money.

At this point, it should be noted that not every female person possesses the *legal capacity* to consent to sexual intercourse. In most states, a female who has not reached a certain minimum age, or who has an abnormally serious mental or physical condition, cannot consent to sexual intercourse in the eyes of the law. This element of legal capacity will be discussed in greater detail later in this chapter in connection with statutory rape.

When a woman who does not have the legal capacity to consent nevertheless agrees and engages in sexual intercourse, the agreement does not constitute a valid consent under law. However, it does not seem logical that the act of forcible rape can be committed when a woman has agreed to have sexual intercourse, whether or not she has the legal capacity to consent. Forcible rape seems impossible in this situation, because *any* agreement or willingness on the part of the woman (whether or not it constitutes a legal consent) would seem to eliminate the presence of force. Some courts have followed this theory, while a number have not.

General Criminal Intent

A male person who has sexual intercourse with a female person with force and without her consent generally will bear criminal responsibility for forcible rape. Forcible rape is viewed as a "cause-and-result" crime, as is criminal battery. Indeed, forcible rape is in actuality an explicit type of criminal battery, in which contact with a particular part of the victim's body is required.

Proof that the male offender did in fact penetrate his female victim's vagina by force and without her consent normally demonstrates the offender's presumed criminal intent. It cannot be overstressed that every person is presumed by law to intend the natural and probable consequences of his acts. Older statutes used to require that the male possess an "intent to ravish" his victim at the moment of penetration. Few statutes still require a specific criminal intent such as this.

In most states, a husband cannot commit forcible rape on his legal wife, since she is prevented by law from withdrawing her general consent to have sexual intercourse with her husband during their marriage. Difficulties arise, however, when forcible rape occurs between parties who are divorced or who have lived together in a "common-law" type of marriage. Most courts have permitted forcible rape convictions in all instances in which the couple were not legally married at the time of the penetration. This reasoning may be sound when applied to divorced couples, since a divorce must surely indicate the ex-wife's withdrawal of consent to have sexual intercourse with her former husband. In the case of common-law marriages, however, courts should look beyond the existence of a mere certificate. A common-law marriage is still regarded as valid by some states. If the couple has lived together in an apparent marriage in one of these states, their relationship is regarded as being just as permanent as a marriage entered into by formal ceremony. Hence, the common-law wife may have generally consented to having sexual intercourse with her common-law husband to the same extent as a woman who was married in a wedding ceremony.

Statutory Rape

The elements of statutory rape can be outlined as follows:
A. The Criminal Act:
1. sexual intercourse
2. by a male person with a female person
3. who does not have the legal capacity to consent
B. The Criminal Intent:
4. no criminal intent required

Statutory rape, like forcible rape, requires sexual intercourse by a male person with a female person. These two requirements are the same for both types of rape. A discussion of these elements appears in the previous section.

Lack of Legal Capacity to Consent

Statutory rape is significantly different from forcible rape in at least two respects. First, the element of *force* that is required for forcible rape is not necessary for statutory rape. Second, statutory rape does not depend on the absence of consent by the victim.

Statutory rape occurs when a male person has sexual intercourse with a female person who does not have the *legal capacity to consent* to sexual intercourse. In every state, a female person who has not reached a certain minimum *age* (defined in the statute) does not have the legal capacity to consent to sexual intercourse. In many states, a female person who has a seriously abnormal *mental or physical condition* does not have the legal capacity to consent to sexual intercourse.

Statutory rape was not a crime at common law. The elements of this crime therefore vary from state to state, because they depend on the language of each particular statute. In most states, a girl acquires the legal capacity to consent to sexual intercourse on her sixteenth birthday. The age of consent ranges from twelve to eighteen years of age among the states.

In a few states, a girl who has a reputation for being of "unchaste" character may legally consent to having sexual intercourse at a younger age than may an ordinary girl. In these states, the objective of statutory rape laws is to protect "innocent" girls. A girl who was not a virgin prior to the present act of statutory rape may nonetheless be of "chaste" character. In most states that attempt to evaluate the character of the girl involved, she is not considered "unchaste" unless she has had sexual intercourse on several different occasions with several different partners. In many states, however, the girl's reputation for chastity does not affect her incapacity to consent. In these states, statutory rape may be committed in a house of prostitution.

The fact that a girl is married does not affect her legal capacity to consent to sexual intercourse with a man other than her husband. Normally, however, a couple may engage in sexual intercourse without the husband's committing statutory rape even though the wife has not reached the age of consent, if the marriage is recognized by the law of the state.

The statutes of a few states require that the girl be both penetrated and "abused" in order for statutory rape to occur. "Abuse" is not the same thing as force. In most of these states, "abuse" of the girl's sexual organs is presumed by law to occur routinely as a result of normal sexual intercourse. In some of these states, however, statutory rape cannot be proven unless unusual injury to the girl's sexual organs can be shown.

As mentioned, statutory rape may be committed in many states even if the female has reached the age of consent, if she has an abnormally serious mental or physical condition. Most of these states do not clearly define the meaning of either a mental or a physical condition. Ordinarily, a woman may legally consent to having sexual intercourse even if she has lower than average intelligence. However, a woman who is severely retarded in either mental or physical development may not have this legal capacity. A woman who has been institutionalized or declared to be mentally incompetent may also lose her capacity to consent to sexual intercourse.

At common law, a woman who had an abnormally serious mental condition was *presumed* to lack the legal capacity to consent to intercourse. This presumption could be disproven, or refuted, however, by evidence that the woman did in fact agree to sexual intercourse as a result of her "animal instinct." The courts in American states have consistently refused to recognize an "animal instinct" as having any bearing on a woman's legal capacity to consent to sexual intercourse.

It is important to clarify, however, that forcible (rather than statutory) rape may occur even though the victim has not reached the age of consent or suffers from a seriously abnormal mental or physical condition. When the element of *force* is present and the female *does not consent* to the sexual intercourse, forcible rape occurs. In the absence of force, statutory rape occurs if the female does not have the legal capacity to consent, even if she agrees to the sexual intercourse.

Lack of Criminal Intent

The crime of statutory rape is a notable *exception* to the general rule that no person bears criminal responsibility for any criminal act unless it can be shown that he possessed a criminal intent at the moment he committed the act. Most statutory rape statutes say expressly that a criminal intent (general or specific) on the part of the offender is *not* an element of criminal responsibility for this crime. In most instances when the statute has not been this explicit, courts have interpreted the statute in this fashion.

Some statutes do state that the offender must have some knowledge that his victim has a seriously abnormal mental or physical condition if this condition rather than the victim's age forms the basis for the charge of statutory rape. Few statutes require knowledge by the offender that his victim is not old enough to consent.

As with those crimes that do require a general rather than a specific criminal intent, an offender's intent to commit the act of statutory rape may be considered to be apparent from his willingness to commit the act. Many courts have reasoned that a man who voluntarily has sexual intercourse with a woman who is not his wife *assumes the risk* that she may not have the legal capacity to consent. By assuming this risk, the theory goes, the man assumes criminal responsibility for his deed if the woman does not in fact have the legal capacity to consent, and mistake as to age is no excuse.

A few courts have looked beyond the criminal act and explored the *reasonableness* of the man's belief that his victim was old enough to consent. These courts have let the jury consider two vital questions in determining a man's criminal responsibility for statutory rape: (1) Did he honestly believe the girl was over the age of consent? (2) Would a reasonable man honestly believe the same girl was over the age of consent under the circumstances surrounding the criminal act?

Where the jury is permitted to consider the reasonableness of the offender's belief, its decision may be influenced by several kinds of evidence. The girl's physical appearance may indicate her apparent maturity, which may conflict with her actual maturity. Or her social sophistication may be measured by the circumstances surrounding the act, such as the time, the place, and the girl's behavior.

Sodomy Offenses

The elements of sodomy can be outlined as follows:
    A. The Criminal Act:
        1. "deviate" sexual intercourse

2. (*a*) by a male person with a female person or
   (*b*) by a male person with a male person or
   (*c*) by a male person with an animal
B. The Criminal Intent:
3. a general criminal intent

"Deviate" Sexual Intercourse

The act of "deviate" sexual intercourse, as defined by law, is required to constitute the act of sodomy. "Deviate" sexual intercourse is quite different from ordinary sexual intercourse. Under most statutes, deviate sexual intercourse occurs whenever a male person penetrates his penis into the anus of any male or female person. Under most statutes, also, deviate sexual intercourse occurs whenever a male person penetrates the vagina of a female animal or the anus of a male or female animal.

As with ordinary sexual intercourse, any amount of penetration, however slight, accomplishes the act of deviate sexual intercourse in the eyes of the law. No seminal emission is required, but minimum amount of penetration must be proven.

The traditional common-law crime of sodomy had a much narrower meaning than it has now under many statutes. Strictly speaking, sodomy is committed only when a male person penetrates his penis into another male or female person's anus. Thus, sodomy did not originally encompass either the crime of *bestiality* or that of *buggery*. At common law, a male person committed bestiality by penetrating a female animal's vagina, and he committed buggery by penetrating a male or female animal's anus. Today, sodomy is commonly recognized by most states as including both bestiality and buggery.

Under many contemporary statutes, deviate sexual intercourse may consist of more than sodomy, bestiality, or buggery. Thus, "sodomy" has taken on an even wider meaning in some states. By statute in a number of states, deviate sexual intercourse occurs whenever a male person inserts his penis into the mouth of another male or female person. The technical name for this act is *fellatio*. Courts in Kentucky and Texas have held that fellatio does not constitute sodomy, but other courts have reached the opposite conclusion.

Deviate sexual intercourse has been extended by some states to include contact between the mouth or tongue of a male or female person and another female person's vulva (external genital area). This act is technically known as *cunnilingus*. A few states also have enlarged the scope of deviate sexual intercourse to include the penetration by a male person of his penis into the vagina of a deceased female person. This act is technically known as *necrophilia*.

It is important to note that cunnilingus and necrophilia have seldom been labeled "sodomy," although they are often placed within the framework of deviate sexual intercourse. Therefore, in states that still retain a sodomy statute, neither cunnilingus nor necrophilia is prohibited by that statute. They may, however, be prohibited by a separate statute. Some states have eliminated the word *sodomy* and created an overall statute regarding "deviate sexual conduct." In these states, cunnilingus and necrophilia are sometimes included with the other forms of deviate sexual intercourse.

Between Males, a Male and Female, or a Male and Animal

Deviate sexual intercourse may encompass a wide variety of activities between persons or between a person and an animal. Note that deviate sexual intercourse may occur between persons of the opposite sex or persons of the same sex. In other words, deviate sexual intercourse may include homosexual as well as heterosexual conduct.

Sodomy may be committed by (1) a male person with a female person, (2) a male person with a male person, *or* (3) a male person with an animal. Conspicuously absent from this assortment of activities are two additional possible combinations—deviate sexual intercourse by (1) a female person with another female person and (2) a female person with a male or female animal. Each of these acts is known to have occurred—the former occurring quite frequently.

The reason for this gap in the law is historical. When the English Parliament was .debating passage of England's first homosexual statute (sodomy was a common-law crime, not governed by statute), Queen Victoria personally dismissed the suggestion that sexual conduct between two women be explicitly prohibited. She firmly insisted that women of England would not think of doing any such thing! Apparently due to Queen Victoria's naiveté, lesbian conduct never became a serious crime in England or in the United States. Indeed, lesbian conduct seldom became even a minor crime.

Under many statutes, ironically, deviate sexual intercourse constitutes a criminal act even when engaged in by husband and wife. Only a few states have recognized a marital exception to sodomy, while most states either expressly or implicitly recognize a marital exception to rape. Moreover, *both* parties to deviate sexual intercourse may be partners in criminal activity if both are living human beings. Thus, both a husband and his wife may commit the criminal act of sodomy, even in the privacy of their own bedroom.

The element of force required for forcible rape is seldom required for sodomy or deviant sexual conduct. However, if one person perpetrates an act of deviate sexual intercourse on another person by force, some statutes provide for firmer punishment on conviction. Only Illinois and Connecticut have decriminalized *consensual* deviate sexual intercourse between homosexual adults. *Consensual* means that both parties have consented to the act. Other states have decriminalized deviate sexual intercourse between consenting marital partners.

General Criminal Intent

Sodomy and deviate sexual conduct are both generally viewed as cause-and-result crimes. Proof that either or both (when there are two) living human beings voluntarily participated in an act of deviate sexual intercourse normally demonstrates the offenders' presumed criminal intent. Unless one person uses force against the other person, both are generally presumed to have possessed a general criminal intent by reason of having participated in the illegal activity.

Other Sexual Offenses

Most states have enacted statutes to create sexual offenses other than forcible rape, statutory rape, and sodomy. Frequently, people consider such crimes as adultery, bigamy, fornication, and incest to be sexual offenses. These crimes involve sexual conduct but cause no harm to any person's body, so they cannot be classified as crimes against the person. They will be discussed in Chapter 14 as offenses against the family.

Certain offenses involving sexual behavior clearly involve harm or potential harm to the victim. These offenses include seduction, sexual misconduct, and sexual abuse.

Seduction

An offense known as "seduction" has been created by statute in many states. Seduction was not a crime at common law, so the wording of seduction statutes varies from state to state.

A male person may commit the offense of seduction by having sexual intercourse with a woman whom he has promised to marry in order to induce her to surrender her chastity. Hence, sexual intercourse is the first element of this offense, and the offense cannot take place unless the offender does have sexual intercourse with the victim. Nor does the offense occur unless prior to having sexual intercourse with the victim the offender promised to marry her.

Even if the other conditions are fulfilled, seduction does not take place unless the victim has never been married and is of previously chaste character. This generally means that she must have been a virgin before having sexual intercourse with the offender. Virginity may not be required, however, such as when the victim has had sexual intercourse only with another person who falsely promised to marry her!

The offense of seduction is not committed if the female surrenders to the male out of passion or lust or for any reason apart from his promise to marry her. Usually, the victim's reason for surrendering to the offender at the time of their first sexual encounter is crucial. Therefore, the fact that she may subsequently surrender to his advances as a result of passion will not matter.

In most states, once the man does in fact marry the woman, the marriage bars prosecution for seduction. In some states, once the man makes a bona fide offer to marry the woman, this bars prosecution for seduction, even though she refuses to accept his offer. As a rule, seduction is not prosecuted unless the male offender, rather than the female victim, refuses to go through with the marriage he has promised.

Under most seduction statutes, it does not matter that the offender honestly intended to fulfill his promise to marry the victim at the time he made the promise or at the time he had sexual intercourse with her. In this respect, seduction is akin to statutory rape in that the offender may bear criminal responsibility for this offense without proof that he had a criminal intent. Thus, seduction is one of those few crimes for which absolute criminal responsibility may be imposed by statute even in the absence of criminal intent.

Seduction is different from statutory rape, of course, because the female victim of seduction must be old enough to consent, and must in fact have consented, to sexual intercourse. Some states do require the victim of seduction to be under a certain age—such as eighteen. This age is usually higher than the age of consent that determines whether statutory rape is committed. Although the victim of seduction does actually consent to sexual intercourse, her consent is obtained through her reliance on a marriage that does not take place. Her consent is therefore obtained by means of an *implied* coercion.

Sexual Misconduct

Many states have enacted statutes creating the offense of "sexual misconduct." The wording of these statutes varies considerably from state to state, and so does the conduct required to commit this offense. Sexual misconduct is often committed when one person touches another person's body in an area that the law forbids touching, with an intent to arouse or gratify the sexual desire of himself (or herself), the person who is touched, or both. In some states, this offense takes place only when the two people are not husband and wife. Under some statutes, sexual misconduct occurs only when one or both persons are under a certain age, such as fourteen, sixteen, or eighteen.

Most sexual misconduct statutes do not clearly specify what areas of a person's body may not lawfully be touched for sexual gratification. Some statutes refer vaguely to "private" parts. Statutes that are specific usually prohibit one person from touching any other person's genital organ or a female person's breast area. Many sexual misconduct statutes prohibit both males and females from touching these areas of another person's body, whether the person whose body is touched is male or female. Thus, this conduct is forbidden between two persons of the opposite sex as well as two persons of the same sex.

Under many of these statutes, sexual misconduct may be committed when one person uses his or her genitals, hand, finger, lips, tongue, or some other organ to touch the prohibited area of another person's body. A few statutes provide that sexual misconduct occurs only when the prohibited area of another's body is unclothed, or when one person reaches underneath another's clothing to touch the prohibited area. Under some statutes, however, one may commit sexual misconduct by touching the prohibited area of another's body on top of the clothing that covers the area.

At least one person must intend to arouse or gratify the sexual desire of one or both of the people involved. Otherwise, sexual misconduct is not committed. Thus, sexual misconduct is rarely committed when a physician examines or treats the genital area or the breast of a patient during the practice of medicine.

It is not necessary that both persons intend to arouse or gratify a sexual desire as long as one of them possesses this intent at the moment contact between their two bodies is made. Unless both persons so intend, however, only the person possessing this intent can be prosecuted for sexual misconduct.

Note that either an intent to arouse or an intent to gratify the sexual desire of one or both persons is required, but that these sexual desires need not be both aroused and gratified. Thus, sexual misconduct may be committed even though neither person reaches an orgasm or sexual climax.

It should be stressed that sexual misconduct is not committed by routine kissing of another person's lips, face, or neck. This is true whether the two persons are of the opposite or the same sex. Similarly, this offense is not committed when two people shake hands or embrace each other for a normal length of time.

Masturbation seldom constitutes sexual misconduct, because most sexual misconduct statutes clearly involve conduct between two or more persons. Thus, one who touches areas of his own body for self-gratification seldom commits sexual misconduct. This offense may be committed if one person masturbates in public view, however, under some statutes.

Sexual Abuse

Quite a few states have created the statutory offense of "sexual abuse," instead of or in addition to the offense of sexual misconduct. Like sexual misconduct, sexual abuse may apply to different kinds of behavior in different states. Ordinarily, sexual abuse occurs only when one person touches a prohibited area of another person's body *without* the consent of the person whose body is touched. In this respect, sexual abuse differs from sexual misconduct, which as a rule is committed *with* the consent of the person whose body is touched.

A person may commit sexual abuse by touching someone else's body in a way that would constitute sexual misconduct, except that the person whose body is touched refuses to consent or is unable to consent. Thus, one who touches the prohibited area of another's body may commit sexual abuse if the victim resists being touched. This offense may take place, also, if the victim is too young to consent to sexual contact, having not reached a specified age. Furthermore, this offense may occur if the victim is asleep or otherwise unconscious when the sexual contact is made, or if the victim is mentally incompetent or physically incapacitated so that he or she is unable to resist. One who makes the victim intoxicated from alcohol or drugs may commit sexual abuse by touching a prohibited area of the victim's body.

In a few states, a person who commits the criminal act of forcible rape or statutory rape may bear criminal responsibility only for sexual abuse if he himself is a minor at the time the act takes place. In these states, a male person under a certain age, such as fourteen, sixteen, or eighteen, is not considered old enough to be criminally responsible for rape. By committing rape, he may be convicted only of sexual abuse in these states.

CHAPTER 8

Criminal Homicides

Criminal homicides are offenses that involve a person's death. Homicides are the most serious criminal injury offenses. As such, homicides are more serious forms of assault and battery, since a person must be physically hurt in order to be killed. Assault and battery are lesser included offenses to murder, manslaughter, and most other criminal homicides. The seriousness of homicide offenses depends upon the presence or absence of aggravating or mitigating circumstances surrounding commission of the crime. In any case, the victim is just as dead. However, murder may be reduced to manslaughter because the offender acted in the "heat of passion." Or, a homicide may be murder instead of manslaughter because the offender acted "in cold blood."

Criminal homicides include murder, manslaughter, and homicide from criminal negligence. In addition, suicide and attempting suicide are discussed in conjunction with criminal homicides.

Murder

The elements of murder can be outlined as follows:
A. The Criminal Act:
   1. the killing
   2. of another living human being
B. The Criminal Intent:
   3. (*a*) a specific intent to kill or
      (*b*) a specific intent to do serious bodily harm or
      (*c*) during the course of committing a felony

Killing

The act of murder may not be very different from the act of criminal battery, but battery becomes murder at the moment the victim dies of his wounds. The crime of murder cannot be committed unless the victim dies. Moreover, murder cannot be committed unless the victim dies as a result of wounds caused by another person. This is true of all crimes resulting in the victim's death, such as murder, manslaughter, and criminally negligent homicide. These crimes are known collectively as criminal homicide.

Two questions frequently arise in conjunction with this element of murder and all criminal homicides. When does death of the victim occur? Within what time span after the offender's attack must the victim die?

Death has been defined medically as the absence of heartbeat, or the absence of respiration, or the cessation of brain activity. Courts have referred to death as "the destruction of all the senses" or the lack of consciousness, understanding, and reason. Nevertheless, for the purpose of determining criminal homicide, death is usually presumed to occur at the moment the victim's heart stops beating. Obviously, if cardiac rhythm is restored, even by artificial means, the victim's life is revived and death has not occurred.

At common law, the English courts required that the victim die within *one year and one day* following the offender's attack, in order for the offender's act to constitute murder or any other form of criminal homicide. This rule continues in most states today. If the victim lives a year and two days or longer after being assailed, the offender's attack constitutes only criminal battery.

A killing may take place by either an act or an omission on the part of the person who causes death. However, in order to commit murder or any criminal homicide by *omission,* the offender must be under some *duty* to keep the victim alive, and he must fail to do his duty. As mentioned in Chapter 1, for example, the mother of a minor child (or in many states either parent, both parents, or a legal guardian) is under a duty to feed and care for the child. If the child starves, the mother (or parent or guardian) fails to do her duty. If death results from starvation, the mother (or parent or guardian) may, by omission, have committed some form of criminal homicide.

As another example, the watchman at a railroad crossing is generally under a duty to stop pedestrian and automobile traffic from crossing the tracks as a train approaches. If this watchman falls asleep or intentionally fails to warn passing pedestrians or motorists that a train is approaching, he fails to do his duty. The omission may constitute some form of criminal homicide if a pedestrian or a motorist dies from collision with the train.

Another Living Human Being

The crime of murder requires the killing of another living human being. It never is murder to stab a dead person; nor is it murder to kill any living thing other than a human being. It is not murder, for example, to kill an animal or a plant. The major question that arises in conjunction with this element of murder is: *When does life begin?*

At early common law, a fetus was considered "alive" thirty days following conception. Thirty days was later increased to eighty days. Later still at common law, a fetus was considered to be alive only after it had *quickened* (wiggled in the womb), an event that normally occurs sixteen to twenty weeks after conception. By the middle of the seventeenth century, however, it was not murder at common law to destroy a fetus before the fetus was "born alive." Most present statutes require a *live birth* before a fetus is considered a living human being.

Sometimes it may be difficult to determine whether a fetus is or is not born alive. Normally, a fetus is not considered to be alive until it is completely expelled from its mother's body. Even after it has been separated from the mother's body, a fetus is not considered to be alive until or unless it shows some signs of independent vitality—such as respiration or blood circulation. Some states require additional evidence that the fetus is alive, such as crying. A few states have required that the umbilical cord be cut before the fetus is considered to be alive, but most states do not view this as a necessary element of life.

An attack on a pregnant woman that results in "death" of an unborn fetus but that does not result in death of the mother is criminal battery—not murder or any other form of criminal homicide, in most jurisdictions. The removal of a fetus from the mother's womb with a specific intent to destroy the fetus may constitute the crime of abortion. Some states continue to classify criminal abortion as a form of criminal homicide. However, if the fetus is not considered to be alive, it cannot logically be killed. Therefore, criminal abortion is more reasonably classified as a crime against public health. It may justifiably be considered a crime against the public health, also, because of the risk it may pose to the mother's health and life.

Specific Intent to Kill

The offender's *intent* at the moment of his act or omission is crucial in the classification of criminal homicides. All criminal homicides involve the killing of another living human being. Intent is often the element that marks the difference between (1) murder, (2) manslaughter, and (3) homicide from criminal negligence.

The killing of another living human being with a *specific intent to kill* at the moment of the act or omission constitutes the crime of murder, unless mitigating circumstances reduce the crime to manslaughter. Sometimes it is easy to show a specific intent to kill, and sometimes this task may be extremely difficult or impossible. Usually a specific intent to kill may be inferred from the offender's behavior, words, and other circumstances surrounding the moment at which the victim was assailed, such as the offender's expression: "I am going to kill you."

As emphasized earlier, throughout the criminal law a person is presumed to intend the natural and probable consequences of his acts, in the absence of contrary evidence. Thus, when an offender aims a weapon at a person and kills the person, the offender is presumed to have intended to cause the victim's death (in the absence of contrary evidence). This presumption is reinforced if the offender uses a *dangerous* ("lethal" or "deadly") *weapon* to kill his victim. (For a discussion of dangerous weapons, see Chapter 5 under "Aggravated Battery.") Of course, it is possible for an offender to show that he used a dangerous weapon *without* an intent to kill, but with an intent to *frighten* his victim or to inflict a *nonfatal* wound. In many states, the burden of proof is on the prosecution to prove beyond a reasonable doubt that the offender intended to kill rather than merely to frighten or injure his victim.

Even if no dangerous weapon is used by the offender to kill his victim, a specific intent to kill may be shown by other circumstances surrounding the act. For example, a heavy male offender who strikes a child, a woman, or a frail male victim may be presumed to have possessed a specific intent to kill; furthermore, repeated blows from an offender's fists or feet will generally indicate a specific intent to kill (in the absence of contrary evidence in both cases). Obviously, any kind of statement uttered by the offender at any time (before, during, or after the fact) admitting to a specific intent to kill the victim would almost conclusively show the presence of a specific intent to kill.

Specific Intent to Do Serious Bodily Harm

The killing of another living human being with a *specific intent to do serious bodily harm* in the mind of the offender at the moment of his act constitutes murder, unless mitigating circumstances reduce the crime to manslaughter. Usually it is easier to show that an offender possessed a specific intent to do serious bodily harm than it is to show that he possessed a specific intent to kill. As with a specific intent to kill, intent to do serious bodily harm may be inferred from the offender's behavior, words, and other circumstances surrounding the moment at which the victim was assailed.

A question frequently arises concerning the meaning of "serious bodily harm." *Serious* bodily harm means something much more than mere bodily injury. It means bodily injury that falls short of death—but barely so. For example, an offender who kicks his victim in the head two hundred times, intending only to make the victim permanently feeble-minded, is nevertheless criminally responsible for murder if the victim dies from the injuries.

As with a specific intent to kill, a specific intent to do serious bodily harm may properly be inferred from the offender's possession of a dangerous weapon at the time of the attack on the victim. Or, it may become obviated as a result of an offender's conduct which causes death to another person. Such a specific intent may be inferred as a result of an offender's *willful* or *wanton* disregard of an *extreme* risk to human life. If the offender *willfully* disregards an extreme risk to human life, this means that he was consciously aware of the hazard but chose to ignore its implication. If the offender *wantonly* disregards an extreme risk to human life, this does not mean that he was actually aware of the hazard, but it does mean that he should have been aware of it, because a reasonable man would have recognized the hazard as an extreme risk to human life. Some states require that an offender willfully rather than wantonly disregard such a risk in order to be criminally liable for murder.

An offender who shoots bullets into a house without determining whether or not the house is inhabited by people *willfully* disregards an extreme risk to human life. If death results from his act, this offender may bear criminal responsibility for murder.

An offender who transports dynamite or nitroglycerin in a semitrailer through a congested city street, a tunnel, or over a bridge where heavy traffic flows may *wantonly* disregard an extreme risk to human life. If his cargo explodes and death results to a bystander, he may bear criminal responsibility for murder. In a state that requires willful rather than wanton disregard of the hazard, the truck driver in this example would not be criminally responsible for murder unless he consciously disregarded an ordinance (of which he had knowledge) that prohibited transportation of explosives at the time and place of the explosion.

Killing in the Course of Committing a Felony

The killing of another living human being may constitute the crime of murder even if the offender possessed *neither* a specific intent to kill *nor* a specific intent to do serious bodily harm to the victim. The killing of another living human being may constitute murder if the offender, at the moment he fatally wounds the victim, is in the process of *committing* or *attempting* to commit a felony. This is the *felony-murder rule,* which was explained in Chapter 3.

At common law, a person who caused the death of another person during the course of committing or attempting to commit *any* felony bore criminal responsibility for murder. Later, in England and in most of the United States, the felony-murder rule became more limited in its application, applying only to certain types of felonious activities. In addition, it came to encompass only those deaths that "naturally and probably" resulted from the offender's felonious conduct.

In most states, therefore, the felony-murder rule applies only to felonies that are in themselves "inherently dangerous," such as robbery, arson, forcible rape, and sodomy. Aggravated battery and kidnapping may also be included in some states. In a few states, the felony-murder rule applies to such common-law felonies as larceny and burglary, even though these crimes are not viewed as being "inherently dangerous."

Nevertheless, the felony-murder rule does not apply generally to crimes such as embezzlement and false pretenses, because these crimes are not common-law felonies (though they are felonies by statute in many states), nor are they "inherently dangerous." A person who is engaged in committing a misdemeanor cannot be criminally responsible under the felony-murder rule, but he may bear criminal responsibility under the misdemeanor-manslaughter rule (see the next section of this chapter, "Manslaughter").

By limiting the felony-murder rule to situations in which death results "naturally and probably" from the offender's felonious conduct, most states have eliminated an offender's criminal liability for *unforeseeable* death that may result from commission of a felony. One should note the difference between *unforeseeable* and *unforeseen,* however. If death results from an offender's conduct during the course of committing a dangerous felony, he may be held criminally responsible for murder although he *himself* did not actually foresee the possibility of death. This can happen if an ordinary person with reasonable intelligence would be expected to foresee the possibility of death under the circumstances.

For example, an armed robber who points a loaded revolver or shotgun at his victim *should* foresee that the weapon *could* accidentally discharge. Similarly, a person who sets fire to a building *should* foresee that a fireman or another rescuer *could* be killed while trying to extinguish the blaze.

If two or more persons *conspire* to commit a dangerous felony, then both or all offenders are individually responsible for death caused by an act of one of them. However, the felony-murder rule extends *only* to death that results from an act committed by someone involved in committing a dangerous felony. A felony offender can never be responsible under the felony-murder rule for death inflicted by *someone else* (other than a co-conspirator) during the course of his felony. Some courts and some legislatures have viewed this as a gap in the felony-murder rule.

To fill in this gap, several states have enacted "vicarious liability" statutes, which provide that a person who commits a dangerous felony may be criminally responsible for *any* death that results during or immediately after the commission of the felony (see Chapter 3). Thus, an armed robber may be *vicariously* liable for murder if, during the robbery, a *policeman* or a *victim* accidentally shoots an innocent bystander while attempting to thwart the robbery.

The theory underlying both the felony-murder rule and the "vicarious liability" doctrine is quite easy to comprehend, although one might doubt its wisdom. Because no person may bear criminal responsibility for murder unless some kind of criminal intent can be shown, a person who commits a felony from which death accidentally results could not be culpable for murder in the absence of the felony-murder or "vicarious liability" doctrine. To prevent this type of offender from escaping responsibility for the more serious felony (murder), the law permits the offender's original felonious intent to become coupled with *two* criminal acts instead of only one. Thus, in both felony-murder and vicarious liability, the offender bears criminal responsibility both for the felony he planned and the death he probably did not plan. In other words, the offender cannot argue the limits of his original felonious intent; he must bear criminal responsibility for all harm that results directly during the course of his felonious plan, whether intended originally or not.

Degrees of Murder

In a majority of states, the crime of murder is divided into two degrees. Murder in the *first degree* is considered a more serious crime than murder in the *second degree*. For this reason, murder in the first degree is often punished more severely than murder in the second degree. The death penalty (capital punishment) has been imposed more frequently for first-degree murder than for second-degree murder.

A number of distinctions exist between murder in the first and second degrees. Because of the marked difference in seriousness and punishment between the two crimes, it is important to understand the reasons for the distinctions.

First-Degree Murder. The intent of the offender at the time of his criminal act frequently makes him *culpable,* or criminally liable, for first-degree murder. Proof that the offender possessed a *specific intent to kill* his victim at the moment of the attack will normally support a conviction for first-degree murder. This is especially true if the circumstances of the crime evidence *premeditation* and *deliberation* on the part of the offender prior to the killing.

The fact that a murder is accomplished by lying in wait for the victim, by torture, or by poison commonly suggests the presence of premeditation and deliberation. Thus, this evidence will normally support a conviction of first-degree murder.

In many states, murder that is committed by the offender during the process of committing or attempting to commit certain *specific* felonies constitutes first-degree murder. These specific felonies commonly include arson, burglary, rape, and robbery. In most states, other types of felony-murder will not constitute first-degree murder.

Second-Degree Murder. Generally speaking, all types of murder that do not fall within the scope of first-degree murder are considered second-degree murder. Second-degree murder is less serious than first-degree murder, but still more serious than manslaughter.

An offender who possessed a specific intent to do *serious bodily harm* (rather than to kill) at the time of the killing will ordinarily bear criminal responsibility for second-degree murder but not for first-degree murder. Similarly, an offender who possessed a specific intent to kill his victim, but who acted *without* premeditation and deliberation may sometimes bear criminal responsibility only for second-degree murder.

In states that follow the felony-murder rule, murder that is committed by the offender during the process of committing or attempting to commit an "inherently dangerous" (but nonspecific) felony constitutes second-degree murder. In short, felony-murder that does not constitute first-degree murder usually constitutes second-degree murder. "Vicarious liability" for the death of another person would seem to warrant a conviction for second-degree murder at most.

Manslaughter

The elements of manslaughter can be outlined as follows:
    A. The Criminal Act:
        1. the killing
        2. of another living human being
    B. The Criminal Intent:
        3. (*a*) a specific intent to kill or do serious bodily harm mitigated by extenuating circumstances or
            (*b*) with gross recklessness *or* gross negligence or
            (c) during the course of commiting a misdemeanor

Like the crime of murder, manslaughter cannot be committed unless a living human being is killed. These elements are explained earlier in this chapter. Both of these elements are exactly the same for manslaughter as for murder.

Specific Intent Mitigated by Extenuating Circumstances

A person who kills another living human being while possessing either a specific intent to *kill* or a specific intent to do *serious bodily harm* generally commits murder, unless his criminal responsibility is mitigated by the presence of *extenuating circumstances* at the time of his criminal act. The lingering question in any discussion of manslaughter is: What extenuating circumstances are thought to be sufficient to mitigate or reduce murder to manslaughter?

Traditionally, manslaughter was considered to be the killing of another living human being without "malice aforethought." It is important to realize, however, that no uniform definition of "malice aforethought" has ever existed. Thus, the presence or the absence of "malice aforethought" may well be inconsequential in distinguishing manslaughter from murder—at least in a modern age that requires specificity.

Very few circumstances are ordinarily considered sufficient to mitigate or reduce murder to manslaughter. "Heat of passion" at the time of the killing is often considered a proper extenuating circumstance; *mistaken claim of right* sometimes is.

"Heat of Passion." A person who kills another living human being with a specific intent either to kill or to do serious bodily harm does not bear criminal responsibility for murder in many states if he killed the victim in the "heat of passion." Quite obviously, the phrase "heat of passion" connotes the presence of an *emotional disturbance* in the offender's mind at the time of his criminal act. Passion in this sense is generally intense anger amounting to rage, but it may also consist of intense fright amounting to terror. Whatever the passion may be, it must be sufficient to induce a reasonable man to kill, or it will not be sufficient to reduce murder to manslaughter.

"Heat of passion" is really a temporary loss of self-control on the part of the offender at the moment he kills the victim. It can be created only by some kind of *provocation*. This provocation must have been so strong that it could be expected to cause any reasonable man to lose his self-control under the same circumstances, but not sufficient to excuse criminal responsibility altogether.

The classic example of provocation that is almost universally sufficient to reduce murder to manslaughter is one's sudden discovery of his or her spouse in the act of committing adultery. In this situation, it is usually manslaughter and not murder for the "innocent" spouse to kill the "guilty" spouse, the paramour, or both. Sometimes a person's *belief* that his or her spouse is having an affair may be sufficient to reduce to manslaughter the killing of the suspected spouse, even if the belief is erroneous, so long as the belief was reasonable. This kind of mitigation does not extend outside of marriage and does not include common-law couples, engaged parties, or divorced persons.

Another example of provocation that is almost as classic as the adultery example is a situation in which a person kills another while resisting an *illegal* arrest. A killing that is done to avoid a *legal* arrest seldom mitigates murder to manslaughter, but may reduce first-degree murder to second-degree murder.

If two persons are engaged in mutual combat (a fight), and one kills the other as a result of an intent formed during the struggle, the stress of the situation is sometimes considered a reasonable provocation. Similarly, if the offender kills the victim in retaliation for a battery inflicted by the victim on the offender immediately before the killing, this frequently constitutes provocation. However, a blow from the victim's fist can never constitute reasonable provocation if the offender kills the victim with a dangerous weapon rather than with his own fists. (An unprovoked attack on the "offender" by the "victim" with a dangerous weapon would probably *justify* the killing altogether, as the "offender" would be acting in self-defense. See Chapter 4.)

Words alone, in the absence of some bodily action, cannot constitute a reasonable provocation to kindle the "heat of passion." However, a person may be provoked by conduct that threatens to inflict or does inflict injury on another person, such as his wife or child, who stands in a close personal relationship to him. In addition, a person may be provoked by a third person (other than the victim) so as to kindle the "heat of passion" and reduce a subsequent murder to manslaughter.

Once a person has become provoked, however, the "heat of passion" that is thereby created cannot last forever. A person's criminal responsibility for a homicide will not be mitigated on account of the "heat of passion" if he had time to "cool off" between the moment of provocation and the moment of the killing. In some states, a person's criminal responsibility for a killing may not be mitigated even though he did *not* have enough time to cool off (because he required more time than the average man), if a reasonable man under similar circumstances would have had ample time to regain his composure.

Mistaken Claim of Right. A person who kills another living human being with a specific intent either to kill or to do serious bodily harm does not bear criminal responsibility for murder in many states if he kills the victim under a "claim of right" but is "mistaken." A person who kills under a mistaken claim of right honestly believes that he has a "right" to kill the victim under the circumstances that he honestly believes exist. However, the killing is not excused or justified, because the circumstances are not as the offender believes them to be.

A mistaken claim of right may include a mistaken claim of self-defense, a mistaken claim of defense of another person, a mistaken claim of property defense, or a mistaken claim of coercion, duress, or necessity. (A *legitimate* claim of self-defense, defense of another person, defense of property, coercion, duress, or necessity would ordinarily justify or excuse criminal responsibility for homicide altogether. See Chapter 4.)

In order for a claim of self-defense to justify a homicide, the person who causes another person's death must be *free from fault* in provoking his adversary. If the offender originally provoked the victim toward violence, but afterward killed the victim to save his own life, the homicide cannot be justified. It may be reduced from murder to manslaughter, however, because the victim's provoked hostility serves as a mitigating circumstance.

In addition, a claim of self-defense will not excuse a homicide as being justified unless the person who causes death *reasonably* (although not necessarily correctly) believes that he must use deadly physical force to prevent fatal or serious bodily injury to himself. If the person who causes death *unreasonably* believes that his adversary is about to inflict fatal or serious bodily injury on him, a claim of self-defense will *not* excuse killing the adversary. Moreover, if the person who causes death *unreasonably* believes that deadly physical force is necessary to prevent fatal or serious bodily injury to himself, a claim of self-defense will *not excuse* killing the adversary. In either of these last two situations, however, the homicide will usually be reduced from murder to manslaughter because of the killer's *honest but unreasonable* belief.

Under similar reasoning, murder should be reduced to manslaughter if the killer honestly, though unreasonably, believes that deadly physical force is necessary to prevent another person from immediate fatal or serious bodily harm, or to prevent a felony from being committed, or to prevent a fleeing felon from escaping while in immediate flight from the scene of a crime.

In addition, it should be manslaughter and not murder for a person to kill another innocent person, under coercion or duress, in order to save his own life. The new Minnesota criminal code contains this provision.

Gross Recklessness or Gross Negligence

In many states, a person who kills another living human being may bear criminal responsibility for manslaughter if the victim's death results from the offender's *gross recklessness* or *gross negligence*. A person whose grossly reckless or grossly negligent conduct results in another person's death may be convicted of manslaughter in many states, even though he did not possess a specific intent to kill or to do serious bodily harm at the time of his act.

Gross recklessness and gross negligence are much different from ordinary negligence. Indeed, very few states permit a person to be convicted of manslaughter as a result of ordinary negligence —even if death to another person does result. Ordinary negligence customarily occurs when a person takes an unreasonable risk of injury; a risk that a reasonable, prudent person would not be expected to take under similar circumstances. On the contrary, gross *negligence* usually requires a *high risk* of death or serious bodily injury. In addition, gross *recklessness* normally requires that the offender be *conscious* of the high risk of death or serious bodily injury that his conduct creates. Some states require gross recklessness rather than gross negligence in order to support a manslaughter conviction. A person may create a high risk of death or serious bodily harm, for example, by failing to install proper fire escapes for an apartment building he owns or manages. If death results because tenants or visitors in the building are unable to escape a fire, a conviction of manslaughter may be supported.

Under most circumstances, a person who does create a high risk of death or serious bodily harm is indeed aware of that fact. The most notable exception to this general statement, however, would be the intoxicated motorist. A person who operates a motor vehicle while intoxicated almost always creates a high risk to all persons in his path, although during his drunkenness the motorist may not be aware of the risk he creates.

Killing in the Course of Committing a Misdemeanor

The killing of another living human being may constitute the crime of manslaughter although the offender possessed no specific intent to kill or to do serious bodily harm, and although his conduct was neither grossly reckless nor grossly negligent, if he causes the death of anyone during the course of *committing* or *attempting* to commit a misdemeanor. The *misdemeanor-manslaughter rule,* as this doctrine is commonly called, is the counterpart to the felony-murder rule that was discussed earlier in this chapter. (The misdemeanor-manslaughter rule is also discussed in Chapter 3.)

In some states, a person may bear criminal responsibility for manslaughter if he causes the death of another person while committing or attempting to commit *any unlawful act*. Not all unlawful acts are classified as misdemeanors, of course, and in a majority of states, death that results accidentally during the course of an unlawful act that is *not* a misdemeanor *cannot* support a conviction of manslaughter without proof of gross recklessness or gross negligence.

In many states, also, death that results accidentally from *some* misdemeanors will not support a manslaughter conviction under the misdemeanor-manslaughter rule. In these states, only misdemeanors that are dangerous in themselves can support such a conviction. The two most obvious misdemeanors of this type are criminal assault and criminal battery—especially the latter. Thus, if a person is in the process of committing criminal battery and the victim dies from the offensive contact, the assailant may be convicted of manslaughter without proof of any specific intent to kill or to do serious bodily harm. As with the felony-murder rule, the offender cannot argue the limits of his original criminal intent; he must bear criminal responsibility for all harm that results from his original criminal plan, whether intended originally or not.

On the other hand, a person who utters a loud shriek would bear no criminal responsibility even if another person dies as a result of the sudden noise, unless proof is shown that the noise-maker possessed a specific intent to kill or to do serious bodily harm. This is true although a loud shriek may constitute a misdemeanor ("disturbing the peace" or "criminal nuisance"), since noise-making is not considered dangerous in itself.

No state has established a vicarious liability rule that would encompass death resulting during the course of a misdemeanor but not caused by someone involved in the criminal activity. Vicarious liability seems limited to the felony situation—at least for the moment.

Types of Manslaughter

The *intent* of the offender at the time of his criminal act normally determines the type of manslaughter for which he may be culpable or criminally responsible. While murder is usually divided into two degrees—first and second—manslaughter is generally divided into *voluntary* manslaughter and *involuntary* manslaughter.

Voluntary manslaughter is considered more serious than involuntary manslaughter, and for this reason it is ordinarily punished more severely. It is important, therefore, to understand the reasons for a distinction between the two crimes.

Voluntary Manslaughter. To bear criminal responsibility for voluntary manslaughter, an offender normally must have possessed a specific intent to *kill* or to do *serious bodily harm* at the moment he killed the victim. The theoretical difference between voluntary manslaughter and second-degree murder hinges on the presence or absence of *extenuating circumstances*. Two persons may commit identical killings; yet one offender may bear criminal responsibility for second-degree murder while the other is criminally responsible only for voluntary manslaughter. The killer who is responsible for voluntary manslaughter, in theory, must have killed his victim in the "heat of passion" or under a mistaken claim of right, as explained earlier. These extenuating circumstances are often sufficient to mitigate or reduce second-degree murder to voluntary manslaughter.

In practice, however, most juries probably have little idea of the legal distinction between second-degree murder and voluntary manslaughter, despite instructions from the court. If two offenders committed identical crimes while possessing a specific intent to kill or to do serious bodily harm, the jury may convict one offender of second-degree murder and the other of voluntary manslaughter for illogical reasons. A jury may, for example, take pity on a youthful offender and not take pity on a more mature offender. Frequently, juries are inclined to convict a female offender of voluntary manslaughter just because she is a woman, although they would convict a male offender of second-degree murder under identical circumstances. Furthermore, statistics show that many juries have convicted black offenders of second- (or even first-) degree murder, when white offenders have ordinarily been convicted only of voluntary manslaughter under identical conditions.

Involuntary Manslaughter. In the absence of proof that the offender possessed a specific intent to kill or to do serious bodily harm at the time he killed his victim, a conviction for voluntary manslaughter is not justifiable. If a criminal homicide is committed on account of the offender's gross recklessness or gross negligence, as defined earlier, under the better view this offender may bear criminal responsibility only for *involuntary* manslaughter. Similarly, if death results accidentally during the course of a misdemeanor or other unlawful act, a conviction under the misdemeanor-manslaughter rule should be for *involuntary* rather than voluntary manslaughter.

A criminal homicide that results from gross recklessness or gross negligence or a criminal homicide under the misdemeanor-manslaughter rule is not likely to support a conviction of voluntary manslaughter. On the other hand, the extenuating circumstances may be so great under certain circumstances as to warrant convicting an offender for involuntary manslaughter even though he did in fact possess a specific intent to kill or to do serious bodily harm at the moment he killed his victim. Thus, the person who kills with a specific intent to kill or to do serious bodily harm may be convicted of either voluntary or involuntary manslaughter, depending on the way in which the jury views the extenuating circumstances. On the contrary, the person who kills *without* a specific intent to kill or do serious bodily harm should *never* be convicted of more than involuntary manslaughter, if a distinction is to be maintained consistently between voluntary and involuntary manslaughter.

As with the distinction between second-degree murder and voluntary manslaughter, the distinction between voluntary and involuntary manslaughter is theoretical and not always understood or followed by many juries, despite instructions by the court. Some juries may disregard their duty to evaluate the offender's intent or to measure the extenuating circumstances surrounding the criminal act. Instead, these jurors may be influenced by their prejudices or sympathies.

Homicide from Criminal Negligence

The elements of homicide from criminal negligence can be outlined as follows:

A. The Criminal Act:
   1. the killing
   2. of another living human being
B. The Criminal Intent:
   3. during the course of criminally negligent behavior

Like the crimes of murder and manslaughter, the crime of homicide from criminal negligence cannot be committed unless a living human being is killed. These elements are discussed earlier in this chapter. Both of these elements are exactly the same for murder, manslaughter, and homicide from criminal negligence.

Killing in the Course of Criminally Negligent Behavior

A person who causes another person's death during the course of ordinary negligent behavior cannot as a rule be convicted of either murder or manslaughter. Ordinary negligence does not constitute a specific intent to kill or to do serious bodily harm. Nor can such an intent be implied, as ordinary negligence is not the same as a disregard for extreme risk to human life. As explained earlier, ordinary negligence is different from gross negligence. While ordinary negligence customarily involves an *unreasonable* risk of injury, gross negligence usually involves a *high risk* of death or serious bodily injury.

To prevent the person who causes another's death through *ordinary* negligence from avoiding criminal responsibility under many circumstances, some states have enacted statutes that criminalize the act of homicide if it is committed with *criminal* negligence. Ordinary negligence does not always constitute criminal negligence. Thus, a person would not bear criminal responsibility in every instance in which he caused another person's death. However, criminal negligence may require no more than an unreasonable risk of injury (the standard for ordinary negligence), coupled with some *violation of any criminal law,* however slight. Thus, if a person causes the death of another person during the course of ordinary negligent behavior, *and* if at that moment he is violating any criminal law, he may bear criminal responsibility for the victim's death.

Death resulting during the course of the offender's criminally negligent behavior may be labeled differently in each state. It may, for example, be termed "criminally negligent homicide" (as in New York), "culpable homicide" or "vehicular homicide" (as in California), or "negligent homicide" (as recommended in the Model Penal Code).

The main purpose for criminalizing homicide from criminal negligence is to reduce the number of highway fatalities that occur daily as a result of criminal negligence in the operation of motor vehicles. If death results to another person because the offender is speeding, passing illegally, or recklessly driving a motor vehicle, this may constitute homicide from criminal negligence. If death results to another person because the offender is operating a motor vehicle while intoxicated, the offender almost always bears responsibility for homicide from criminal negligence (except that in a few states this constitutes involuntary manslaughter by statute). The new Wisconsin criminal code provides that a person may bear criminal responsibility for homicide from criminal negligence if death is caused by a vicious animal in the offender's control or if death results from the offender's "accidental" use of a weapon while intoxicated.

Suicide Offenses

Two offenses exist regarding suicide: assisting suicide and attempting suicide.

Assisting Suicide

In several states, a person who aids, abets, or in any way assists another person in committing suicide may be guilty of murder in either the first or second degree. One may assist another person in committing suicide in a number of ways. A person who furnishes another with the means for committing suicide—a weapon, poison, pills, and so on—aids and abets the suicide if he knows what this equipment will be used for when he furnishes it. One may also commit this offense if he is present when another person commits suicide but does nothing to prevent the other person from killing himself. Thus, one may commit the offense of assisting suicide by either an act or an omission. Although no inducement on the offender's part is necessary for this offense, a person may commit this offense by counseling someone else to commit suicide, if the person does in fact commit suicide.

Attempting suicide is not a criminal offense in some states, and in these states, as a rule, one does not commit a criminal offense by aiding, abetting, or otherwise assisting another person in committing suicide.

Attempting Suicide

In many states, attempting suicide is a criminal offense. A person is guilty of attempting suicide when he intentionally tries to end his own life but fails. Attempting suicide was a misdemeanor at common law and remains a misdemeanor in some states that have retained the common law as a body of law. Only a few of the states that have abolished the common law and replaced it with statutes have made attempting suicide a crime.

In states where attempting suicide is a criminal offense, however, one who endangers or causes injury to another person while attempting to commit suicide may be guilty of a felony. He may be guilty of manslaughter under the misdemeanor-manslaughter rule if he causes another person's death while attempting to commit suicide. Thus, for example, a person who crashes his automobile into an automobile driven by another person in an unsuccessful effort to kill himself may be guilty of manslaughter if he lives but the other person dies. If neither the person who attempts suicide nor any bystander dies, however, no form of criminal homicide takes place. Attempting suicide itself is not a form of criminal homicide.

Suicide

Suicide was a felony at common law, although it is no longer a criminal offense in any state. Even at common law, only one who *intentionally* took his own life was criminally responsible for suicide. As suicide was subject to the same defenses as any other criminal offense, an insane person was not considered to possess the capacity to form a criminal intent and, therefore, was not criminally responsible for suicide.

It may seem strange for suicide to have been a criminal offense, since the person who succeeds in killing himself is not alive to be punished. In England for many centuries, however, a person who was considered criminally responsible for suicide was punished posthumously. He was denied burial in a church cemetery, and instead his body was laid to rest along the highway with a stake through its heart! Moreover, as suicide was a felony at common law, the offender's heirs could not inherit his property, which was forfeited to the Crown.

Modern legal theory holds that suicide cannot be a criminal offense, since the person who succeeds in killing himself cannot be punished in this world. Thus, punishment may not be imposed in the name of the state.

part 3

Offenses Against Property and Against the Person and Property

CHAPTER 9

Theft Offenses

Theft, also known as larceny, is the most basic offense that involves the unlawful acquisition of property. It is not the only offense of this kind. Other offenses such as robbery (Chapter 14), embezzlement and false pretenses (Chapter 10) involve particular methods by which one person acquires another's property unlawfully.

Theft is viewed as being a lesser included offense to crimes such as embezzlement, false pretenses, and robbery. This is true because in order for a person to commit one of these three offenses he must also commit theft. Thus, it will be important to remember when reading subsequent chapters in Part Three of this book that when embezzlement, false pretenses, robbery, and numerous other offenses are committed, theft is committed as well.

The seriousness of a theft often depends upon the value of property that has been stolen. In addition, the seriousness of a theft may be determined by the method used to steal the property. Once property has been stolen, frequently it is shuffled among different persons in order to disguise its true identity and prevent recapture by whoever is entitled to the property. Consequently, additional offenses may be committed such as receiving or concealing stolen property.

Theft offenses that are discussed in this chapter include larceny or theft, receiving stolen property, concealing stolen property, theft from the person, theft from a building, and theft from a motor vehicle.

Larceny or Theft

The elements of larceny (theft) can be outlined as follows:
A. The Criminal Act:
1. the taking
2. and carrying away
3. of personal property
4. from another person's possession
B. The Criminal Intent:
5. a specific intent to steal

Taking

The act of larceny or theft cannot occur unless one person takes personal property from another person's possession. A person takes an item of personal property when he assumes control and dominion over the property for himself. One assumes control and dominion over property when he gains the ability to move the property by himself (or on his direction). This is known technically as a *caption*.

A person usually takes control of property when he grasps it with his hand or his fingers, since he then has the power to move the property. For example, one generally takes control of a coin or a jewel by picking it up. With heavy mechanical property, one may not succeed in taking control until he touches a vital part of the property. For example, one does not usually take control of a motor vehicle merely by touching its door; one must touch the starter. A person might take control of a vehicle by affixing a chain to its bumper in order to tow it away.

Property does not always have to be touched to be controlled, however. A person may take control of property that operates by remote control by touching the controls. One may take control of an animal such as a horse by standing near it with a carrot, thus enticing the animal to obey or follow. Similarly, a person may take control of a small animal or bird by holding it to prevent it from escaping. Or one may take control of a larger animal by erecting a fence around it to restrain its movements.

One does not succeed every time he tries to take control of property. For example, a person may strike someone else's hand, causing the second person to drop an item of property onto the ground. If the first person fails to locate the fallen property (perhaps because it is dark), he cannot be said to have taken control of it. In this example, however, the person who struck the other's hand may take control of the fallen property without picking it up. He could step on it, for example, to prevent the person who was carrying it from picking it up.

Carrying Away

The act of larceny or theft cannot occur as a rule unless one person takes and carries away personal property from another person's possession. A person may take control over property and not carry it away. One carries away property that he has taken at the moment he begins to move the property any distance from the place where he found it. This movement is known as an *asportation*.

Property does not have to be moved any substantial distance in order to be carried away. A person must succeed in moving the property at least a slight distance, however, or he cannot be said to have carried it away. Movement of property for only a few inches will generally fulfill the requirement that the property be carried away.

Property that has been taken need not literally be "carried" away in order for an asportation to occur. One who has taken control of property may carry it away by pushing it or by pulling it.

One may carry away a horse by riding it or an automobile by driving or towing it. A pickpocket cannot be said to have carried away another person's wallet unless he removes the wallet from the victim's pocket, although he may take control of the wallet when he touches it inside the pocket.

Courts have held that an asportation occurs when one person places a false address label on another person's package, causing a delivery man to carry it away to the wrong address. In this example, the taker does not move the package himself, but he directly causes the box to be delivered (carried away) to the wrong address.

Although most states still require property to be taken and carried away in order for theft to occur, a few states have abolished the element of carrying away. The new Pennsylvania, Texas and Illinois penal codes do not include asportation as an element of the act of larceny. In these states, therefore, theft may occur whenever one takes (without carrying away) personal property from another person's possession.

Personal Property

One person must take and carry away personal property from another person's possession in order for the act of larceny or theft to take place. Personal property includes all property except real estate.

Property has traditionally been classified as either real property or personal property. *Real* property includes all land, as well as everything that is permanently (or almost permanently) affixed to land for as long as it remains attached to the land. Thus, real property includes substances that are naturally connected to the earth, such as minerals, bodies of water, and growing plants. Trees, crops, and other kinds of vegetables are considered real property as long as they continue to grow in the soil. Houses and other buildings are classified as real property, provided they are built to remain on a particular tract of land.

All property that is not classified as real property is known as *personal* property. All man-made articles that can be carried away are personal property, as are all animals and other living things that have the power to move by means of their own locomotion. In addition, minerals and vegetables become personal rather than real property the moment they are removed from the soil. Thus, oil ceases to be real property and becomes personal property as soon as it has been siphoned from the ground. Crops cease to be real and become personal property when they are harvested. Trees cease to be real and become personal property when they are cut down. In the same fashion, a house or other building ceases to be real estate when it is torn down, and the materials (wood, bricks, and so on) that were part of it become personal property. Mobile homes (trailers) and all vehicles—including automobiles, boats, airplanes, and so on—are examples of personal property. Personal property may be moved from one location to another quite freely.

At common law, it was not considered theft or larceny for one to cut down a tree or tear up a crop on another person's real estate, if the intruder carried the tree or crop away with him as soon as he removed it from the soil. A common-law act of larceny did occur, however, if the intruder cut down a tree or tore up a crop from another person's premises, left the premises without carrying the plant away, and then returned to carry off the plant. Most states have solved this problem by reasoning that all real property (including loam or soil itself) becomes personal property at the moment when it ceases to be part of the earth. Thus, a crop becomes personal property when one pulls it out of the soil, whether or not the crop is carried away and no matter when it is carried away.

At common law, also, only personal property that was thought to be *valuable in itself* could be taken and carried away in an act of larceny. Thus, larceny could not be committed at common law by taking and carrying away another person's stocks, bonds, checks, deeds, promissory notes, or other documents. These items were thought to represent value, but were not considered valuable in themselves. In all states today, a document is thought to be worth at least as much as the value of the paper and ink of which it is made. Thus, theft or larceny may occur when one steals a document, although the item itself may be worth only a fraction of a cent. By statute in some states, the value of certain important documents—such as documents of title (deeds, certificates), credit cards, and negotiable instruments (checks and bank drafts)—is declared to be higher than the cost of the document itself.

Only *tangible* personal property could be taken and carried away in an act of larceny at common law, but property need no longer be tangible to be stolen. Gas, electricity, labor, and services are all considered to be personal property.

Another Person's Possession

The act of larceny or theft cannot occur unless one person takes and carries away personal property from another person's possession. Thus, personal property must have been in some person's possession immediately prior to the moment when someone else takes it and carries it away, or else larceny or theft does not take place.

Property does not have to be taken and carried away from another person's body to constitute theft. Indeed, a person may possess property without constantly carrying the property with him. Nor does property have to be taken and carried away from the possession of its owner to constitute theft. A person may (rightfully or wrongfully) possess property that he does not own.

There is a vital difference between possession and ownership of property. A person *possesses* all property that lies within his exclusive dominion and control. Property lies within a person's dominion as long as he continues to supervise the property to make certain that it remains within his control. Normally, a person possesses all personal property that he places on land that he owns, as long as the personal property remains there. One may possess personal property that is not located on land that he owns, as long as he continuously controls and supervises this property wherever it is located.

A person who *owns* property has the initial legal right exclusively to possess, use, and enjoy his property. An owner of property may surrender this initial right by agreeing to let someone else possess his property, or by abandoning the property without intending ever to exercise further control over it, or by forfeiting the property through a legal proceeding.

One person may own property that he lets someone else possess, just as one may possess property that another person owns. A thief may possess property that he has stolen, as long as he continuously controls and supervises it. A thief does not own the property he steals, however, since he never has any legal right to possess, use, or enjoy it.

Normally, larceny or theft does not occur when a person takes and carries away property that he himself owns. Under certain conditions, however, one may commit larceny or theft by taking and carrying away property that he owns but that he has delivered into someone else's possession for safekeeping. This is generally true only if the owner has agreed not to take back the property, at least for a period of time. For example, a person may commit larceny or theft by taking and carrying away personal property that he owns but that he has pawned or mortgaged, if he earlier surrendered possession of the property so that another person (one who loaned him money) could hold it as security for the repayment of a debt.

Not all personal property is owned, and not all personal property is possessed by anyone. Some personal property is neither owned nor possessed by anyone, and some is not presently possessed by anyone, although an absentee owner may hold legal title to it. Property cannot be possessed without being owned, since any person who possesses property automatically owns it unless someone else does.

Property may, however, be owned without being presently possessed by anyone. Such property is known as either *lost* or *mislaid* property. Property is *lost* when the last person to possess it accidentally loses control of it by carelessness. Property is *mislaid* when the last person to possess it knowingly gives up control over it and intends but forgets to repossess it later.

Property that no person either owns or possesses is known as *abandoned* property. Property is abandoned when the last person to own it (as well as the last person to possess it) knowingly gives up control over it forever. Only the owner of property can abandon it. Even if the owner of the property does abandon it, the property does not become abandoned unless no one else takes control over it. This is true because the first person to take control of abandoned property becomes its new owner, and the property ceases to be abandoned. Although only the owner of property can abandon it, anyone (including a thief) who possesses property can lose or mislay it. For this reason, both lost and mislaid property may have been stolen, but abandoned property cannot have been stolen, since abandoned property is neither owned nor possessed by anyone.

When someone assumes control over *lost* or *mislaid* property, larceny or theft may or may not occur. It does *not* occur if the one who takes and carries away the property does not take possession of it away from someone else. Sometimes lost or mislaid property is possessed by someone other than the finder, but often it may not be. In some states, for example, lost or mislaid property automatically becomes the possession of the person who owns the land on which the property is found. Thus, in these states, the finder of lost or mislaid property may commit larceny or theft by taking and carrying the property away from the land on which he found it. Even in these states, however, the person who owns land on which lost or mislaid property is found does not necessarily become owner of this property, if the property is earmarked or labeled, or if the owner of the property can reasonably be determined.

Larceny or theft can never occur when someone takes possession of abandoned property, because no one else possesses the property or has any right to control it. Thus, a person who takes control and dominion over abandoned property becomes both its new owner and its new possessor. He becomes its owner until he sells it or gives it away, and he becomes its possessor until he surrenders exclusive control and dominion over it.

Specific Intent to Steal

No person can be criminally responsible for taking and carrying away personal property from another person's possession unless he can be shown to have intended to *steal* the property at the moment he took control of it. Theft is not a "cause-and-result" crime. Thus, one does not automatically bear criminal responsibility for taking and carrying away personal property from another person's possession. A specific criminal intent must be proven.

An *intent to steal* is defined generally as a person's intent to deprive another person permanently of the latter's right to exercise exclusive dominion and control over property that he owns or has a right to possess. Thus, one may have an intent to steal if his objective is to deprive another person of the possession of property. This is ordinarily true regardless of whether the person who takes property intends to gain a benefit for himself.

Sometimes it may be difficult to determine whether one who has taken property from another's possession intended to deprive the latter of possession forever. As a rule, proof that the taker intended at the time to deprive another of possession for an unreasonably long period of time will be sufficient to show an intent to steal. Thus, one may be considered to have had an intent to steal property even though he may not actually have intended to deprive someone else of possession forever.

On the other hand, a person is not criminally responsible for theft if he takes and carries away personal property from another person's possession with the intent to use the property temporarily and then return it to the person from whom he took it. The intent must be to return the property within a reasonable time, however. Moreover, the intent must be to return the property unconditionally. An intent to return the property only upon the fulfillment of a condition that the taker has no right to impose is considered an intent to steal the property. In addition, most states require that a person who takes property intending to return it must appear to be capable of returning the property unharmed. Thus, a person who takes property intending to use it recklessly cannot be said to intend to return the property.

A person who takes and carries away property from another's possession with an intent to return the property cannot bear criminal responsibility for theft even if he later becomes unable to return the property. The intent at the time of the taking determines the criminal responsibility of the offender. Thus, a person who takes property with an intent to return it unconditionally can never be criminally responsible for theft, even though some unexpected obstacle prevents him from returning the property later.

Someone who finds identifiable (earmarked or labeled) property that has been lost, mislaid, or stolen is criminally responsible for theft if he intends to steal the property at the moment he picks it up and discovers the owner's identity. However, the finder of this property bears no criminal responsibility for theft if he intends to return the property at the moment he picks it up and discovers its owner's identity, even if he decides afterward to steal the property by keeping it.

Similarly, a person to whom property is misdelivered by accident is not as a general rule criminally responsible for theft if he receives the property thinking it was sent to him, and then decides to steal it when he discovers the mistake. A few courts have held that one bears criminal responsibility for theft even if he receives misdelivered property quite innocently, if he decides to steal the property at the moment he opens a package and discovers the contents.

One who takes and carries away personal property from another person's possession with an intent to steal it is criminally responsible for theft even if he becomes frightened sometime later and decides then to return the property. Again, it must be stressed that intent at the time of the taking, and not a subsequent change of intent, determines criminal responsibility for theft. The criminal intent (if required) must always exactly coincide with the criminal act, or one can never bear criminal responsibility for the act.

There is disagreement concerning the criminal responsibility of a person who takes and carries away property from another person's possession with an intent to restore the *equivalent value* of the property, rather than to return the actual property itself. Some courts have held that an intent to restore the equivalent value of property is not an intent to steal, provided the property that is taken was *offered for sale* at the time of the taking, either by its owner or by the person from whose possession the property is taken. Most courts agree that an intent to return the equivalent value of property that has not been offered for sale is an intent to steal. This is especially true if the property is unique and has no monetary value, or if the owner or possessor has rejected offers to buy the property. Indeed, a victim who prefers to keep rather than to sell his property should not be compelled to "sell" the property to a thief who has already taken possession of it.

As a rule, a person who takes and carries away personal property from another person's possession under a *reasonable claim of right* is not criminally responsible for larceny or theft. Two difficulties arise at this point, however. The first is to determine what constitutes a reasonable claim of right. The second is to determine the taker's criminal responsibility, if any, if he honestly believed he had a claim of right but if his belief was unreasonable.

Generally speaking, a person takes property under a *reasonable claim of right* when, at the time of the criminal act, he honestly believes (1) that the property has been *abandoned,* (2) that he is taking back his own property from the possession of a thief who stole it, (3) that the person from whom he takes the property gave him *permission,* or (4) that the person who owns or possesses the property owes him (the taker) a *debt.*

As mentioned, property that has actually been abandoned does not belong to anybody. Therefore, any person may lawfully take control of abandoned property. A problem arises when one takes and carries away property that he believes has been abandoned, when in fact the property has not been abandoned but has been lost, mislaid, or stolen. Unless the property is earmarked or labeled, one cannot generally be criminally responsible for taking it and carrying it away, providing the property is found on public land or on land owned by the finder. If the property is found on land owned by a person other than the finder, it cannot legally be abandoned in many states and can be stolen if the finder takes it and carries it away without the permission of the landowner.

Some states require that a person who finds property (even if he finds it on his own land) must make an attempt to trace its ownership. Under this type of statute, a person may be criminally responsible for theft *if* he removes the property from the spot where he found it without attempting to trace ownership and *if* the property turns out not to have been abandoned.

Most states permit an owner or a person who has a right to possess property to recapture the property from the possession of a thief who has stolen it. A problem arises here when one takes property from another's possession, believing the property was stolen from him, when it turns out that the property was not stolen after all. Many courts will consider the reasonableness of the person's belief that he was merely taking back what he believed to be stolen property. On the contrary, one who is neither the owner nor the rightful possessor of stolen property will be criminally responsible for theft if he takes and carries the stolen property away from the possession of a thief who stole it from someone else. In theory, a first thief has a better right to possess stolen property than a second thief!

A person who believes that he has either the owner's or the possessor's permission to take and carry away property will not usually be criminally responsible for theft. It may be difficult, however, for a person to show that he believed he had been given another's permission, when in fact he had not. Most courts will at least look at the reasons why a person believed he had another's permission to remove property.

One does not generally bear criminal responsibility for taking and carrying away property from the possession of another person who owes the taker a debt, as long as the value of the property taken *does not exceed* the amount of the debt. Even if no debt is actually owed, some courts will permit a person to avoid criminal responsibility if evidence shows that he honestly believed a debt was owed to him. When one removes property from another's possession to collect a debt, he may very well be considered criminally responsible for theft to the extent that the value of property taken is greater than the value of the debt that existed or that he thought existed.

Degrees of Larceny

In most states, larceny or theft is divided into two categories, *grand larceny* (grand theft) and *petit larceny* (petit theft). In some states, petit larceny is known as "petty" larceny. The distinction between grand and petit larceny often depends on the dollar value of the stolen property. Thus, theft of property worth over $50 may constitute grand larceny, while theft of property worth $50 or less may constitute petit larceny. The distinguishing value may be higher in some states, ranging from $60 to $100 or even $250. The nonmonetary value of the stolen property may also have a bearing on what type of larceny is committed. Thus, theft of public documents or public records may constitute grand larceny, regardless of the monetary value of the property.

A few states divide larceny into more than two categories by subdividing grand larceny into two or more degrees. These states distinguish between grand larceny in the first, second, and third degrees. In any event, petit larceny is a misdemeanor in most states, while all degrees of grand larceny constitute felonies in nearly every state. The greater the value of the stolen property, however, the more serious the felony may become. Hence, one may commit grand larceny in the second degree, for example, by stealing property valued at over $500 or over $1,000. In some states, such as New York, a person may commit grand larceny in the first degree by stealing property as a result of extortion or blackmail. These criminal offenses will be discussed in Chapter 14.

The value of property is not necessarily determined by its cost to its owner at the time of purchase. Value is often determined by the *market value* of property at the time and place of the theft. The market value of property is the amount its owner could obtain by selling the property on the open market. The market value of unique property, such as valuable paintings, may depend on the price one buyer is willing to pay, because the property cannot be sold on the open market.

Separate items of property may be *aggregated,* or counted together, to determine the overall value of several items of property together. Property that is stolen at the same *time* and *place* from the same *victim* may always be aggregated. Property that is stolen at different times and places from different victims may never be aggregated. The difficulty occurs when different items of property are taken (1) at the same time or place from different victims or (2) at different times or places from the same victim. Under either of these conditions, property that is taken as part of a continuing plan or scheme may be aggregated in many states.

Receiving Stolen Property

Receiving stolen property is a separate offense from that committed by stealing the property. The offense of receiving stolen property, often known simply as "receiving," is worded differently under statutes in various states.

The criminal act of receiving is committed when a person accepts actual possession of property that in fact has been stolen. Thus, one commits the act of receiving by accepting dominion and control of stolen property. One who buys stolen property commits the act of receiving, but so also does a person who accepts stolen property as a gift.

One may commit the act of receiving without actually touching the property with his own hands, if someone else takes possession of the property on his behalf as a result of a prior agreement. Similarly, one may commit the act of receiving without intending to keep the stolen property for himself. Thus, a person who accepts possession of stolen property on behalf of someone else commits the act of receiving.

Not everyone who possesses stolen property is criminally responsible for the offense of receiving, however. Under most receiving statutes, a person bears criminal responsibility for this offense only by accepting possession of property that he *knows* has been stolen, and even then only if he *intends* to deprive the owner or rightful possessor of the property permanently.

Thus, a person who accepts stolen property without having any reason to believe that it is stolen does not bear criminal responsibility for receiving. Nor does one who accepts possession of property that he knows is stolen bear criminal responsibility, if at the moment he accepts the property he intends to return either the property or its equivalent value to the person from whom the property was stolen. In addition, one who knowingly accepts possession of stolen property may not be criminally responsible for receiving, if he accepts the property under a reasonable claim of right. (For a discussion of what constitutes a reasonable claim of right, see the previous section on "Larceny or Theft.")

Some statutes have been written to eliminate the element of knowledge as a necessary requirement for criminal responsibility for receiving. These statutes have usually been held unconstitutional because they are in violation of the Fourteenth Amendment,[1] which holds that no state shall "deprive any person of life, liberty, or property without due process of law." Courts have held that these statutes violated this due process clause. Note, however, that absolute knowledge that property has been stolen is not always necessary for one to bear criminal responsibility for receiving. One who has reason to believe or to suspect that property may have been stolen can be criminally responsible for receiving, if he accepts possession of the property without checking its ownership.

In many states, the proprietor of a pawnshop is required by law to check with the local police before making loans on certain kinds of property. For example, a statute may require the proprietor to check out the serial numbers of property that is marked by number. By failing to comply with this requirement, one who runs a pawnshop may become criminally responsible for receiving if the property he accepts turns out to have been stolen.

Even one who accepts possession of property that he knows or believes has been stolen does not always bear criminal responsibility for receiving. He must be shown to have possessed an intent to deprive the owner or rightful possessor of the property permanently at the *moment* the property came into his possession. Thus, a person who innocently receives property that he only later learns is stolen cannot be criminally responsible for receiving stolen property. He may, however, become criminally responsible for *concealing* stolen property.

Concealing Stolen Property

Concealing stolen property is a separate offense from stealing the property. In most states, moreover, concealing stolen property is a separate offense from receiving stolen property. This offense, often known simply as "concealing," is worded differently under statutes in various states.

The criminal act of concealing is committed when a person hides property that in fact has been stolen. One who hides stolen property on land he owns or anywhere else under his control commits the act of concealing. Yet there is no requirement that the property be hidden on the offender's land or that he keep the concealed property under his control. Of course, one cannot commit the act of concealing unless at some moment he possesses the stolen property. The act of concealing may still have been committed, nevertheless, if the offender gives up possession of the property after concealing it, as when he buries it and walks away.

As with receiving, one may commit the act of concealing without actually touching the property with his own hands, if someone else takes possession of the property on his behalf as a result of a prior agreement. Similarly, one may commit the act of concealing without intending to hide the stolen property for his own use. He may be hiding the property for the use of someone else, or he may be going to sell the property after it "cools off."

To commit the act of concealing, the offender need not actually hide the stolen property in the sense of placing it in a secret location where no person can see it. The act of concealing is accomplished when the offender or someone acting on his behalf prevents the owner or rightful possessor of the property from learning of its whereabouts. As long as the stolen property is kept away from its owner or rightful possessor, the property is concealed, regardless of how many other persons are permitted to view it.

Not everyone who hides stolen property is criminally responsible for the offense of concealing. Under most statutes, a person bears criminal responsibility for this offense only by hiding property that he *knows* has been stolen, and even then only if he *intends* to deprive the owner or rightful possessor of the property permanently.

Thus, a person who hides stolen property but has no reason to believe that it is stolen does not bear criminal responsibility for concealing. Nor does one who hides property that he does know is stolen, if at the moment he hides it he intends to return either the property or its equivalent value to the person from whom the property was stolen. In addition, one who knowingly hides stolen property may not be criminally responsible for concealing if he conceals the property under a reasonable claim of right. (Claim of right is discussed earlier under "Larceny or Theft.")

Unlike the receiving of stolen property, the concealing of stolen property may be an *ongoing* act. In other words, one receives stolen property only at the moment when he first accepts possession of the property. One continues to conceal stolen property as long as it remains under his control and supervision. Hence, a person may become criminally responsible for concealing stolen property when, at any time during the course of possessing the property, he intends to deprive the owner or rightful possessor of the property permanently. In this respect, a person who does not bear criminal responsibility for receiving may very well be criminally responsible for concealing. This would be true, for example, if the offender accepts possession of stolen property without knowing that it is stolen, but upon learning that fact decides to keep it away from its owner permanently. This would be true, also, if the offender accepts property that he knows has been stolen, intending to return the property or its equivalent value later, but while he possesses the property decides to keep it away from its owner permanently.

Other Theft Offenses

In addition to larceny or theft, receiving stolen property, and concealing stolen property, other theft offenses have been created by statute in some states. They include theft from the person, theft from a building, theft from a motor vehicle, and theft of a motor vehicle.

Theft from the Person

Several states have enacted statutes creating a special offense known as theft from the person. The elements of this offense are basically the same as those of larceny or theft, except that the property must be taken from the victim's person. Hence, theft from the person covers such criminal activities as picking pockets and purse-snatching. This offense is different from robbery, however, since no force or threat is required (see Chapter 14).

Theft from the person may take place whenever a person steals property that is attached to the victim's body or that is under the immediate control of the victim at the time it is stolen. Thus, theft of any property from the pocket of clothing that the victim is wearing at the time of the theft may constitute this offense. Theft of property that is not actually on the victim's person may constitute this offense, if the property is close beside the person when it is stolen. If the person is unconscious, however, the property may not be under his immediate control unless it is grasped in his hand.

A person does not bear criminal responsibility for theft from the person unless, at the moment he takes and carries away property from the victim's person or immediate control, the offender possesses an intent to steal the property.

Theft from a Building

In some states, theft from a building is a separate criminal offense created by statute. The elements of this offense are basically the same as those of larceny or theft, except that the property must be taken from a building. This offense is different from burglary, however, since the offender need not have entered the building unlawfully (see Chapter 12). Thus, this offense covers all thefts that take place in a building that is open to the public. This offense would also cover the situation in which the thief is a guest in the victim's home, office, or store and steals property that is inside the building.

Under most statutes, theft from a building may be committed

whenever one takes and carries away property from another person's possession, provided the property is inside a building at the time it is taken. The building does not usually have to be a dwelling or house, although a dwelling is a building. Some statutes provide that this offense may be committed when property is taken from a boat, a mobile home (trailer), or another movable structure. As a rule, this offense does not depend on whether the property was locked up inside the building. The property simply must have been kept within a building rather than in the open.

A person does not bear criminal responsibility for the offense of theft from a building unless, at the moment he takes and carries away property from another person's possession, he possesses an intent to steal the property.

Theft from a Motor Vehicle

A number of states have enacted statutes creating the special offense known as theft from a motor vehicle. The elements of this offense are similar to those of larceny or theft, except that the property must be taken from a motor vehicle, such as an automobile, a truck, a bus, a motorcycle, or a tractor. The property need not be taken from any specific area of the motor vehicle, nor does the vehicle have to be locked at the time the property is stolen. This distinguishes theft from a motor vehicle from burglary of a motor vehicle (see Chapter 12).

A person does not bear criminal responsibility for the offense of theft from a motor vehicle unless, at the moment he takes and carries away property from another person's possession, he possesses an intent to steal the property.

Note that theft *from* a motor vehicle is not the same as theft *of* a motor vehicle. In the former offense, property situated within the vehicle, other than the vehicle itself, must be stolen. In the latter, the vehicle itself must be stolen.

Theft of a Motor Vehicle

Many states have created the offense of theft of a motor vehicle under a variety of different names. "Grand theft auto," "car theft," or "joy-riding" are just a few of many labels for this offense.

The elements of this offense are the same as the basic elements of larceny or theft, except that the property that is taken must be a motor vehicle. Generally, the vehicle must be in working condition, although this is not always required. The vehicle does not have to be registered, however, nor does it have to be locked at the time it is stolen.

A person does not bear criminal responsibility for the offense of theft of a motor vehicle unless, at the moment he takes and carries away the vehicle from another person's possession, he possesses an intent to steal the vehicle. Many statutes provide for different grades of criminal responsibility for different thefts of vehicles. Thus, a person may bear more serious criminal responsibility for "grand theft auto" than for mere "joy-riding." Indeed, "joy-riding" may not be viewed as a form of theft at all under many statutes, since it frequently does not involve intent to steal but involves only an intent to use the vehicle temporarily.

CHAPTER 10

Criminal
Conversion Offenses

Embezzlement, false pretenses, and other criminal conversion offenses involve the unlawful misappropriation of property by a person into whose possession the property has been entrusted. These offenses entail more than simple theft. Breach of trust and deceit are additional elements. However, theft remains a lesser included offense. Conversion offenses are distinguished mainly according to the method of conversion used in the crime. As with many offenses that are related to theft, severity of a conversion offense is likely to be dependant upon the value of the property that is converted.

Conversion offenses that are discussed in this chapter include embezzlement, false pretenses, and consolidated theft offenses.

Embezzlement

The elements of embezzlement can be outlined as follows:

    A. The Criminal Act:
        1. the conversion
        2. of another person's property
        3. by one who lawfully possesses the property
    B. The Criminal Intent:
        4. a specific intent to defraud

Conversion

The act of embezzlement cannot occur unless one person converts another person's property. In order to convert another's property, one must be in possession of the property and seriously interfere with the owner's rights to it. A conversion requires a *willful* interference with the owner's property rights and cannot take place through the negligence of one who possesses the property.

One who is in possession of someone else's property may convert the property in many different ways. He may sell, give away, or mortgage the property without the owner's permission, or he may severely damage the property to the extent that he makes the property less valuable to its owner. One may convert another's property by depleting it (using it up) or by claiming to be the owner of the property himself. A person in possession of someone else's property may convert the property by refusing to give it back to its owner, but as a rule the owner must first demand its return. Under many statutes, a person may convert another's property by placing it in a secret hiding place, intending to misappropriate it at a future time.

Some embezzlement statutes provide that the person in possession of property must convert it "to his own use." This language is misleading, since no state requires the person who converts another's property to gain personally from this activity in order to commit embezzlement. Indeed, persons often commit embezzlement in order to benefit their families or a business that employs them.

Another Person's Property

A person does not commit embezzlement by converting property that he owns all by himself. To be embezzled, property must be owned at least in part by someone other than the person who converts it. In fact, most courts have held that a person cannot commit embezzlement by converting property in which he has any ownership interest. Thus, one cannot usually commit embezzlement by misappropriating more than his share of property that he jointly owns with another person.

Embezzlement occurs most frequently when an agent represents a principal or when a broker represents two or more parties to a business transaction. For example, the classic act of embezzlement occurs when a bank teller receives a depositor's money as an agent for the bank but converts the deposit to his own use. A real estate agent may commit embezzlement by misappropriating a buyer's deposit on the sale of a house. A stockbroker may commit embezzlement by purchasing shares of stock in his own name with a client's money.

Only personal property may be taken and carried away to fulfill the requirements of the act of larceny or theft. But both real property and personal property may be converted to fulfill the elements of embezzlement. For example, the executor of an estate or the guardian of a minor child who has the authority to sell, rent, or mortgage real estate may convert the real property by selling it for less than its market value.

Under most embezzlement statutes, nearly any type of property may be embezzled; certainly money is not the only type. As with larceny, intangible personal property such as stocks, bonds, checks, deeds, and other documents may be embezzled. Even property that has been illegally acquired—such as prize money for a lottery—may be embezzled.

It is a federal offense to embezzle goods shipped in interstate commerce[1] or to embezzle federal funds, federal records, or other government property.[2] It is a federal offense, also, to embezzle any property that has been deposited or delivered in the U.S. Mail.[3]

One Who Lawfully Possesses the Property

A person must lawfully possess someone else's property in order to commit embezzlement by converting it. In this respect, embezzlement is different from larceny or theft. In larceny, the thief takes and carries the property away from the victim's possession. In embezzlement, the embezzler has already been given lawful possession of the property, but while possessing the property he misappropriates it.

Embezzlement is ordinarily committed by an agent, a broker, or a fiduciary (a person in a position of trust) such as an attorney, the legal guardian of a minor child or of an insane person, the executor of a deceased person's estate, a trustee, or a public official.

An employee may embezzle the property of his employer, but as a rule only if someone other than the employer hands him the property. For example, an employee who receives the delivery of a package on behalf of his employer, to whom the package is addressed, may commit embezzlement by keeping the package for his own use. In this example, the employee may also commit embezzlement by giving the package to someone other than his employer. On the contrary, as a rule, an employee cannot commit embezzlement by misappropriating property his employer has handed to him to hold onto but to return later. When an employee receives his employer's property directly from the employer, the employee does not usually receive possession. He merely receives custody (control, but not dominion) over the property. The employer retains possession, since he supervises the employee, who works as his servant. An employee who takes and carries away property his employer has loaned to him may commit the act of larceny or theft, however.

Some embezzlement statutes make a specific exception to the general rule that an employee cannot embezzle property that he has received from his employer. Under these statutes, an employee may commit an act of embezzlement rather than larceny or theft by misappropriating property that belongs to his employer but that is "under his care," whether the property has been handed to him by the employer or by someone else.

Only a person who has been "delivered" or "entrusted" property can convert the property and commit embezzlement. Thus, many courts have refused to recognize the act of embezzlement when a person finds identifiable lost, mislaid, or stolen property, picks up the property intending to return it to its owner, but later decides to steal the property by keeping it. These courts have reasoned that one who finds property never becomes "entrusted" with lawful possession and therefore cannot embezzle this property.

Specific Intent to Defraud

In most states, a person is not criminally responsible for embezzlement unless he intends to *defraud* the owner of property he lawfully possesses at the moment he converts it. Thus, embezzlement is not viewed as a "cause-and-result" crime in these states, and, as a rule, one who lawfully possesses another's property does not automatically bear criminal responsibility for embezzlement whenever he converts the property. A specific intent to defraud must be proven in most states.

There is very little difference between an intent to defraud and an intent to steal. An intent to steal, however, involves a plan both to take away and to deprive another person of possession of property permanently. An intent to defraud does not involve a plan to seize and take away property, since the offender already possesses the property. Instead, the intent to defraud involves a plan to cheat the owner out of his property rights, after the owner has entrusted the offender with the care and supervision of his property. In this respect, an intent to defraud involves a scheme to betray another person's trust. In the case of embezzlement, the offender betrays the trust that the owner of property placed in the offender's hands by agreeing to let the offender lawfully possess the property.

In many states, embezzlement requires an intent on the part of the offender to cheat the owner out of his property permanently, rather than temporarily. In these states, one is not criminally responsible for embezzlement if he intends at the time he converts someone else's property to return it to his victim later on. As in larceny, this principle holds even if some unexpected obstacle later prevents the converter from returning the property as planned. In these states, also, one is not criminally responsible for embezzlement if at the time of the conversion he intends to restore the equivalent value of the property to his victim. However, he may bear criminal responsibility if he does not have the ability to return either the property itself or its equivalent value.

In some states, an intent on the part of the offender to cheat the owner out of his property temporarily is sufficient to constitute the required criminal intent for embezzlement. In these states, even one who converts property intending to return it later or to restore its equivalent value to the victim may nevertheless be criminally responsible for embezzlement. For example, one who possesses another's property may invest it in his own name to profit from the interest and then return the principal to the owner. In this example, there is no intent to defraud the owner permanently, but there is an intent to defraud the owner temporarily.

A few states, including Missouri and Oregon, treat embezzlement as a "cause-and-result" crime. In these states, by statute, a person who voluntarily converts someone else's property (which he lawfully possesses) is criminally responsible for embezzlement even without proof that he possessed a specific intent to defraud the owner (either permanently or temporarily) at the moment of the conversion.

Where a specific intent to defraud is required to create criminal responsibility for embezzlement, a person who converts another's property under a reasonable claim of right cannot as a rule bear criminal responsibility for embezzlement. (For a review of what may constitute a reasonable claim of right, see Chapter 9, which discussed this principle as it applies to larceny or theft.)

False Pretenses

The basic elements of false pretenses can be outlined as follows:
A. The Criminal Act:
1. the untrue representation
2. of a material fact
3. known to the offender
4. but unknown to the victim
5. to deprive another person of an interest in property
B. The Criminal Intent:
6. a specific intent to defraud

Untrue Representation

To commit the act of false pretenses, a person must first of all make a representation that is untrue—in other words, one that is not fully accurate. A spoken lie or "half-truth" is an untrue representation, as is a written falsehood. A representation does not have to be made in the form of an oral or written statement. It may be made by means of a symbol or a token or even by a physical gesture that has a significant meaning and that is commonly understood.

Examples are plentiful of untrue written and spoken representations. The person who writes out a bill of sale pretending to sell property that he does not own makes an untrue representation. So does the owner of an automobile when he tells someone buying his car that it has been driven only twenty thousand miles, when in fact it has been driven substantially more miles. An excellent athlete who disguises his identity or ability when entering an athletic competition may make an untrue representation. Thus, a "scratch" golfer who enters a tournament declaring that he has a "handicap" of 15 makes such a representation. So does the owner of a race horse who enters the animal in competition and declares him to be a five-year-old when in fact he is a three-year-old.

A person who makes a long-distance telephone call and gives the operator the wrong billing number makes an untrue representation. Hence, the act of false pretenses may occur over a telephone line as well as when the offender and victim are face to face. Indeed, the act of false pretenses may be committed on radio or television, as well as by means of a printed or painted sign; a manufacturer who advertises a product as having a special quality when in fact it does not have that quality makes an untrue representation.

As mentioned, a person may make an untrue representation by displaying a symbol or a token. Thus, one who wears a uniform that is commonly associated with a specific activity represents himself as a participant in that activity. This representation is untrue if the person does not take part in the activity normally associated with the uniform. For example, a person who is not a policeman makes an untrue representation by wearing the uniform of a police officer, and a person who is not a soldier makes an untrue representation by wearing an army uniform.

One may make an untrue representation merely by displaying a badge, an emblem, or other insignia. Hence, a person who shows a policeman's badge to someone else represents himself as a police officer. His representation is untrue if he is not in fact a police officer. Similarly, one who shows someone else the identification card of an organization, club, or school represents himself as a member of that group. This representation is untrue if he is not presently a member in good standing of the group whose card he displays.

Material Fact

Only the untrue representation of a *fact* can be the basis for false pretenses. Even then, the misrepresentation must be of a *material* fact. At this point, it is important to understand what a fact is, and to understand the meaning of a material fact.

A fact may be defined as an actual happening in time or space or as a mental or physical event. A fact may be an action that has been performed, or one that has not been performed. Nevertheless, a fact must always involve either a present event or a past event. It can never involve a future event, since a future event has not yet happened so long as it remains a future event. When a future event does happen, it ceases to be a future event and becomes a present and then a past event. For example, it is a fact that Jimmy Carter was inaugurated President of the United States on January 20, 1977. It is a fact that America will be three hundred years old on July 4, 2076. However, it is *not* a fact that America will celebrate her tricentennial on that date, since until the moment arrives we cannot predict with any accuracy whether citizens of the time will see fit to engage in celebration.

Neither an opinion, a prediction, nor a promise ordinarily can constitute a fact. An *opinion* is a person's statement concerning what he believes to be true, rather than what he knows to be true or what is in fact true. As a rule, one does not commit the act of false pretenses by giving someone else a false opinion, since anyone has the right to form his own opinion on any subject. A few courts have held that a false opinion may constitute the untrue representation of a fact if the opinion relates to a matter known only to the person expressing the opinion and if the opinion is expressed dishonestly. The general rule, however, is that an opinion is not a fact.

A *prediction* is a person's statement concerning what he believes will happen at some future time. Thus, one's prediction is a kind of opinion, but it relates to the future rather than to the present. As a rule, one does not commit the act of false pretenses by making a false prediction, since at the time it is made a prediction can be neither proven nor disproven. A person who makes an untrue representation of his ability to make accurate predictions—such as a soothsayer—may commit the act of false pretenses. Still, in this situation the untrue representation relates to the offender's statement about his ability, not to the quality of the prediction itself. Thus, a prediction is not a fact.

A *promise* is a person's pledge concerning his conduct or his course of action for the future. As such, a promise is both a kind of opinion and a kind of prediction. A few courts have viewed a promise as an expression of the present (rather than the future) intention of the person making the promise. These courts have held that one who makes a false promise misrepresents his present state of mind. Most courts recognize the difficulty of determining whether one whose promise turns out to be false intended it to be false at the moment he made it. He may have intended it to be true when he made it, but changed his mind afterward. The general rule, therefore, is that a promise is not a fact.

Not every fact is a material fact. Only the untrue representation of a *material* fact can constitute the basis for false pretenses. Generally, a fact is material only if it is capable of deceiving or misleading an ordinary, rational person who relies on its being true. Thus, many courts have held that a representation that on its face is absurd, irrational, or otherwise insignificant is not a material fact because it should not deceive anyone, since no one should rely on its truthfulness. Other courts have held that a fact is material if it does succeed in deceiving or misleading a particular victim. Certainly, a fact that does not succeed in deceiving or misleading anyone is not material.

Under particular circumstances, any fact may become material. Most facts are not material under all conditions. Certain types of facts are more likely than others to become material, as these facts frequently mislead or deceive people. In other words, people rely more often on the truthfulness of some facts than other facts.

Facts that relate to a person's *identity* or *age* are extremely likely to be viewed as material. A person who pretends that someone else's name or a fictitious name is his own name makes an untrue representation. This untrue representation is material when another person must rely on the truthfulness of this person's identity. Thus, one's misrepresentation of his identity is material when the person to whom the misrepresentation is made has a right to know his real name. For example, an employer, who must depend on persons who work for him, has a right to know his employees' real names. A person who pretends he is older or younger than he is makes an untrue representation. This misrepresentation is material when the person to whom the untrue representation is made has a right to know how old this person is. A bartender, for example, has a right to know whether a person who asks for a drink has reached the legal drinking age.

Facts that relate to a person's *qualifications, skill, expertise, experience,* or *ability to do a specific task* are extremely likely to be material. A person who pretends he is experienced in a certain line of work makes an untrue representation if he has not had the experience he claims to have. This untrue representation is material when the person to whom the misrepresentation is made has a right to rely on this person's experience. For example, an employer seeking to hire someone for a skilled job has a right to know that the person he hires has been trained to do the job.

Facts that relate to a product's *quality* or *selling price* are extremely likely to be material. So are facts relating to a product's *guarantee* or *warranty.* So are facts relating to the *authenticity* of a sample that is represented as being identical to other units of the same product. An untrue representation about a product's characteristics is material when a customer relies on the misrepresentation and is deceived or misled. It is material, also, when a potential customer relies on an untrue advertisement that appears in print or on a television or radio commercial.

It is a federal offense for anyone

(a) who has devised or intends to devise any scheme or artifice to defraud or to obtain money or property by means of a false or fraudulent pretense to transmit or cause to be transmitted by means of interstate wire, radio, or television communication any writing, sign, signal, picture, or sound for the purpose of executing such scheme or artifice.[4]

(b) to fraudulently or wrongfully affix or impress the seal of any department or agency of the United States to or upon any certificate, instrument, commission, document, or paper, or, with knowledge of its fraudulent character, with wrongful or fraudulent intent, to use, buy, procure, sell, or transfer to another any such certificate, instrument, commission, document, or paper, to which or upon which such seal has been so fraudulently affixed or impressed.[5]

(c) to knowingly make any false statement, false representation, false report, or false claim with respect to the character, quality, quantity, or cost of any work performed or to be performed, or materials furnished or to be furnished in connection with the construction of any highway or related project approved by the Secretary of Commerce, or in connection with the submission of plans, maps, specifications, contracts, or cost of construction of any such highway or related project.[6]

Facts that relate to the *financial status* or solvency of an individual or a business are extremely likely to be material. A person or a business makes an untrue representation by claiming to anyone that his or its capital assets are greater than they actually are, or that his or its indebtedness is less than it actually is. This untrue representation is material when it deceives or misleads another person or another business into offering credit or making a loan of money. The untrue representation is not material if it fails to deceive or mislead anyone.

Facts relating to the way in which money given to a charity will be used are extremely likely to be material. A person or an organization that asks for contributions for a *specific charitable purpose* makes an untrue representation if the money will not in fact be used for the stated purpose. A person or an organization that asks for contributions for *any* charitable purpose makes an untrue representation if the money will not in fact be used for charity, or if he (it) keeps the money for himself (itself). This kind of untrue representation is material when a contributor makes a donation and is deceived or misled as to how his money will be used.

The uttering—that is, the writing and passing—of a *worthless check* or the passing of *counterfeit money* constitutes an untrue representation that is material if the check or the money is given to another person as payment for a debt. One who gives a check or money as payment for a debt represents that the check or the money is worth the value written on its face. A worthless check or bogus money has no value, so this representation is untrue. The untrue representation is material when someone accepts the check or the money as payment for a debt but is deceived or misled, since one who accepts money or a check relies on its stated value.

Known to the Offender

A person does not commit the act of false pretenses every time he makes an untrue representation, even if the representation is material and does mislead or deceive another who relies on its truthfulness. One who makes a material untrue representation does not commit the act of false pretenses if he *honestly believes* his representation is true, even if his belief is unreasonable.

One who makes a material untrue representation may commit the act of false pretenses if he *knows* the representation to be untrue. Even if he does not know it to be untrue, he may commit the act of false pretenses if he *believes* the representation is untrue, or if he is *unsure* whether it is true or untrue.

Thus, one who makes a representation believing it to be true does not commit the act of false pretenses even if the representation turns out to be untrue, as long as his belief is genuine. On the other hand, one who makes a material untrue representation may commit the act of false pretenses if he does not genuinely and honestly believe it to be true when he makes it. Likewise, one who suspects that a material representation he makes is untrue may commit the act of false pretenses if he does not care enough about its truthfulness to try to verify it.

Unknown to the Victim

A representation that the victim knows is untrue at the time it is made cannot be the basis for false pretenses. This is the rule regardless of whether the person who makes the untrue representation knows it to be untrue and regardless of whether the fact that is misrepresented is a material fact.

In order for false pretenses to take place, one person (the victim) must rely on another person's untrue representation of a material fact and be misled or deceived. One cannot rely on the truthfulness of a fact that he knows is untrue, and one cannot be deceived or misled by a fact on which he does not rely.

In most states, however, false pretenses may occur whenever the victim is ignorant of the truthfulness of a representation, if the other elements of false pretenses are present. Usually it does not matter that the victim should have been aware of the falsity of the representation. Nor does it matter, as a rule, that a person of ordinary intelligence would not have relied on its truthfulness and therefore would not have been misled or deceived. What matters is that a particular victim is in fact misled or deceived, because he was led to rely on an untrue representation.

Depriving Another Person of an Interest in Property

The act of false pretenses is not completed until the offender successfully deprives another person of some kind of interest in some kind of property. At this point, several questions often arise due to the ambiguity of many statutes. Can real property as well as personal property be obtained by false pretenses? What about intangible personal property? Must the person who is deprived of interest in property be the same person to whom the misrepresentation is made? Must the person who is deprived of interest in property be the owner of the property? Must the offender become owner of the property?

The early English statutes that created the offense of false pretenses applied only to tangible personal property. In short, these early statutes were limited to "money, goods, wares, or merchandises." Thus, early false pretenses statutes covered only that type of property to which common-law larceny statutes applied.

Most modern statutes are ambiguous concerning the type of property that may be involved in a case of false pretenses. Some of these statutes specifically include real property, and others specifically limit application of the statute to personal property. Most statutes fail to specify whether both real and personal property may be involved in false pretenses. Most courts that have interpreted the ambiguous statutes have held that false pretenses should be limited to personal property unless the statute clearly includes real property. On the other hand, most courts have decided that both tangible and intangible personal property may be the subject of false pretenses. Thus, the act of false pretenses may be committed when a person obtains gas or electricity, labor or services, by means of an untrue representation.

The person who is deprived of interest in property as a result of an untrue representation does not have to be the person to whom the misrepresentation was made. Indeed, the person who is deprived of interest in property need not be a human being, but may be a corporation or other organization. Usually, the person to whom the misrepresentation is made must be an agent, partner, officer, or other legally recognized representative of the person who is deprived of interest in the property, however. Thus, a person who makes an untrue representation to a bank teller may commit the act of false pretenses, even though the bank and not the teller is the one that is deprived of interest in property.

In many states, the person who is deprived of interest in property does not have to be the owner of the property. In these states, anyone who possesses property may be the victim of false pretenses. In some states, however, the act of false pretenses is not completed unless the offender obtains legal title to the property, and, of course, one can obtain legal title only from the owner. The best rule seems to be that one who makes an untrue representation may commit the act of false pretenses by depriving another person of whatever interest this person may have in property that the offender obtains. Thus, one who obtains possession of property from another who possesses but does not own the property should be viewed as committing the act of false pretenses when the other elements of this offense are present.

The offender does not have to become the owner of the property he obtains by false pretenses. Indeed, he can never have legal title to property obtained in this unlawful manner, just as a thief never owns the property he steals. As a general rule, the offender may commit the act of false pretenses even though he does not obtain as great an interest in the property as his victim has. Thus, one who makes an untrue representation for the purpose of renting a car may commit the act of false pretenses even though he obtains only a temporary interest as a lessee of the vehicle and the rental agency retains a permanent interest as the lessor.

Specific Intent to Defraud

One does not bear criminal responsibility for false pretenses unless he possesses a specific intent to defraud at the moment he makes an untrue representation. Thus, false pretenses is not viewed as a "cause-and-result" crime. The mere fact that a person makes an untrue representation voluntarily does not automatically make him criminally responsible for false pretenses, even if another person who relies on the representation as being true is deprived of an interest in property. A specific criminal intent must be proven.

An intent to defraud has been discussed earlier in this chapter with reference to the crime of embezzlement. Essentially, it is a plan to cheat an owner or a possessor of property out of the rights that accompany his ownership or possession. As a rule, an intent to defraud must involve a plan to deprive another person of property permanently. Thus, one who makes an untrue representation in order to deprive another person of a property interest temporarily does not bear criminal responsibility for false pretenses. A person who makes an untrue representation to obtain property that he intends to return later on, for example, is not criminally responsible for false pretenses. Nor is one who makes a misrepresentation to obtain property but who intends to return the equivalent value of the property to the person of whom he deprives interest.

As with both larceny and embezzlement, a person who obtains property by false pretenses is not criminally responsible for this act when he makes an untrue representation under a reasonable claim of right. (For a review of what may constitute a reasonable claim of right, turn back to Chapter 9, where this concept was discussed in conjunction with larceny or theft.)

Theft Offenses Consolidated

The offenses of embezzlement and false pretenses were both created by the English Parliament several hundred years ago to plug loopholes in the common-law larceny laws. Hence, these "new" offenses were created to extend the offense of larceny to cover new situations that were unheard of in earlier times when the common law originated. These offenses were created prior to American colonization, and were therefore adopted in most American states.

Recently, a few states have made an effort to consolidate these three crimes—larceny, embezzlement, and false pretenses—into one comprehensive crime. Frequently, but not always, the comprehensive crime has been labeled "theft." The Illinois Criminal Code of 1961 was among the first to create the crime of theft, as follows:

§ 16-1. *Theft* A person commits theft when he knowingly:

(a) Obtains or exerts unauthorized control over property of the owner; or

(b) Obtains by deception control over property of the owner; or

(c) Obtains by threat control over property of the owner; or

(d) Obtains control over stolen property knowing the property to have been stolen by another or under such circumstances as would reasonably induce him to believe that the property was stolen, and

(1) Intends to deprive the owner permanently of the use or benefit of the property; or

(2) Knowingly uses, conceals, or abandons the property in such manner as to deprive the owner permanently of such use or benefit; or

(3) Uses, conceals, or abandons the property knowing such use, concealment or abandonment probably will deprive the owner permanently of such use or benefit.

The 1967 amendment to the California Criminal Code created the consolidated crime of theft, as follows:

§ 484. *Theft Defined* (a) Every person who shall feloniously steal, take, carry, lead, or drive away the personal property of another, or who shall fraudulently appropriate property which has been entrusted to him, or who shall knowingly and designedly, by any false or fraudulent representation or pretense, defraud any other person of money, labor or real or personal property, or who causes or procures others to report falsely of his wealth or mercantile character and by thus imposing upon any person, obtains credit and thereby fraudulently gets or obtains possession of money or property or obtains the labor or service of another, is guilty of theft.

The staff draft of the California Penal Code Revision Project (1971) proposed that the definition of theft be modified, as follows:

§ 1002. *Theft* A person is guilty of theft when:

(a) He takes or obtains property of another, without the consent of such other, with intent to deprive him thereof; or

(b) He transfers an interest in, or exercises control over property of another which has been entrusted to him, with intent to fraudulently appropriate the property to an unauthorized use; or

(c) He obtains the possession of property of another by means of a false representation or pretense, with intent to deprive him thereof; or

(d) He obtains property of another by means of a false representation or pretense, with intent to defraud any person; or

(e) He comes into control of property of another which he knows to have been lost, mislaid, or delivered under a mistake as to the nature or amount of the property or the identity of the recipient, and, with intent to deprive the owner thereof, he fails to take reasonable measures to restore the property to the person entitled to have it; or

(f) He receives, retains, or disposes of property of another, knowing that it has been stolen; or

(g) He obtains services with intent not to pay for them; or

(h) He damages, removes, conceals, encumbers, or transfers property subject to a conditional sales contract or other security agreement with intent to hinder enforcement of that agreement; or

(i) He is a contractor who fraudulently appropriates to his own use money or other property paid to him in connection with a particular contract without having paid for the labor or materials furnished for that contract.

Notice that each of these three examples of the consolidated theft offense merges larceny, embezzlement, and false pretenses, and that the Illinois law and the staff draft of the California revision also include receiving and concealing stolen property. The requirement that the offender have possessed a criminal intent at the time he committed the criminal act is retained. This intent is no longer specified as an intent to steal, however; instead, it is an intent to deprive the owner permanently of the use or benefit of his property. Does this mean that an intent to temporarily deprive the rightful possessor of property fulfills the required intent for theft? In this respect, and in others, many theft statutes are not fully clear.

CHAPTER 11

Fraud Offenses

Fraud offenses involve deceit in addition to theft or at least potential theft. In this respect, fraud offenses resemble criminal conversion offenses. Unlike conversion offenses, however, fraud offenses do not necessarily entail a breach of the victim's trust by the offender. If the criminal plan that accompanies most fraud offenses unfolds without detection, theft may result. However, such fraud offenses as forgery and counterfeiting may take place without the actual occurrence of any theft. Thus, theft does not have to be a lesser included offense to crimes of fraud. The severity of fraud offenses depends, as a rule, upon the techniques used in the crime and the value of the property that is intended to be stolen.

Fraud offenses that are discussed in this chapter include forgery, counterfeiting, criminal simulation, credit fraud offenses, and other deceptive practices such as uttering counterfeit items, issuing or passing a bad check, deceptive business practices, and use of slugs.

187

Forgery

The basic elements of forgery can be outlined as follows:

A. The Criminal Act:
1. (*a*) the false making or
2. (*b*) the material alteration of any writing
3. which appears to be the basis for legal liability

B. The Criminal Intent:
4. a specific intent to defraud

False making

A false making of a written document may take place when one person signs another person's name without the latter's permission, or signs a fictitious name, or signs his own name in an illegitimate capacity. The act of forgery may be committed by writing in pencil, ink, crayon, or by typewriter, printing, engraving, or by pasting letters on a document.

A person may sign another person's name on a document, and in this way accomplish a false making. It does not matter that the person who falsely signs another's name is a close relative or friend of the person whose name is signed, if the person who signs the name is not authorized to do so. As a rule, one authorizes another person to sign his name by giving the other person a *power of attorney*, in the form of a signed, written document. In many states, however, one may orally authorize another to sign his name. A person who signs someone else's name, relying on the latter's oral permission, takes the chance that he may not be able to prove that he received permission.

One may also accomplish a false making by signing a fictitious name on a document. One signs a fictitious name when he signs the name of a nonexistent person, or when he signs the name of a person whom he does not know exists. For the purpose of forgery, the person need not be a living human being. Thus, one may sign another person's name or a fictitious name by signing the name of a dead person, or by signing the name of a corporation or an unincorporated organization.

Under certain conditions, a false making may take place when a person signs his own name if he signs it in an illegitimate capacity.

For example, one who signs his name as an agent of another without authority to act as the other's agent may create a false making. Similarly, one may create a false making by signing his own name to a document that he knows is invalid, as when one signs a deed to convey property that he has previously conveyed to someone else.

A person may commit forgery by means of a false making when he signs his own name to a document while pretending to be someone else who has the same name as his. Thus, one who impersonates another and signs their common name may commit forgery, even though the name he signs belongs to him as well as the other person.

Whenever a person signs the name of another person or a fictitious person, or signs his own name pretending to be someone else with the same name, the act of forgery may be committed, even though the offender misspells the forged name. However, when a person misspells the forged name so badly that an ordinary observer would not recognize its relationship to the name of the person whose signature it is supposed to be, forgery does not occur.

Material Alteration

A material alteration of a written document, although different from a false making, may also constitute forgery. A document may become altered when someone changes its written content in any way, by addition or by erasure. Thus, one may commit forgery by either adding or erasing dates, names, words, or numbers in a written document. One may alter a document even by changing its content after it has been forged previously.

Not every type of alteration is a material alteration, however, and only a material alteration constitutes forgery. An alteration is considered to be *material* when the addition or the erasure changes the legal significance of the document. Thus, one who adds the name of a witness to a document when no witness is required by law commits an alteration, but the alteration is not material. On the contrary, a person who changes the description of property or the amount of money referred to in a document, for example, commits a material alteration.

Generally, a document can be altered (and therefore forged)

only after it has been completed (that is, signed) in its original form. For this reason, a person who induces another person to sign a document by misrepresenting the content of the document does not commit forgery in most states. This conduct usually constitutes the criminal act of false pretenses (Chapter 10) or of some statutory offense such as the obtaining of a genuine signature by fraud.

Written Documents

Nearly any written document can be subject to an act of forgery. Thus, documents ranging from a bankbook, a check, a deed, a promissory note, or a prescription for drugs—to list just a few of many examples—may be forged.

A person does not commit forgery by altering the content of his own business records, unless another person has an interest in those records. Thus, one who changes the date of an appointment on his own personal calendar in order to disguise his whereabouts on that date does not commit forgery. However, one who makes a false entry in his bankbook may commit forgery, since the bank has an interest in the amount of all deposits recorded in the book. Similarly, an employee who makes alterations in his employer's business ledgers to cover up an embezzlement, for example, may commit forgery, since his employer has an interest in those records.

One may commit forgery by falsely making or by materially altering a receipt, even though this changes the content of a past obligation rather than a present or future obligation. Thus, one who alters a cancelled check may commit forgery. However, forgery is not committed when a person writes a private memorandum to himself, even if the content of this memorandum is false.

It is a federal offense to falsely make or alter many documents that are issued by the United States government. For example, it is a federal offense to falsely make or alter a passport,[1] a visa,[2] naturalization and citizenship papers,[3] a certificate of discharge from the armed forces,[4] or a money order from the Post Office.[5] Only Congress has the authority to make or alter these documents. Similarly, it is a federal offense to falsely make or alter any of a number of documents issued by a foreign government, when the making or the alteration is done within the territory of the United States.[6]

Apparent Basis for Legal Liability

Any written document that *is* the basis for legal liability may be subject to forgery in every state. In many states, any written document that *appears* to be the basis for legal liability, whether or not it is in fact, may also be subject to forgery. However, a document that neither is nor appears to be the basis for legal liability cannot be forged in any state.

A written document can be the basis for legal liability only when it creates or terminates rights or interests that can be enforced in the courts. Thus, for example, one who writes a love letter and signs someone else's name to it does not commit forgery, since the letter neither creates nor terminates the legal rights or legal interests of anyone. However, one who includes a promise to marry in a forged love letter may commit forgery, at least in states where an offer of marriage gives rise to legal liability. In some states one who breaks his promise to marry another person may be sued for damages.

Letters of introduction and letters that contain someone's opinion on a given subject may be subject to forgery in some states but not in others. There has been disagreement concerning whether credentials may be forged. Many courts have decided that one who falsely makes or materially alters the credentials of a public officer commits forgery, since this affects the public interest. Thus, one who creates a credential that identifies him as a police officer may commit forgery.

In most states, a document need only appear to be the basis for legal liability to be subject to forgery. Thus, one who creates or alters a document that looks as if it is the basis for legal liability but that has some technical defect still may commit forgery. For example, the false making of a deed to land may constitute forgery even if the deed is not the basis for legal liability because no revenue stamp was attached to it. Similarly, a document may be subject to forgery even if it requires completion to be the basis for legal liability. Thus, one who falsely signs the name of a married man to a mortgage may commit forgery, even though the state law requires a married man's wife to cosign the document before it is valid.

A document that is void on its face cannot be subject to forgery, since it neither is nor appears to be the basis for legal liability. Thus, one who makes or materially alters a document that says nothing either before or after the alteration does not commit forgery.

Specific Intent to Defraud

A person does not bear criminal responsibility for forgery unless he can be shown to have possessed a specific intent to defraud at the moment he falsely made or materially altered the written document. Thus, forgery is not viewed as a "cause-and-result" crime, and a general criminal intent is not sufficient to make anyone criminally responsible for forgery. More than the fact that a person voluntarily made or altered a document is required to convict him of forgery; a specific criminal intent to defraud must be proven.

When the specific intent can be shown to have existed in the offender's mind at the time of his act, his criminal responsibility for forgery is complete. It does not matter that no one was actually deceived. Nor does it matter that the offender did not actually receive any financial gain from his attempts. Indeed, one may bear criminal responsibility for forgery even though, at the time of his criminal act, he did not have in mind any particular person to defraud.

A person who falsely makes or materially alters public documents is often presumed to intend to defraud the public at large. This is true with respect to a birth certificate, a marriage or divorce certificate, or the recording of a deed or mortgage. Similarly, one who falsely makes or materially alters a driver's license or a license of any other kind that is issued by a state may be presumed to intend to defraud the public in the absence of contrary evidence.

A person would not be criminally responsible for forgery, however, if the evidence showed that he falsely made or materially altered a written document merely to exhibit it as a specimen rather than to use it for any fraudulent purpose.

Counterfeiting

The basic elements of counterfeiting can be outlined as follows:
A. The Criminal Act:

1. *(a)* the false making or
   (b) the material alteration
2. of a spurious item
3. to resemble a genuine item
4. (issued by a government)
B. The Criminal Intent:
5. *(a)* a general criminal intent or
   (b) a specific intent to defraud

False Making

A person commits the act of counterfeiting by either falsely making or materially altering a spurious (ungenuine) item to resemble a genuine item. Essentially, then, the act of counterfeiting is the same as that of forgery. However, forgery is usually restricted to the false making or material alteration of a *written* document. Counterfeiting, too, sometimes includes the false making or material alteration of a written document—such as paper money—which is mass-produced by printing. Otherwise, counterfeiting involves the false making or the material alteration of items other than written documents.

The false making of an item takes place at the moment the false item begins to resemble its genuine counterpart. The false item does not have to be identical to the genuine one in size, shape, color, or detail. It must bear a clear and obvious resemblance to the genuine item, however, to the extent that it may be mistaken for the real thing. Thus, a person who makes a slug look similar to a genuine quarter dollar may commit counterfeiting, although the false quarter looks shabbier, duller, or more worn than the average genuine quarter. It is general resemblance, rather than perfection of resemblance, that characterizes the false making of an item to resemble a genuine one.

Material Alteration

Just as forgery may be committed by materially altering the writing on a document, counterfeiting may be committed by materially altering the design on a nonwritten item. Not every alteration is material, however. To be material, the alteration must change either the value or the significance of the altered item. The change in value or significance may be either for better or for worse. Obviously, such a change is usually made to increase rather than decrease the value of an item.

One may commit counterfeiting by plating a silver coin with gold so that the coin may be mistaken for a gold coin of greater value. Counterfeiting may be committed by joining together the uncancelled portions of two used stamps to give the appearance of one uncancelled stamp.

Counterfeiting would not be committed, however, merely by writing insignificant words on a dollar bill. Although this might be an alteration, the alteration would not be material as long as the writing did not change the apparent value of the bill. Defacing money is a separate federal offense, however.

A Spurious Item

A person who makes or materially alters one item so that it resembles another item commits the act of counterfeiting only if the item he makes or alters is *spurious*—that is, only if it does not have both the same value and the same significance as the genuine item it resembles. Usually a spurious item is worthless and has no value at all. This is not always true, however. For example, a counterfeit ten- or twenty-dollar bill may be worth more to a collector than genuine currency of the same denomination. Still, the counterfeit bill is spurious, because it was not made on authority of Congress and therefore has no significance as legal tender.

Of course, one does not commit counterfeiting by making or altering a genuine item when he has authority to do so. Thus, a person who works at the U.S. Mint and who prints money on the authority of Congress does not commit counterfeiting. Even one who works at a mint may commit counterfeiting, however, if he prints more money than Congress has authorized him to print, since the excessive bills would not be genuine items.

Resemblance to a Genuine Item

Neither the false making nor the material alteration of any item can constitute counterfeiting unless the item that is made or altered resembles a *genuine* item. A genuine item may be any tangible property that has an independent value and significance and that is presently in existence. One may commit counterfeiting by falsely making or materially altering an item to resemble a genuine item that once existed but no longer exists, such as an ancient coin. Counterfeiting is not committed, however, when a person creates an item that does not resemble any other item of value or significance.

In this respect, counterfeiting is different from forgery. One may commit forgery by falsely making or materially altering any written document that is the basis for legal liability. The forged document does not have to bear a resemblance to a genuine document that represents the same legal liability.

Counterfeiting usually takes place when a person falsely makes or materially alters some kind of money. In earlier times, counterfeiting was often committed by making spurious coins. Most coins are no longer valuable enough to make counterfeiting profitable, however, and today counterfeiting generally occurs when someone falsely makes or materially alters a Federal Reserve note ("paper money") or some other negotiable instrument such as a United States Savings Bond. Creating a spurious coin still constitutes counterfeiting, however.

Issuance by a Government

In a broad sense, counterfeiting may be committed whenever a person falsely makes or materially alters an item to resemble *any* genuine item. As a rule, however, this offense has a much narrower meaning. Counterfeiting usually takes place only when one falsely makes or materially alters an item to resemble a genuine item that has been *issued by a government.*

In this sense, stamps, savings bonds, and other items issued by the U.S. government, in addition to money, may be counterfeited. It is a federal offense for anyone to make or to materially alter any of the following items: (1) the Great Seal of the United States, or the seal of any U.S. court, department, or agency,[7] (2) gold or silver coins or bars that resemble minted coins of the United States,[8] (3) any stamp that resembles a stamp issued by the United States,[9] or (4) any deed, power of attorney, order, certificate, receipt, contract, or other writing for the purpose of obtaining or of enabling another person either directly or indirectly to obtain or receive any sum of money from the United States or from any of its officers or agents.[10]

It is also a federal offense to make or materially alter an item to resemble a coin or currency issued by any foreign government, when the manufacture or alteration is done within the territory of the United States, or if the counterfeited item is brought within the territory of the United States.[11]

The offense of counterfeiting may be punished by state laws as well as by the federal government. Indeed, some states make it a state offense for one to make counterfeit money or other government securities within the state. Hence, counterfeiting may be both a state and a federal offense. Some states have extended the offense of counterfeiting to cover the false making or the material alteration of any item that contains the state's seal or the seal of a state agency. Thus, one who without authority imprints the seal of a state on a spurious driver's license or on a spurious race track ticket, for example, may commit counterfeiting.

General Criminal Intent

The common law made a sharp distinction between the criminal intent required for forgery and that required for counterfeiting. At common law, a person was criminally responsible for forgery only if at the moment of his act he possessed a specific intent to defraud. On the contrary, one was criminally responsible for counterfeiting if he possessed a general criminal intent.

Counterfeiting was viewed as a "cause-and-result" crime at common law, and it usually is still viewed as such under most counterfeiting statutes. When only a general rather than a specific criminal intent is required, then one who voluntarily makes or alters a spurious item to resemble a genuine item bears criminal responsibility for counterfeiting. When only a general criminal intent is required, it does not matter that the person who makes the spurious item intends that it be used only as a specimen of his craftsmanship or as a mere decoration.

Most federal statutes that regulate counterfeiting require only a general rather than a specific criminal intent. Thus, for example, one who falsely makes or materially alters any coin to resemble those minted by the United States or any foreign government bears criminal responsibility for counterfeiting if his criminal act was voluntary.[12] So also does one who voluntarily makes or alters a spurious stamp to resemble those issued by the United States or any foreign government.[13] In the case of a stamp, however, one is not criminally responsible for counterfeiting when he prints the likeness of a stamp in an album or a magazine for stamp collectors.[14]

Specific Intent to Defraud

Although most federal statutes that regulate counterfeiting require nothing more than a general criminal intent, one very important federal statute requires a specific intent to defraud. This is the statute that forbids the making or altering of any obligation or other security of the United States[15] and includes counterfeiting of a Federal Reserve note ("paper money") or a United States Savings Bond. Thus, one who voluntarily makes a spurious item to resemble paper currency is not criminally responsible for counterfeiting unless he possesses an intent to defraud. One who voluntarily makes a spurious item to resemble a coin bears criminal responsibility for counterfeiting even if he possesses no intent to defraud.

Criminal Simulation

Many states do not have an offense known as "counterfeiting." Even where counterfeiting is a state crime, this offense usually applies only to the creation of a spurious item to resemble a genuine item that is issued by a government—federal, state, or foreign. Every day, however, spurious items are created to resemble genuine items other than those issued by a government. The offense of "criminal simulation" prohibits this conduct in most states.

Generally, a person may commit the offense of criminal simulation by either making or altering *any* object so that it appears to have an antiquity, rarity, source, or authorship that it does not really have. Under some criminal simulation statutes, this offense is committed only when the object takes on a greater value or significance as a result of the untrue appearance.

The intent required to make a person criminally responsible for criminal simulation varies from state to state. As a general rule, a specific intent to defraud is required. Some statutes require that the offender also have a knowledge of the true character of the object.

Credit Fraud Offenses

Most states have enacted statutes to create a variety of criminal offenses relating to the fraudulent use of items relating to credit. The names of these offenses vary widely from state to state, but the statutes generally refer to the "misuse" of a credit card or a telephone billing number.

It is a criminal act in most states for a person to present a credit card as payment for property or services with knowledge that the card is stolen, has been forged, or has been revoked or cancelled. Similarly, it is a criminal act in most states to give a telephone operator the wrong telephone or credit card number to which to bill a long-distance telephone call.

Generally, no specific criminal intent must be shown in order for a person to bear criminal responsibility for a credit fraud offense. He must be shown to have had knowledge that the credit card or supporting information will be insufficient to meet the obligation. A credit card or supporting information (such as the signature) will be insufficient if the credit voucher (after being stamped by the card and signed) will be dishonored and therefore not paid by the bank which issued the card. Many statutes provide that one who acts in good faith under a claim of right either does not bear criminal responsibility in the first place or at least has an affirmative defense to criminal responsibility. Thus, a person who uses a credit card issued to another member of his immediate family, with the consent of the person in whose name the card is issued, may not bear criminal responsibility. A person who presents a credit card in his own name may not be criminally responsible for a credit fraud offense even if the card has been cancelled or revoked by the issuing company, unless the company has notified him of the cancellation or revocation.

Other Deceptive Practices

In most states, several additional deceptive practices are prohibited by statute. These cannot all be discussed here, but the major ones deserve brief attention.

Uttering Counterfeit Items

One "utters" a counterfeit item when he uses it to pay any debt, with intent to defraud. It is a federal offense to utter a counterfeit obligation or other security of the United States,[16] just as it is a federal offense to utter a counterfeit coin.[17] This offense is separate from the offense of *making* the spurious item. A specific intent to defraud is always required with uttering, however. Thus, an innocent person who receives counterfeit money as change and then proceeds to spend the bogus currency is not criminally responsible for this offense. One may become criminally responsible, however, by using a counterfeit item to pay a debt when he believes or has reason to believe the item is not genuine.

Issuing or Passing a Bad Check

In every state, a person who either issues or passes a bad check commits a criminal act. A check is *bad* when the bank account on which the check is drawn contains *insufficient funds* to cover the full value of the check. The bank account does not have to be empty. Thus, one who writes a check for one hundred dollars on an account containing only fifty dollars issues a bad check.

The person whose name appears on the check *issues* the check, unless his name is forged. Any other person who receives the check and then negotiates it to a third person *passes* the check. A criminal act is committed each time a person issues or passes a bad check.

One may not bear criminal responsibility every time he issues or passes a bad check, however, Under most statutes, one is not criminally responsible for passing a bad check unless, at the moment he passes the check, he knows or has reason to believe that the issuing person's bank account contains insufficient funds. A person who issues a bad check is criminally responsible for this act (1) if he does not have an account in the bank on which the check is drawn or (2) if he does not have sufficient funds to cover the check in the account beginning with the day on which the check is dated and continuing for a reasonable period of time thereafter. Under the Uniform Commercial Code, a person who issues a check is discharged from his obligation to provide sufficient funds to cover the check after twenty days in some states and after thirty days in other states. (Add one extra day for each Federal Reserve Bank through which the check is transmitted.)

As a rule in most states, even within the twenty-one or thirty-one day period, a person who issues a check with insufficient funds to cover it does not bear criminal responsibility for issuing a bad check if he makes the check good within a certain amount of time. In some states, a person is allowed five business days to make the check good; in others, he is allowed up to ten.

Deceptive Business Practices

Under some new criminal codes, such as that in Pennsylvania, a person may commit a crime by engaging in certain deceptive business practices. The Pennsylvania statute reads as follows:

§ 4107. *Deceptive business practices.*
(a) *Offense defined.*—A person commits a misdemeanor of the second degree if, in the course of business, he:
(1) uses or possesses for use a false weight or measure, or any other device for falsely determining or recording any quality or quantity;
(2) sells, offers or exposes for sale, or delivers less than the represented quantity of any commodity or service;
(3) takes or attempts to take more than the represented quantity of any commodity or service when as a buyer he furnishes the weight or measure;
(4) Sells, offers or exposes for sale adulterated or mislabeled commodities;
(5) makes a false or misleading statement in any advertisement addressed to the public or to a substantial segment thereof for the purpose of promoting the purchase or sale of property or services;
(6) makes a false or misleading written statement for the purpose of obtaining property or credit; or
(7) makes a false or misleading written statement for the purpose of promoting the sale of securities, or omits information required by law to be disclosed in written documents relating to securities.

Notice that this statute overlaps the offense of false pretenses to a considerable degree. It specifies very clearly the conduct that is required. A "deceptive" criminal intent is presumed under this Pennsylvania statute, unless the *defendant* proves by a preponderance of the evidence that his conduct was neither knowingly nor recklessly deceptive.

Use of Slugs

Under the language proposed for revision of the Massachusetts Criminal Code, the following conduct should be criminalized:

§ 25. *Use of Slugs.*
  (a) A person is guilty of use of slugs if:
  (1) with intent to defraud, he inserts or deposits a slug in a coin box, turnstile, vending machine or other mechanical or electronic device or receptacle; or
  (2) he makes, possesses or disposes of a slug with intent to enable a person to insert or deposit it in a coin box, turnstile, vending machine or other mechanical or electronic device or receptacle.

CHAPTER 12

Criminal Intrusion Offenses

Criminal intrusion offenses are designed to provide extra protection for property that is prized enough to be enclosed in one way or another. Buildings and vehicles are normally enclosed with sides or walls, doors, windows, and a roof. Fields may be enclosed with fences. The fact that property has been enclosed indicates that someone wishes to set it apart from the public domain.

Burglary, housebreaking, and criminal trespass are accompanied often by the offender's intent to steal property that has been enclosed. However, theft does not have to be the objective of one who commits an intrusion offense. An intruder may harbor some other criminal purpose, such as to destroy the enclosed property or to inflict bodily injury upon someone who is found within the enclosure.

Severity of an intrusion offense depends generally upon the kind of enclosure that has been erected and the time of day or night when the intrusion takes place. It is more serious as a rule for one to intrude into a building than into a vehicle or field, and more serious to intrude anywhere at night than during the day.

Intrusion offenses that are discussed in this chapter include burglary, housebreaking, and criminal trespass.

Burglary

The basic elements of burglary can be outlined as follows:
   A. The Criminal Act:
      1. the breaking and or
      2. the entering
      3. into enclosed property
      4. which another person possesses
   B. The Criminal Intent:
      5. a specific intent to commit a crime therein

Breaking

In many states, a person must break into some kind of enclosed property in order to commit the act of burglary. An actual *breaking* usually takes place only when a person physically moves an obstacle that stands between himself and the inside of property that otherwise is fully enclosed. The obstacle that is moved must be capable by itself of preventing the intruder from entering the property unless he moves it. If any additional obstacle must also be removed before an entry can be accomplished, there has been no breaking.

A breaking can occur only on property that was fully enclosed prior to the breaking. Many states limit the type of property that may be broken into. In some states, only a building may be broken into. In many states, a building or a vehicle may be broken into. In other states, any fenced-off area, such as a swimming pool with a fence and a closed gate, may be broken into, even though the area does not have a closed roof. In the case of a fenced-off area, however, no breaking would occur if someone merely climbed the fence; to break in he also would have to open the gate or cut some wire.

A breaking may occur when one enters a portion of a building that is fully enclosed and is off limits to him, even if the rest of the building is open to him. For example, a servant may break into his employer's bedroom by opening a closed door if he has been told not to enter the bedroom; this is true even if this servant is permitted to enter other rooms in the house. Similarly, one may break into a closed office that opens onto a public foyer or lobby.

Ordinarily, a breaking occurs when a person opens a door or window that was closed before he opened it. To constitute a breaking, a door or window need not have been locked, but it must have been shut fully before it was opened. Usually, this means that a door must have been latched and a window must have been closed. Thus, a closed door or window may be broken into merely by being opened. It is not necessary that the door or window be "broken" in the literal sense of the word. Violence is not necessary in order for a breaking to occur.

No breaking takes place, however, when a person walks through an open doorway or climbs through an open window. Nor does a breaking occur when one finds a door partly open and opens it further, or when one sees a window partially open and opens it wider. In the eyes of the law, an open door or an open window is an invitation for a person to enter the property. Of course, this does not mean that it is an invitation for a person to commit a criminal act after entering the property.

One may break into a building, vehicle, or other structure in many ways other than by opening a door or a window. A breaking occurs when a person makes a hole in a roof with an ax, or when one climbs into a house through a chimney. Although a chimney creates a hole in the roof, this does not mean that a building becomes unenclosed. Normally, an open chimney is not considered to be an invitation for an intruder to enter the building. Thus, by climbing down a chimney, a person may break into a building without moving any obstacle, since the chimney is considered an obstacle in itself.

A "constructive" rather than an actual breaking may take place if the intruder does not move any obstacle that encloses the property but tricks someone on the property into moving the obstacle for him. For example, a person who falsely represents himself as a repairman commits a breaking at the moment an occupant of a house innocently lets him in. In this situation, the intruder does not need to use any physical force to open a door or a window.

Not every state requires a breaking as a necessary element of burglary, and only twelve states require a breaking for every kind of burglary. Seventeen states require a breaking for higher degrees of burglary, but not for lesser degrees. In some of these states, for example, a breaking is required only if the burglary is committed during the day or in a building other than a dwelling. Thus, in these states, no breaking is necessary if the burglary is committed at night or at any time of day or night in a dwelling.

At least twenty-two states have disregarded breaking as an element of the burglary act. In these states, the unlawfulness of the *entry* alone determines whether burglary is committed. A few states, such as North Carolina, forbid anyone to "break or enter" any building unlawfully. No court has determined whether, under this type of statute, burglary can be committed as a result of a breaking without an entry.

Entering

As the law now stands, burglary cannot take place unless someone enters enclosed property. The purpose of making burglary a crime is to protect buildings and other structures from unlawful intrusion. An intrusion cannot occur unless someone enters enclosed property.

An entry takes place at the moment any part of the intruding person's body is extended into the enclosed property. Thus, when the intruding person extends his finger through a window frame, for example, or when he extends his foot through a doorway, his entry into the property is accomplished. Obviously, one enters a structure when he walks, crawls, climbs, or extends his head into it. One may enter a boat house, for example, by swimming into it. In states where a breaking is required, however, burglary may not be committed when one swims underneath walls if they extend only to the surface of the water.

Generally, an entry does not occur when a person extends a tool or other instrument through a door, window, or other opening to a structure. One exception to this rule is when the intruding person extends a tool, such as a hook, into the property in order to grasp some property situated inside. Another exception is when one shoots a bullet into a building.

When both a breaking and an entering are required to constitute burglary, the breaking must take place *before* rather than after the entry. Breaking *out* of a building that has been entered without a breaking does not constitute burglary if both a breaking and an entering are required.

At common law, a person committed burglary only by breaking and entering at *night*. Today, burglary may be committed by daylight as well as at night in every state. In some states, however, one may commit a higher degree of burglary by making an unlawful entry at night.

In states where the seriousness of burglary depends on the time of day when entry occurs, difficulties have arisen concerning the moment when day ends and night begins, as well as when night ends and the next day begins. Most states distinguish day and night according to when the sun rises and sets. In these states, day becomes night at sunset, and night becomes day at sunrise. A few states have declared the transition between day and night to occur one half-hour after sunset and one half-hour before sunrise. By either means of calculation, the hour and minute at which night begins and ends varies according to the time of year.

Enclosed Property

At common law, burglary took place only when a person broke into and entered someone else's *dwelling* place. A dwelling place was considered to be the place where a person permanently lived or resided, usually a house. Only a permanent structure could be a dwelling place at common law, and therefore a temporary structure such as a tent could not be burglarized, since it was not considered permanent enough to be a dwelling place.

Barns, sheds, stables, and other outbuildings situated on the land where a dwelling house stood were considered a part of the house at common law, and therefore could be burglarized. Moreover, any part of a dwelling place could be burglarized at common law, whether or not its occupants were at home at the time it was broken into and entered.

Nowadays, every state has substantially extended the definition of a dwelling house to include hotel and motel rooms and apartments. In most states, burglary may be committed through an unlawful intrusion into many buildings where no person lives, such as public buildings, office buildings, warehouses, stores, and mines. A number of states recognize houseboats, mobile homes (trailers), and other types of movable vehicles as places where burglary may be committed. Whether movable or not, property must be *enclosed* to be burglarized. Thus, breaking into the glove compartment of a convertible automobile would constitute burglary in a number of states, but reaching into a convertible car with its roof open (or any vehicle with an open window) could never constitute burglary.

Another Person's Possession

The act of burglary cannot take place unless a person enters enclosed property that he does not have a lawful right to enter. One always has a lawful right to enter property that he *possesses,* but sometimes it is hard to resolve who is in possession of specific property at a particular moment.

A person who rents a house, another kind of structure, or a vehicle automatically *possesses* it. Thus, a person who rents the house in which he lives does not commit burglary by entering it, even if he has to break into the house because his key has been misplaced. (The same is true of a person who lives in a house that he owns.)

When several people own or rent a house or another building or vehicle together, each of these persons may break into the structure, because each *possesses* it. When several people rent different apartments within the same building, however, each person possesses only his own apartment, not the other apartments. Hence, if one person breaks into an apartment that he does not rent, he may commit burglary, even if this apartment is located in the same building as his own apartment.

The owner of property surrenders possession of the property when he rents it. Therefore, a person may commit burglary even on property he owns if he has rented the property to someone else. A tenant, not the landlord, always possesses the property he rents and occupies.

Specific Intent to Commit a Crime Therein

A person cannot be criminally responsible for burglary unless he can be shown to have possessed an intent *to commit a crime within the structure* that he unlawfully entered. Note that the intruder must be proven to have intended to commit a crime *inside* rather than outside the structure.

The type of crime that must be intended varies from state to state. Some states require that a *felony* be intended, as this was the common-law rule. Most states require only that some crime have been intended, whether the crime constitutes a felony, a misdemeanor, or another unlawful act. In many of these states, however, an intruder who can be proven to have intended commission of a felony may bear criminal responsibility for a higher degree of burglary.

No state views burglary as a "cause-and-result" crime. Thus, the state must prove a specific intent on the part of the intruder to commit a crime at the moment he entered the structure. Some states will *presume* an intent on the part of an intruder to commit a crime if he does not offer any other reasonable explanation for entering the structure. This presumption becomes more conclusive in some states if the intruder carries explosives, a firearm, or another dangerous weapon on his person at the time he enters the structure.

If a specific intent to commit a crime inside a structure is on an intruder's mind at the moment he unlawfully enters the property, the intruder bears criminal responsibility for burglary even if he fails to commit the crime he has planned. Thus, one who unlawfully enters a building intending to steal money he thinks he will find inside is criminally responsible for burglary even if he is unable to find the money, or if he is stopped by the police before he can find it, or if no money lies anywhere inside the building.

On the other hand, a person who plans to break into a structure to steal something inside, but who abandons his plan to steal prior to entering the structure, is not criminally responsible for burglary. Similarly, one who innocently enters a building to satisfy his curiosity but without any intent to commit a crime therein cannot be criminally responsible for burglary even if he decides to steal something he sees after entering the building.

As mentioned earlier, a few statutes clearly limit the type of property that can be burglarized. Thus, if a statute says that only a building may be burglarized, one bears no criminal responsibility for burglary if he breaks into and enters an automobile. Some statutes provide that only a structure containing valuable goods may be burglarized. Under such a statute, one who breaks into and enters an empty building cannot be criminally responsible for burglary.

Housebreaking

As mentioned, common-law burglary could be committed only by breaking and entering the dwelling place of another person at night with an intent to commit a felony therein. Thus, one did not commit burglary at common law by breaking into another's dwelling house during the hours of daylight. Neither did one commit burglary at common law by breaking into and entering a building other than a dwelling house at any time of the day or night. A gap thus existed in the English law, and to fill it, Parliament created the statutory offense known as "housebreaking."

The offense of housebreaking may be committed by breaking and entering into nearly any type of building at any time of the day or night. Thus, the building does not have to be a dwelling house, but may be a warehouse, an office, a store, a church, or virtually any other structure. This offense may be committed either before or after sunset, as the time of day makes no difference. In addition, housebreaking does not require a specific intent on the part of the offender to commit a felony inside the building he breaks into and enters. It is a "cause-and-result" crime and requires only a general criminal intent. Thus, one may become criminally responsible for housebreaking by breaking into and entering a structure voluntarily if he has no legal right to do so.

Statutory provision for an offense of housebreaking is unnecessary in most states, since the offense of burglary itself has become reformed and expanded beyond its common-law limitations. For this reason, few, if any, states presently have an offense known as housebreaking. Nearly every state has an offense known as "criminal trespass," however—patterned after housebreaking, but much broader.

Criminal Trespass

Criminal trespass is a statutory offense that fills many gaps left open by definitions of burglary. Nearly every state has enacted a statute creating the offense of criminal trespass, and the elements of the offense vary slightly from state to state, depending on what intrusions are not covered by the burglary statutes. Criminal trespass is always a less serious offense than burglary and is usually a misdemeanor. It may be a felony under certain conditions, however.

A person may commit criminal trespass by entering a structure even though it is not fully enclosed. This is possible because criminal trespass does not require any breaking, but simply an unlawful entry by one person onto another person's property. Thus, one who walks through an open doorway or an open window may commit criminal trespass. Similarly, a person who remains on another's property after he is expected to leave it may commit criminal trespass.

Under some statutes, a person does not commit criminal trespass except by entering or remaining on another's property after being told to leave, unless the property has been posted with a conspicuous No Trespassing sign in accordance with the statute. While a person who fails to heed such a warning generally commits the offense of criminal trespass, a warning of this sort is not always required under criminal trespass statutes. One who is warned not to enter or who is warned to leave property may become a "defiant" trespasser if he does enter or refuses to leave the property. A "defiant" trespasser may commit a more serious degree of the criminal trespass act than any other kind of trespasser.

Some criminal trespass statutes apply only when a person unlawfully enters property that is at least partially enclosed. Under these statutes, one might commit criminal trespass by entering an open doorway or by climbing through an open window into a building or other structure. Even under a statute that requires the property to be partially enclosed, the property does not as a rule have to be a building. Thus, one may commit criminal trespass by unlawfully entering or remaining within a fenced yard.

Under many criminal trespass statutes, however, property may be unlawfully entered even though it is not even partially enclosed if it clearly appears to belong to someone other than the intruder. Thus, the front lawn of a house usually appears to belong to the person who occupies the house. Similarly, the driveway leading to a building or the parking lot in front of a business generally appears to be part of the nearest building in sight.

A person who commits criminal trespass bears criminal responsibility for his conduct if at the time of his act he possessed the criminal intent required under the appropriate statute. Different criminal intents are required under different statutes. Many require the intruder to enter the property "knowing that he is not licensed or privileged to do so." A person is licensed or privileged to enter another's property if the occupant of the property has given actual or implied consent. Under many state laws, a person who does not fence his property implicitly grants a license or privilege to anyone who enters the property for a purpose that can in any way benefit the occupant. Thus, a postman, a milkman, or even a salesman is ordinarily considered licensed at least to walk up to the front door of a building and ring the doorbell. A person who has nothing to offer or deliver to the occupant might not be licensed or privileged to ring the bell. Even one who does have something to offer or deliver to the occupant is not as a rule privileged to walk inside a private house without being admitted by an occupant, although he may be privileged to walk inside an office to talk with a receptionist.

Some criminal trespass statutes provide that one who enters another's property by subterfuge (trick) or surreptitiously automatically is responsible for criminal trespass unless he has the actual permission of an occupant of the property. Thus, a salesman who enters a house disguised as a telephone repairman may be criminally responsible for this offense. Even a person who is on legitimate business, such as a gas meter reader, may be criminally responsible for criminal trespass if he sneaks into or onto property rather than entering the premises in a normal manner.

CHAPTER 13

Property
Destruction Offenses

Property destruction offenses are committed when a person inflicts harm upon property. The property may be real estate such as a house or a barn, or it may be personal property such as a vehicle, jewelry, or other belongings that are movable. Indeed, everyone holds a property interest in his own reputation, and this can be destroyed by harmful words.

These offenses may be distinguished according to the type of property being destroyed or by the method of destruction. Harmful words that are used to injure someone's reputation may constitute the offense known as criminal libel. When a building or a vehicle is destroyed by being set on fire, the offense of arson may be committed. The offense of criminal mischief may take place when either real estate or movable property is tampered with in an effort to impair functioning of the property.

Severity of a property destruction offense may depend upon the replacement value of the property. However, arson is regarded as being an especially serious crime because of the danger that fire poses to the entire community in addition to an individual victim.

Property destruction offenses that are discussed in this chapter include arson, criminal mischief, and criminal libel.

Arson

The basic elements of arson can be outlined as follows:
 A. The Criminal Act:
  1. the burning
  2. of property
  3. (*a*) that another person possesses or
   (*b*) that one possesses
 B. The Criminal Intent:
  4. (*a*) a general criminal intent (if another person possesses the property) or
   (*b*) a specific criminal intent (if the offender possesses the property)

Burning

The act of arson cannot take place unless property is burned. In most states, a burning is viewed as occurring when property is both set on fire and charred. A few states consider property to be burned when it is ignited, whether or not it becomes charred.

To be charred, the property must suffer some permanent damage from the fire. Thus, property that suffers temporary discoloration from smoke or from a scorch is not usually charred. Property is considered to be charred if damage caused by fire cannot readily be repaired once the fire has been extinguished. As a rule, property is considered to have burned if even the slightest portion of the property has been reduced to carbon.

Property does not, therefore, need to have been totally damaged or destroyed in order to have been burned. A very slight amount of damage will generally be sufficient, so long as this damage is permanent rather than temporary. Similarly, a building is considered to have been burned if any portion of the building has been set on fire and charred. Thus, the burning of a floor, wall, door, window frame, or even a shingle on the roof will constitute the burning of a building. The structure need not be burned to the ground.

Only fires that are set by a human being constitute a burning within the definition of arson. When lightning strikes a building, or when an animal starts a fire, arson does not take place. When a person sets property on fire, however, arson may take place regardless of the method or the means used by the person to ignite a fire.

At common law, arson could be committed at any time of day. In this respect, arson differed from burglary, which could be committed only at night at common law. Under a number of statutes, however, a higher degree of arson may be committed when property is set on fire at night. Still, no state limits the act of arson to any particular time of day or night.

Property

At common law, only the burning of a dwelling place could constitute the act of arson. However, barns, sheds, stables, and other outbuildings situated on the land where a dwelling house stood were considered a part of the house. Thus, at common law, only property that could be subject to burglary could be subject to arson.

By statute, most states have extended the concept of arson to include most other buildings besides dwelling houses. Office buildings, warehouses, stores, schools, churches, and other permanent structures can generally be subject to arson. Moreover, structures that are more or less permanent, such as mobile homes (trailers) and houseboats, may also be subject to arson. A few states have broadened their arson statutes to include the burning of motor vehicles. Nevertheless, the burning of most personal (rather than real) property does not constitute arson.

Arson may take place even if the property that is burned is not fully enclosed at the time of the burning. Thus, a house with an open door or an open window may be subject to arson, although it could not be subject to burglary. This is true because the purpose of an arson statute is to protect certain types of property from destruction, whereas the purpose of a burglary statute is to protect enclosed property from intrusion.

The burning of personal property in the vicinity of a building does not constitute arson unless this personal property itself can be subject to arson under a particular statute. Nor does the burning of personal property become arson merely because a fire spreads accidentally to a nearby building. Normally, the act of arson occurs only when a person sets fire directly to a portion of a building or other permanent structure that can be subject to arson.

Another Person's Possession

As a basic rule, a person commits arson only by burning property that someone else possesses at the time of the burning. Thus, one who sets fire to property that he possesses himself does not, under this rule, commit arson. Arson is generally viewed as an offense against the possession of property, rather than against property itself.

A person who sets fire to property that another person possesses may commit arson even if he owns the property that he burns. For example, the owner of an apartment building may commit arson by setting the building on fire if he has rented the building to one or more tenants. A tenant who rents an apartment from a landlord temporarily possesses the property during the course of his lease. Hence, a landlord has no right to burn his tenant out of the latter's possession.

As a basic rule, a tenant would not commit arson by burning his apartment, since he is in possession of the apartment. By statute in some states, however, a tenant may commit arson by burning an apartment or other property that he rents. Under this type of statute, the tenant is viewed as destroying his landlord's right to repossess the property at the termination of the lease.

General Criminal Intent

As a basic rule under law, all fires are presumed to have been started accidentally from natural causes. Even when a fire appears to have been started though human effort, the presumption continues that the fire was started accidentally. Only when the evidence clearly shows that a person voluntarily and nonaccidentally set a fire does this presumption change.

When a person is shown to have voluntarily and nonaccidentally set fire to property while knowing the property belonged to someone else, the offender is presumed to have acted with a general criminal intent. In this respect, arson is viewed as a "cause-and-result" crime. Arson is never viewed as a "cause-and-result" crime, however, when the person who set the fire also possessed the property that was burned. Thus, while a *general* criminal intent is usually sufficient to make a person bear criminal responsibility for burning property in someone else's possession, a *specific* criminal intent is necessary to show that a person is criminally responsible for burning property in his own possession.

Specific Criminal Intent

At common law, one could never bear criminal responsibility for arson by setting fire to property in his own possession. By statute in many states, however, there are two exceptions to the common law rule. First, a person who sets fire to property in his own possession *specifically intending* to let the fire spread to a neighbor's property may be criminally responsible for arson. Second, a person who sets fire to his own property *specifically intending* to collect on an insurance policy may be criminally responsible for arson. In either situation, when a person sets fire to property in his own possession, a general criminal intent is not sufficient to make him bear criminal responsibility for arson. A specific criminal intent must be proven.

When a person can be shown to have set fire to property in his possession in order to let the fire destroy a neighbor's property, the person is not relieved of criminal responsibility merely because the fire is extinguished before it reaches the neighbor's property. Similarly, a person who is shown to have set fire to his own property to collect its insurance value is not relieved of criminal responsibility merely because he does not succeed in obtaining the insurance money. Most states do not relieve a person of criminal responsibility even if the insurance policy turns out to have been invalid or not in force at the time of the burning, if the offender thought his policy was valid and in force. Michigan, however, requires that the policy have been both valid and in force at the time of the burning, or one who sets fire to his own property intending to collect its insurance value does not bear criminal responsibility for arson.

Criminal Mischief

The offense of arson usually is limited to the burning of a building or certain kinds of personal property, such as a motor vehicle. Arson does not cover the burning of most types of personal property. Arson never covers the damaging of property by any means other than fire. For this reason, most states have enacted statutes to create the offense of "criminal mischief." This offense is labeled "malicious mischief" in some states, but the word *malicious* is misleading, since few such statutes require the offender to possess a malicious intent in order to bear criminal responsibility for the offense.

Under most statutes, a person commits criminal mischief by causing damage to, or by destroying, property belonging to another person. Any amount of damage will usually be sufficient to constitute the act of criminal mischief, and the property does not have to be destroyed. When property is destroyed, however, a higher grade of the criminal mischief offense may be committed.

Nearly any kind of property may be subject to criminal mischief, as long as it belongs to someone other than the person who causes the damage. Thus, one may commit criminal mischief by doing harm to a building, to land, to tangible personal property, or to intangible personal property. The harm need not be permanent and may be repairable without difficulty, but criminal mischief still may take place. The injury to the property does not have to be caused by fire or any other particular means. The property may be damaged or destroyed without any risk of danger to any human being, and still criminal mischief may occur. Thus, one may commit criminal mischief by writing graffiti on the wall of a washroom, for example, as well as by breaking a window or crashing an automobile into a tree. Or one could commit criminal mischief by opening a gas line or a steam pipe so that its contents pour out and are wasted.

In some states, a person may commit criminal mischief by tampering with property belonging to someone else. This conduct constitutes a separate offense known as "criminal tampering" in a few states, such as New York. One tampers with property when he meddles with it in such a way and to such an extent that a person who has a right to use the property becomes inconvenienced. Property may be tampered with and not be damaged or destroyed. Thus, a person who shuts off someone else's water pipe or electric current tampers with property, although no property is destroyed or even damaged.

Generally, a person who commits criminal mischief bears criminal responsibility for this offense if he voluntarily tampers with or damages property but has no right to do so. Some statutes provide that a person is not criminally responsible for criminal mischief when he reasonably believes he has a right to tamper with or damage the property, even if he actually has no such right. Generally speaking, a person has a right to do what he pleases with peoperty he owns or property in his possession, unless he has agreed not to damage or tamper with it. However, certain things— such as gas or water meters—may be on a person's property but he may be prohibited by law from tampering with them.

Some statutes make a person criminally responsible for criminal mischief only when he intentionally, knowingly, or recklessly damages or tampers with property without the right to do so. Under a few statutes, one may bear criminal responsibility for criminal mischief by damaging or destroying someone else's property through criminal negligence. A few statutes provide that a person may bear a higher degree of criminal responsibility by damaging or tampering with property in such a way that he creates a risk of danger to a human being than he would by doing the same thing without creating this risk.

Criminal Libel

The Basic elements of criminal libel can be outlined as follows:
A. The Criminal Act:
1. the publication
2. of a defamation
3. (*a*) in writing
   or
   (*b*) by broadcast

    4. without privilege [or truth]
  B. The Criminal Intent:
    5. with a general criminal intent

Publication

Some form of publication is required for the act of criminal libel to take place. A publication is nothing more than a meaningful communication that one person makes to at least one other person. A publication is made when one person communicates with another person or with many other persons, so long as at least one of the persons to whom the publication is made understands its meaning.

A publication may consist of a word, a symbol, a picture, or a gesture, but it usually is made in the form of a statement. The statement may be a sentence or only a phrase. It may be spoken, written or printed. Not every spoken word or written letter constitutes the act of criminal libel, however.

One may make a publication secretly or publicly. Thus, a person may make a publication by whispering in another's ear, or by shouting, or by talking on the telephone or into a radio microphone. A written publication may be made in the form of a note, a letter, a poster, a newspaper, or a magazine.

A person may make a publication without communicating an original idea. Whenever one person communicates in any understandable way with another person, a publication is made. Thus, one who tells another some news that he has learned from someone else republishes the news by means of this new publication. How frequently a publication is made depends upon the number of times it is communicated by a specific person, rather than how many times it is heard by a different listener. Thus, a person may make only one publication by speaking to a thousand persons, or he may make a thousand publications by speaking to one person a thousand times.

Defamation

Only the publication of a defamation can result in the act of criminal libel. Indeed, this offense is labeled criminal defamation in some states. For this reason, it is important to understand the meaning of a defamation.

A *defamation* is a publication that causes actual damage to the reputation of any person other than the one who makes the publication. Thus, one does not commit criminal libel by making a publication which damages his own reputation without damaging anyone else's reputation. Nor does one commit the act of criminal libel by making a publication which could damage only the reputation of the person to whom the publication is made, since no actual damage would result unless the publication is made to a third person.

Many kinds of publications may be damaging to a person's reputation. It is defamatory, for example, to suggest that a person is dishonest, immoral, professionally incompetent, or that the person has a loathsome disease. Not every disease is considered loathsome. This distinction is generally reserved for diseases such as leprosy and venereal diseases, although any form of mental illness might be considered loathsome. A publication is defamatory if it causes a person to be held in contempt, hatred, scorn, or ridicule, or if it tends to impair his standing in the community where he lives.

One may commit the act of criminal libel even by defaming the reputation of a person who is dead, under most statutes. A publication which defames a deceased person may embarrass his surviving relatives, friends, or business acquaintances. One may commit criminal libel, also, by making a publication which is defamatory to a person other than a living or dead human being, such as a family, organization, or corporation.

A publication may defame a person without referring to the person directly by name, as long as the identification is clear to at least one person other than the one making the publication and the one to whom it refers. The defamatory context of the publication must be clear and meaningful, however, since innocent words cannot be regarded as being defamatory.

Writing

Traditionally, the publication of a defamation was known as *libel* if the publication was written, but it was known as *slander* if the publication was spoken. Slander is not a criminal offense, although it results in defamation. The reason why libel may be a crime and slander may not be relates to the greater *durability* of libel than of slander. Ordinarily, the written communication is in existence for longer than the spoken communication. A written publication exists until it is erased or until the material containing the writing is destroyed. A spoken publication no longer exists at the close of the speech in which it is made, unless it is tape recorded. Even the tape recording of a spoken publication is not a criminal offense as a rule, although the publication may well damage someone's reputation.

The rule to remember is that *any* written publication which is defamatory may be the subject of criminal libel, while *not every* spoken publication which is defamatory may be the subject of this offense. Until a few decades ago, a spoken communication could never be the subject of criminal libel. The introduction of radio and television has changed this rule.

Broadcast

Even a spoken publication may be the subject of criminal libel under certain conditions, if it defames another person's reputation. Thus, a spoken publication which is broadcast over radio or television may be the subject of criminal libel in states where criminal libel is an offense.

While an ordinary spoken communication may be much less durable or permanent than a written communication, a spoken communication which is broadcasted over the mass-media becomes quite durable. Indeed, a spoken publication which is made over television to the entire nation or world may damage a person's reputation to a far greater extent than a letter which is sent to only one person.

A publication may defame a person's reputation without being written or spoken, if the publication is made as a gesture. A gesture may be broadcasted over television. It may also be broadcasted without television. Thus, one who hangs another person in effigy makes a publication which defames the reputation of the one who is ridiculed. This publication may be broadcasted when the symbol is hung for onlookers to observe. Hence, a defamatory publication may be broadcasted by sound or by sight, with or without the use of radio or television.

Privilege

The Federal Constitution provides that a member of either house of Congress "shall not be questioned in any other place" as a result of a speech or other communication which he makes during the course of any Congressional function. This privilege is both *absolute* and *complete*. As this privilege is absolute, it gives protection without regard to the truth or falsity of the publication, and without regard to the senator's or the congressman's knowledge of its truth or falsity. As the privilege is complete, the congressman or senator is protected even if the publication is not pertinent to the proceeding during which it is made. The privilege extends to all committee and sub-committee functions, in addition to communications made on the floor of Congress. Many states have extended a similar privilege to state legislators, by state constitution or statute.

An *absolute* privilege extends to the executive and judicial branches of the federal government, but this privilege is not complete. Thus, the President of the United States and his assistants may make defamatory publications without regard to their truth or falsity, and with or without knowledge that a defamatory publication is true or false. Similarly, a judge, attorney, party, witness, or other official in any judicial proceeding also has an absolute privilege to make a defamatory publication during the course of a proceeding. Neither the executive nor the judicial privilege is complete, however, since it does not cover a defamatory publication which has no relationship to the official proceeding or function where it is made. A privilege which is not complete does not exist unless the defamatory publication is pertinent to the official proceeding or governmental function at which it is made.

As a rule, a municipal official such as a city councilman, a mayor, or a city manager has only a *qualified* privilege. A qualified privilege is neither absolute nor complete. One who has a qualified privilege does not commit the act of criminal libel by making a defamatory publication which is pertinent to an official proceeding, whether it is true or false, provided that he believes the publication to be true. The privilege which is qualified does not exist if the publication is false and the person who makes it knows or has reason to believe it is untrue.

At common law, a private citizen could commit criminal libel by making any defamatory publication, whether it was true or false. This rule is different in most states today. Ordinarily, even a private citizen is privileged to make a defamatory publication if the publication is *true,* and if there is some *social interest* in having the truth disclosed. A few statutes provide that a defamatory publication which is true can never be the subject of criminal libel, even if there is no social interest in having the truth disclosed. While this might be the better rule, the laws of many states still look to the social interest of a defamatory publication.

A publication is usually considered to be of social interest if it is newsworthy. Any current event which takes place before the public eye is newsworthy, unless there is some unusual reason for keeping the event a secret. Furthermore, the public has a right to know of events or conditions which affect the character of any public official or candidate for public office. Even a lower echelon official, such as a policeman, fireman, or government office worker, may be considered a public official. A newspaper, television or radio station as well as a private citizen enjoys the privilege of criticizing a public official even at the expense of defaming his reputation, provided the defamation is true. Mere belief that it is true may not be sufficient if the defamatory publication is in fact false.

General Criminal Intent

By voluntarily publishing a defamatory communication, a private citizen — including a newspaper, radio or television station — may be presumed by law to possess a general criminal intent to commit criminal libel. Hence, this offense is viewed as a "cause-and-result" crime in most states. No specific intent to cause damage to the victim's reputation need be proven, nor does any evidence of malice have to be shown.

The voluntary act of publishing a defamatory communication gives rise only to a presumption of a general criminal intent. This presumption may be refuted or counteracted by evidence that the person who made the publication used *reasonable caution* to be sure the publication was true. Evidence of recklessness on the part of the person who makes a defamatory publication may make him criminally responsible for libel, as of course would any evidence of malice or of an intent to publish what he knew to be untrue. Ordinary negligence, however, does not as a rule create a general criminal intent which is sufficient to make a person bear criminal responsibility for libel.

CHAPTER 14

Crimes Against the Person and Property

In Chapters 6-13, each crime that was discussed caused harm or potential harm either to a person or to property but not to both. In this chapter, crimes are discussed that cause harm or potential harm to property as well as to at least one person at the same time. This is true primarily because by committing robbery, blackmail, kidnapping for ransom, mutiny, piracy on the seas or piracy in the air, the offender uses the victim(s) to help him to unlawfully acquire property.

Because these crimes threaten people and property at the same time, most of them are regarded as being very serious offenses. These crimes become especially serious when accompanied by use of explosives or firearms. Most of the offenses discussed in this chapter are punished more severely than any property offenses, because of the offender's inherent threat to inflict serious bodily harm or death upon the victim(s). They are punished as seriously as forcible rape and mayhem, and are surpassed only by murder.

Assault is a lesser included offense to each of the crimes in this chapter. Battery is likely to be a lesser included offense to each of these crimes except blackmail, depending upon the offender's conduct in each instance. If the offender is successful in unlawfully acquiring the desired property, then theft will become a lesser included offense to each of these crimes as well.

Robbery

The basic elements of robbery can be outlined as follows:
A. The Criminal Act:
   1. larceny
   2. *(a)* from the victim's person or
      (b) from the victim's presence
   3. *(a)* by force or
      (b) by threat
B. The Criminal Intent:
   4. a specific intent to steal

Larceny

Robbery contains all the elements of larceny, plus *two* additional elements. Larceny (see Chapter 9) consists of (1) the taking (2) and carrying away (3) of personal property (4) from another person's possession (5) with a specific intent to steal. The two additional elements in robbery are that the personal property must be taken and carried away (1) from the victim's person or presence and (2) by force or by threat.

The Victim's Person or Presence

One requirement for the act of robbery is that property must be taken by one person from another person's possession. In this respect, the act of robbery is the same as the act of larceny. In addition, however, property must be taken either from the victim's person or from his presence to fulfill the requirements for robbery. The fact that property must be taken from the victim's person or presence, rather than simply from his possession, distinguishes robbery from larceny.

Property is on one's *person* if it is in his hand, attached to his body, or in the pocket of clothing that he is wearing. Thus, whatever property a person carries in his hand at any given moment is considered to be on his person. Similarly, the clothes one wears on any part of his body, as well as property in the pockets of the clothes, is considered to be on his person.

In the act of robbery, property also can be taken from the victim's *presence*. Property is in a person's presence if at any given moment it is within his immediate area of control. It may be within his eyesight, but it does not have to be. The area a person immediately controls, however, cannot extend beyond the very limited distance that he can physically defend at any particular time.

It may be important to note that property on one's person is also in his presence. Property may be in one's presence, however, but not on his person. Moreover, property may be in someone's possession and be neither on his person nor in his presence. When someone takes property from the victim's possession but not from either his person or his presence, the act of larceny may be committed, but the act of robbery is not.

Force

Even if property is taken from the victim's person or from his presence, this alone does not constitute the act of robbery. The property must also be taken either by force or by threat.

Property is taken from a victim by *force* when it is physically removed from his person or from his presence against his will. It is taken against his will when it is taken without his consent, provided the victim is aware that his property is being taken from him. The act of robbery is not committed when someone removes property from an unconscious victim, unless the offender (or someone acting on his behalf) causes the victim's unconsciousness. Thus, one who removes an article of property from the person or presence of a drunk he finds lying unconscious does not commit robbery. But a person who clubs his victim over the head, or one who administers drugs or alcohol in order to make his victim lose consciousness, does commit robbery if he steals property from the victim's person or presence.

Difficulty sometimes arises in determining the degree of force that is necessary to constitute the act of robbery from a conscious person. Normally, a victim who is conscious must be aware that his property is being taken away from him, or robbery is not committed. As a rule, a person does not commit the act of robbery by picking a wallet from the victim's pocket, for example, as long as the victim does not realize that his property is being taken away from him. However, robbery will take place at the moment the victim begins to offer any resistance to the taking of his property. Thus, a person who struggles to prevent a pickpocket from taking his wallet turns the theft into the act of robbery.

In order for an offense to constitute robbery, force must be used by the offender against the victim either before or while he steals the property, not afterward. Robbery is not committed if the victim becomes aware that his property has been stolen only after it has been taken. This does not apply to a victim who has been rendered unconscious by the offender, of course, since the act of knocking the victim unconscious occurred prior to the theft, even though the victim may not have become aware of the theft until he regained consciousness.

Threat

Unless the property is taken from the victim's person or presence by force, it must be taken from his person or presence by threat in order to constitute robbery. A threat consists of any physical expression created by one person for the purpose of scaring another person. Usually, a threat consists of spoken words, but it can just as easily consist of a facial expression, clenched fists, a written note, or one of countless other methods of communication.

To contribute to the act of robbery, a threat must succeed in causing the victim to apprehend or foresee the possibility of harm if he refuses to surrender his property. A threat by the offender to do immediate bodily harm to the victim is sufficient to constitute the act of robbery, as is a threat by the offender to do immediate bodily harm to someone else who stands in a close relationship to the victim. Thus, a threat to do immediate bodily harm to the victim's wife, child, or parents would usually be sufficient, provided the person against whom harm is threatened is physically in the vicinity of the victim. This is necessary, because only a threat to do *immediate* harm applies in the case of robbery. A threat to do harm in the distant future does not fulfill this element of robbery, although it may constitute the act of blackmail, which will be discussed in the next section.

Unlike the act of criminal assault, the act of robbery may be committed by means of a threat to do harm other than bodily harm. A threat by the offender to harm the victim's property may be sufficient if the property that is threatened with harm is valuable to the victim. Thus, a threat to destroy the victim's house or automobile is usually sufficient to support a charge of robbery when the other elements of the crime are present.

Every person has a property interest in his reputation. In numerous instances, an offender threatens his victim with being accused of some crime. Generally, a threat by the offender to accuse his victim of committing a crime is not considered serious enough to support the act of robbery except when the offender threatens to accuse the victim of having committed sodomy (see Chapter 7). This threat is considered sufficient to constitute this element of robbery, since an accusation of sodomy can be extremely damaging to any person's reputation.

Any threat that would be sufficient to instill fear in an ordinary person is viewed as being sufficient to fulfill this element of robbery. The offender is not excused from robbery merely because his particular victim is too brave to become frightened. Similarly, a threat to do most types of bodily or property harm is sufficient to fulfill this element of robbery if the victim does become frightened, even though the threat is made in such a way that an ordinary victim would not become frightened. The design of the threat is crucial in determining its significance in the act of robbery. If the threat is designed to frighten the victim, the threat will fulfill this element of robbery unless it is considered so trivial that no person could be scared by it.

Specific Intent to Steal

No person can be criminally responsible for robbery unless he can be shown to have intended to *steal* the property he took and carried away from someone else's person or presence by force or by threat. Hence, both robbery and larceny require the same specific intent to steal. Neither robbery nor larceny is viewed as a "cause-and-result" crime. Thus, one does not automatically bear criminal responsibility for taking and carrying away personal property from another's person or presence, even if force is used or a threat is made.

An *intent to steal* has been discussed in detail in Chapter 9 with reference to larceny. It is generally defined as a person's intent to deprive another person permanently of the latter's right to exercise exclusive dominion and control over property he owns or has a right to possess.

In most states, an intent on the part of the offender to return either the property or its equivalent value is considered to indicate the absence of an intent to steal. However, the offender's intent at the moment of his criminal act determines his criminal responsibility for robbery, as it does for larceny. In most states, a person who takes property under a reasonable claim of right is not criminally responsible for robbery any more than he is for larceny. Since the victim is present during a robbery and not during a larceny, however, the robber can never reasonably believe that he has the victim's permission to take the property, nor can he ever believe that the property has been abandoned.

In a few states, one may bear criminal responsibility for robbery when he takes and carries away property from the person or presence of a *thief* or a victim who the offender believes owes him a *debt*. In these states, the element of force or threat is viewed as being so dangerous that even the *owner* of property should bear criminal responsibility if he uses or threatens violence. Hence, these states seem to recognize criminal responsibility for robbery even when the property is taken under a reasonable claim of right, although they would not recognize criminal responsibility for larceny under the same claim of right. In most states, however, the intent to steal is the same for both larceny and robbery. For a greater understanding of these exceptions to an intent to steal, see the section on the criminal intent required for larceny in Chapter 9.

Blackmail or Statutory Extortion

The basic elements of blackmail or statutory extortion can be outlined as follows:

A. The Criminal Act:

1. *(a)* the demand or
   (b) the acquisition
2. of property from another person
3. by threat of future harm
B. The Criminal Intent:
4. *(a)* a general criminal intent or
   (b) a specific intent to steal

Demand or Acquisition

The act of blackmail or statutory extortion cannot take place unless one person either *demands* or *acquires* possession of property from another person by threat of future harm. Under the blackmail statutes of a few states, the criminal act is not completed unless the offender actually takes possession of property from the victim. In most states, however, the act of blackmail is completed as soon as the offender makes a demand for the property by communicating a threat to the victim.

Under statutes requiring that the offender actually take possession of the property in order to complete the act of blackmail, this offense cannot be committed so long as the victim refuses to give up possession of the property the offender demands. In most states, however, blackmail does not depend on whether the victim surrenders possession of the property, once the offender makes his demand.

To constitute the act of blackmail under some statutes, the demand must be made in writing. Most statutes do not include this requirement, however, and permit the demand to be made either in writing or orally. As a rule, the demand does not have to be made directly to the victim but may be made to a third person who is told to convey the message to the victim. When the demand is made to the victim himself, it still does not have to be made personally; it may be delivered by telephone, message, or mail. It is a federal offense for a person to commit blackmail over the telephone or through the United States mails.[1]

Property from Another Person

The act of blackmail consists of one person's demand or acquisition of property from another person. Normally, the property that is demanded or acquired belongs to the person from whom it is demanded or acquired—in other words, it belongs to the victim. However, the property does not have to belong to the victim himself in order for blackmail to be committed. For instance, the property may belong to a third person and simply be under the control of the victim who is blackmailed; or the blackmailed victim may be ordered to steal property from someone else and subsequently to surrender it to the blackmailer or extortionist. It is possible, moreover, for the property that is demanded or acquired to belong to the blackmailer himself and not to the victim. This ownership factor does not affect the act of blackmail, but it may affect the existence of the required criminal intent, which will be discussed shortly.

Threat of Future Harm

During the act of blackmail, the victim is threatened with some form of future harm. It is primarily in this way that blackmail is distinguished from robbery, for the victim of a robbery is threatened with the prospect of immediate (usually physical) injury. Another difference is that the robbery victim is threatened to such an extent that he parts with his money or property without consent, while the victim of blackmail is generally viewed as consenting to the surrender of his money or property as part of a conscious effort to avoid the occurrence of the future harm that has been threatened. Of course, the victim's "consent" is not legally binding, and he retains legal title to the "surrendered" money or property, since he parts with his assets under duress.

At common law, two types of future threats were considered to support a conviction for robbery instead of blackmail if accompanied by the demand or the acquisition of someone else's property. These threats were: (1) the threat to destroy the victim's house and (2) the threat to accuse the victim of sodomy, regardless of the truth of the allegation. Virtually all other threats of action to take place at a future time were considered to support blackmail but not robbery convictions at common law. Today, in most jurisdictions, even a threat to destroy the victim's home or to accuse him of sodomy would not support a conviction for robbery but only a conviction for blackmail (or the related offense of extortion, which includes blackmail in some states).

The threat to do future harm to a person may vary in its content. Future harm may be physical harm, but it does not have to be. Thus, blackmail may be committed when one person communicates to another that the latter's life or health will be endangered unless certain property is surrendered. In addition or instead, blackmail may be committed when one person communicates to another that the latter's reputation will be disgraced or defamed or that a secret affecting the victim will be exposed unless property is surrendered. Normally, the truth of the defamation or the secret is immaterial as far as blackmail is concerned. Thus, blackmail may be committed when an extortionist threatens to announce that the victim has committed a crime, for example, or that the victim is adopted or illegitimate, or that the victim is homosexual, regardless of whether or not the announcement is true. Such an allegation by itself, however, does not constitute blackmail unless accompanied by (or more likely preceded by) a demand for or an acquisition of property as a condition for maintaining silence.

In many states, one particular kind of a threat does not constitute blackmail if the threat is communicated under certain conditions. A person to whom a civil debt is owed as a result of criminal conduct may threaten to prosecute the offender criminally unless the debt is paid. In order for this threat not to constitute blackmail, the debt must be real and it must have arisen as a direct result of the criminal offense for which prosecution is threatened. This exception ordinarily applies to the collection of the value of a worthless check by the person who accepted it as payment for goods or services or in return for cash. The person against whom prosecution is threatened must be guilty of the alleged crime or this exception does not apply. Several states, including California and New York, do not recognize this exception to their blackmail-extortion statutes. In these states, courts have determined that the law does not intend the use of criminal process as a means of collecting a debt. Instead of threatening criminal prosecution, persons to whom a debt is owed in these states can threaten to bring a civil suit and proceed to bring suit if the debt is not paid. In no state is the crime of blackmail committed when one person threatens to bring a civil suit against another, since the beginning of litigation other than criminal prosecution is not viewed as causing harm to the defendant.

One additional but unusual exception to the ordinary elements of blackmail should be noted. In at least one state, Iowa, the collection of a just debt at gunpoint has been prosecuted successfully as blackmail, even though this conduct would have constituted robbery had the victim not been indebted to the assailant. Blackmail ordinarily is not viewed as a lesser included offense to robbery, but in Iowa it seems to have been used to prosecute robbery committed with diminished criminal responsibility.

General or Specific Intent

In many jurisdictions, a specific intent to steal must be shown in order to support a conviction for blackmail, just as such a specific intent is ordinarily required to support a conviction for larceny (theft) or robbery. In other jurisdictions, a general criminal intent alone is sufficient. Since a general criminal intent usually may be presumed from the threatening conduct, the extortionist's state of mind becomes significant more often under statutes that require proof of a specific intent to steal.

In most jurisdictions, the lawful owner or the rightful possessor of property is privileged to recapture that property from anyone who has acquired control of it unlawfully, provided the recapture is accomplished *peaceably*. Does this mean that the victim of a theft or a robbery, for example, may recapture the stolen property by means of blackmail? In most jurisdictions, the answer to this question is no, since a general criminal intent may be supported by evidence of threats, which do not constitute peaceable behavior. In a few states, however, a person may be privileged to recapture property that he owns or has a right to possess, even by committing blackmail. Particularly under statutes requiring proof of a specific intent to steal, the rightful owner or possessor of the property may avoid bearing criminal responsibility for blackmail even if he has demanded or acquired the property from another person's control by threatening future harm. This is true because normally a person is not considered to harbor an intent to steal property that he owns or has a right to possess, even if he takes and carries away this property from someone else's actual possession.

Intent to steal is generally defined as a person's intent to deprive another person permanently of the latter's right to exercise exclusive dominion and control over property he owns or has a right to possess. Intent to steal has been discussed in detail in Chapter 9 with reference to larceny and earlier in this chapter in conjunction with robbery.

Kidnapping for Ransom

Kidnapping for ransom, unlike some other forms of kidnapping, may be considered as an offense against both the person and property. Elements of kidnapping are considered in Chapter 6.

Kidnapping for ransom involves the transportation of another person against his will with a specific intent to hold the victim for ransom or reward. In this crime, the transportation of the victim constitutes an offense against the person, while the intent to hold the victim for ransom or reward constitutes an offense against property. In effect, the victim of a kidnapping for ransom (or others, such as his family, from whom ransom or reward is demanded) is offered a choice by his captors: he must part with some property such as a sum of money, or part with his life or physical well-being.

The definitions of *ransom* and *reward* vary slightly from state to state, but the general meaning of these two words is plain and almost universal. One intends to hold another person for ransom or reward if he plans to obtain *anything of value* from *anyone* as a result of the kidnapping. Money or currency always constitutes value, whether the currency is American or foreign. Securities, real estate, or any type of property also constitutes value. Value need not always be tangible, however. A person's intent to hold his victim for ransom or reward may become apparent if the offender plans or offers to release the victim in exchange for a specific *favor*.

To show that an offender has planned to hold his victim for ransom or reward, it is not necessary to show that the ransom or reward was actually paid, nor even that it was ever demanded. The offender must simply be proven to have carried out the transportation for the *purpose* of obtaining a ransom or reward. The demand or the acquisition of the ransom or reward by means of a threat constitutes the separate offense of blackmail or statutory extortion, discussed in the previous section.

Mutiny and Piracy on the High Seas

Mutiny and piracy are two separate offenses that are related to robbery and that may be perpetrated so as to include kidnapping as well. Each of these offenses involves the forcible interference with control of a ship by its master. The master (captain) of a ship is viewed legally as possessing the exclusive right to exercise lawful control over the vessel's destination and over the conduct of all persons aboard. During the tenure of his command, the master of a ship alone has the right to determine what activities will and will not take place aboard the ship, and the ship becomes his property. Depriving the master of a ship of his exclusive right to control activities aboard ship, if done forcibly and in his presence, may constitute the crime of mutiny or piracy, depending on who the offender or offenders are. Mutiny and piracy have been known as offenses committed "on the high seas," a holdover from the era dominated by tall ships of sail. However, mutiny and piracy may be committed while a ship is sailing on an inland body of brackish or fresh water—such as the Great Lakes—as well as on the ocean; and these offenses may be committed when a ship is lying in port as well as when it is under way.

Mutiny

Mutiny occurs when one or more crew members aboard a ship forcibly impede or prevent the ship's master from exercising his lawful control over the vessel. A ship has only one master at one time. The master of a ship is the individual to whom command responsibility for a vessel has been delegated by the ship's owner or by a representative of the owner, as indicated in the ship's sailing papers. The captain of a vessel, who serves as its master of record, may delegate his authority to an authorized representative (such as the first mate or executive officer) during his absence from the vessel. On such an occasion, this authorized representative of the captain becomes the ship's master *pro tempore* until the captain's return.

If any crew member, including even a subordinate officer, forcibly impedes or prevents the ship's master from exercising control over the vessel's destination or over conduct of persons aboard the ship, the crime of mutiny may take place. A member of the crew may bear criminal responsibility for mutiny by participating actively in the forcible overthrow of the master's control or by standing by passively and permitting another to divest the master of his control by force. This offense thus may be perpetrated by commission or by omission, since every crew member aboard a ship has a duty to assist the master in retaining the exercise of control over the vessel.

It may be important to distinguish mere insubordination from mutiny. A crew member may become insubordinate merely by refusing or failing to execute the master's orders. To be criminally responsible for mutiny, however, a crew member must take actual control of the vessel away from the master, or witness another crew member doing so without assisting the master in maintaining control. Therefore, a ship's pilot who is ordered to steer west but who steers east instead would be insubordinate but not necessarily mutinous, unless he forcibly prevented the master from changing course on discovery of the error.

Piracy

Piracy occurs when one or more rebellious persons board a ship and make an effort by force to impede or prevent the ship's master from exercising lawful control over the vessel. Unlike mutiny, which may be committed only by the crew, piracy is perpetrated by one or more persons having no right even to board a vessel but doing so in order to assume control of the ship by force. Normally, a pirate seizes a vessel in order to plunder its cargo, to convert the ship itself for his own use, or to take the crew into his own service. Motives of the pirate are immaterial, however. This crime is complete as soon as the intruder boards a vessel and makes an effort to interfere with the master's exercise of control over it.

In relation to both mutiny and piracy, it may be helpful to elaborate on the meaning of control of a vessel. A mutinous crew or a pirate may interfere with control of a vessel by delaying its voyage, changing the direction of its voyage, causing it to take on or part with cargo, or compelling the crew to perform or to abstain from service—all contrary to the wishes of the ship's master. Neither mutiny nor piracy is committed when a ship's master is persuaded to alter his wishes peaceably, but upon the threat or use of force, effort to overcome the master's control may become mutiny or piracy. Holding the master or a crew member at gunpoint would constitute sufficient force, but it is not necessary. Threatening the security of the ship by implying that a bomb may be detonated would constitute force, as would a threat to hurl a crew member or the master himself overboard unless the master complies with the directive of a mutineer or pirate. Normally, the force or threat of force must be imminent, as in the case of robbery. The threat of future harm by means of blackmail or extortion would as a rule constitute insufficient force for either mutiny or piracy, since the master of a ship would not be expected to give up control over the vessel except on peril of imminent death or serious bodily harm.

Air Piracy ("Skyjacking")

Air piracy is virtually identical to piracy on the high seas except that it is perpetrated on an aircraft instead of a vessel. Air piracy occurs when any person makes an effort by force to impede or prevent the pilot of an aircraft from exercising lawful control over the plane. Air piracy has become known informally as "skyjacking" because the act of air piracy is similar to hijacking. Under the laws of many jurisdictions, hijacking is a special form of robbery, often committed by intercepting a vehicle such as a truck or a train in order to steal its cargo. Air piracy is frequently committed in order to cause the plane to be landed in a jurisdiction where it can be held for ransom, but a demand for ransom is not a necessary element of this offense.

The crime of air piracy is complete whenever control over an aircraft by its authorized pilot is jeopardized by force or threat of force. As in piracy, the force or threat of force must be imminent and sufficient to imperil the life or physical well-being of a person aboard the aircraft. Since an aircraft is very sensitive to shockwaves, particularly when in flight, display of virtually any firearm or explosive device aboard the plane may support a conviction for air piracy.

CHAPTER 15

Preparatory and Ancillary Crimes

The offenses that have been considered up to this point are known collectively as substantive crimes. Each substantive crime consists of elements that are different from those of any other substantive crime. In this chapter, several preparatory and ancillary crimes are introduced. These offenses, also known as "inchoate" crimes, are harmful in relation to the substantive crime(s) that they inspire or compound.

Preparatory offenses consist of criminal solicitation, criminal facilitation, and criminal attempt. These crimes are labelled as being preparatory because the person who is doing the soliciting, facilitating, or attempting does not perform a completed substantive crime. Ancillary crimes include criminal conspiracy, the condition of being an accessory either before or after the fact, and criminal complicity (an accomplice is an accessory to a crime during its commission). While preparatory offenses must precede actual commission of a substantive crime, ancillary offenses may precede, accompany, or follow a substantive crime.

The severity of a preparatory or an ancillary crime is likely to depend upon the seriousness of the substantive crime with which it is associated. For instance, attempted murder is more serious than attempted theft. In addition, conspiracy is more serious than other inchoate crimes because it involves collaboration of two or more offenders, and the law presumes that two offenders working together are more dangerous than one working alone.

Preparatory Offenses

Preparatory offenses are crimes that may, but do not necessarily, result in fulfillment of the purpose for which the criminal activity was planned. Criminal solicitation, criminal facilitation, and criminal attempt are examples of preparatory offenses. As a rule, these offenses are not prosecuted as such if the contemplated criminal activity actually takes place as planned. However, the criminal solicitor or the criminal facilitator may well be prosecuted as an accomplice or even a conspirator if the purpose of the planned criminal activity is achieved. Preparatory offenses have been created essentially to prevent persons who have participated in the planning of unexecuted criminal activity from escaping criminal responsibility. Since preparatory offenses are intended to punish persons who have become involved in incomplete (sometimes called *inchoate*) criminal conduct, the punishment for these offenses is ordinarily somewhat less severe than the punishment that would be provided upon conviction for completed substantive crimes, such as those already discussed in Chapters 5-14.

Criminal Solicitation

It is uncertain whether criminal solicitation was an offense at common law prior to the early nineteenth century. At that time, it became a misdemeanor at common law for one person to solicit—that is, to ask or encourage—another to commit any felony or to commit a misdemeanor that would breach the public peace, obstruct justice, or otherwise injure the public welfare.

Under the Model Penal Code, a person commits the act of criminal solicitation when he "commands, encourages, or requests another person to engage in specific conduct which would constitute [a crime]." Thus, the criminal act is complete when the request is made, whether or not the person to whom the request is made actually commits the crime he is asked to commit. The request may be made orally or in writing. It may be made directly, or it may be made to a third person who is asked to convey the message to the person the solicitor wants to commit the crime. The request may be for someone to commit either a felony or a misdemeanor.

One begins the act of criminal solicitation when he commands, induces, entreats, or otherwise attempts to persuade another person to commit a particular felony. The criminal act is not complete, however, unless the person to whom the request is made commits some *overt act* in response to the solicitation. Thus, criminality depends on something besides mere speech. Furthermore, the solicitor must persuade another person to commit a crime, not merely encourage him to do so.

Both the Model Penal Code and the proposed Federal Criminal Code Revision require the solicitor to request another person to commit a "specific" or a "particular" crime. The proposed Federal Code Revision requires that the crime be a felony, while under the Model Penal Code it may also be a misdemeanor. Still, one does not commit the offense of criminal solicitation by merely asking another person to engage in vague criminal behavior; one must clearly define the behavior to the person who is asked to commit the crime.

Normally, the person who solicits another to commit a crime bears criminal responsibility only if he makes the request for the purpose of *promoting* or *facilitating* the commission of the crime. The circumstances under which the solicitation is made must strongly indicate that the solicitor is *serious* about having the person to whom he makes the request actually do what is asked. Thus, one who offers to pay or otherwise to reward the other person normally appears to be serious in his request to have this person carry out the crime. Of course, a person may be criminally responsible for criminal solicitation without offering payment or reward as long as his seriousness is evident. However, one who commits criminal solicitation only as a joke or to observe the reaction of the person he solicits would not generally bear criminal responsibility for this offense.

In seven states, it is an offense for one person to seriously solicit another person to commit any crime—felony or misdemeanor. In three states, it is an offense for one to seriously solicit another to commit a felony, but not for one to solicit another to commit a misdemeanor. In most states, however, there is no offense known as "criminal solicitation." Instead, the solicitor may be criminally responsible as a *conspirator* if the person he asks to commit a crime agrees. He may be criminally responsible as an *accomplice* if the crime he solicits is committed successfully. In the majority of states, however, a person who seriously solicits another to commit a crime bears no criminal responsibility at all if the person he solicits declines to commit the crime. The statutes in these states are based on the view that one who unsuccessfully solicits another to commit a crime poses no danger to society, since the person who is solicited refuses to commit the crime and the solicitor indicates his own unwillingness to commit the crime by asking someone else to do it.

Criminal Facilitation

Criminal facilitation is an offense that has been created by statute in a number of states. It differs from criminal solicitation in that the facilitator must do something more than merely ask another person to commit a crime. Under most statutes, a person commits the act of criminal facilitation by providing substantial *assistance* to another person to enable the latter to commit a crime. Some criminal facilitation statutes require that one person supply another with either the *means* or the *opportunity* to commit a crime.

The act of criminal facilitation is not completed unless the person who receives the assistance actually commits the crime the facilitator helped him commit. Furthermore, one who helps another commit a substantive crime does not commit the offense of criminal facilitation if the person who commits the crime could have obtained similar assistance from another person in a lawful manner. Thus, a gunsmith who supplies a purchaser with a firearm will not be criminally responsible for criminal facilitation provided the gunsmith is unaware of the purchaser's criminal plan, and provided the purchase is authorized by state and Federal law.

Under most statutes, one who commits the offense of criminal facilitation bears criminal responsibility only if he assists another person who he *knows* is going to commit a crime. Some statutes make a person criminally responsible for this offense only if he knows that the person he helps plans to commit a felony, and then only if the person who receives the help actually does commit a felony. As a rule, one who commits the offense of criminal facilitation does not bear criminal responsibility unless the person to whom he gives assistance actually commits the very crime the facilitator believes will be committed at the time he gives his assistance. Some statutes, however, make a facilitator criminally responsible if the person who receives the assistance commits a crime *similar* to the one the facilitator thinks will be committed.

Criminal Attempt

Criminal attempt was not a crime under the early common law. This offense probably was created by the English Court of the Star Chamber in the sixteenth century. When the Star Chamber was abolished after 1640, the theory of criminal attempt lingered on as a common-law offense. Today, most states have enacted statutes regulating the attempted commission of all crimes.

In many states, different statutes regulate the attempt to commit different crimes. Thus, one statute may regulate a person's attempt to commit murder, while another may regulate one's attempt to commit robbery. Under the Model Penal Code, criminal attempt is created as a specific criminal offense. One may commit criminal attempt under the Model Penal Code by means of any act or omission that represents a *substantial step* toward the completion of any substantive crime. Indeed, the Model Penal Code describes the major kinds of conduct that may constitute such a substantial step:

> (a) lying in wait, searching for or following the contemplated victim of the crime;
>
> (b) enticing or seeking to entice the contemplated victim of the crime to go to the place contemplated for its commission;
>
> (c) reconnoitering the place contemplated for the commission of the crime;

(d) unlawful entry of a structure, vehicle or enclosure in which it is contemplated that the crime will be committed;

(e) possession of materials to be employed in the commission of the crime, which are specially designed for such unlawful use or which can serve no lawful purpose of the actor under the circumstances;

(f) possession, collection or fabrication of materials to be employed in the commission of the crime, at or near the place contemplated for its commission, where such possession, collection or fabrication serves no lawful purpose of the actor under the circumstances;

(g) soliciting an innocent agent to engage in conduct constituting an element of the crime.

Thoughts alone can never constitute criminal attempt, and in this respect criminal attempt is no different from any other criminal offense. To commit the offense of criminal attempt, the offender must begin to act or fail to act in a way that may result in the commission of a crime. Statutes vary concerning how close the offender must come to committing the actual crime. Some courts have held that a person does not commit criminal attempt unless he comes *dangerously close* to fulfilling his criminal plan. Other courts have ruled that the act or the omission required to constitute criminal attempt must be one that in the *ordinary course of events* would lead to the commission of the target crime, except for the unexpected intervention of some nonrelated obstacle. Some courts will not recognize the act of criminal attempt as taking place unless at least *one basic element* of the target crime is present. A basic element is an event that is indispensable to a particular substantive crime, as a "taking" is to larceny or theft. In some states, this indispensable element must be completed by the offender at a location that is physically near the scene where he plans to commit the substantive crime, and at a time that is near the time when he plans the crime. In a few states, one cannot commit criminal attempt unless his conduct serves *no other purpose* than the commission of a crime.

A person bears criminal responsibility for criminal attempt only if at the time of his conduct he has at least a *general* criminal intent. In states that have a single offense known as criminal attempt covering the attempt to commit all crimes, a *general* criminal intent is sufficient to make a person criminally responsible. Thus, a person whose conduct reveals an attempt to commit larceny (theft) or some other substantive crime that requires a *specific* criminal intent could still be criminally responsible for the catchall offense of criminal attempt. In order for an offender to bear criminal responsibility for an attempt to commit a particular crime, however, he must be shown to have had the *specific* intent, if any, that is required for that crime. Thus, a person bears criminal responsibility for attempted larceny (theft) or attempted robbery only if he is shown to have had a *specific* intent to steal. Similarly, one bears criminal responsibility for attempted embezzlement or attempted forgery only if he is shown to have had a *specific* intent to defraud. Most states do not have a catchall criminal attempt offense covering the attempt to commit any crime. Instead, as mentioned, most states have a variety of separate offenses such as attempted larceny (theft), attempted robbery, and attempted murder. As both larceny (theft) and robbery require a specific intent to steal, so do attempted larceny (theft) and attempted robbery require specific criminal intent. Murder requires a specific intent to kill, so attempted murder, too, requires specific intent to kill.

Possible Parties to a Crime

A crime cannot take place without a principal actor, who is normally referred to as the principal criminal offender, or more simply as the *principal*. However, principals are frequently assisted by other persons who provide aid and support as criminal activities are carried out. Persons who assist principal offenders are known as *accessories* or *accomplices* and bear criminal responsibility for complicity in the criminal conduct in which they participate. Principals, accessories, accomplices, and other persons sometimes agree to participate in criminal activity, in which case the agreement itself may make them into *conspirators*. Principals, accessories, accomplices, and conspirators are all possible parties to a crime.

Principals

A person who engages in criminal conduct by act or omission and who possesses the required criminal intent at the same moment is a *principal* criminal offender. Of course, two or more persons may act or fail to act jointly in conduct that constitutes a crime. In this situation, if each person has the required criminal intent at the time of the crime, each becomes a principal criminal offender. In other words, any person who commits a criminal offense directly is a principal offender if his intent is such thát he bears any criminal responsibility at all for the crime.

Generally, a person must be present at the scene of a crime when it occurs in order to be a principal offender. However, it is possible for one to be "constructively" present at the scene without actually being there. For example, a person who uses another as an intermediary in the commission of a crime may be criminally responsible as a principal. This is often true when the intermediary is an innocent person who does not have a criminal intent but has been duped into criminal conduct. It may also be true when the intermediary is incapable of forming a criminal intent by reason of his youth or mental incompetence. Similarly, one who sets a criminal event in motion may be a principal offender even if he isn't present to see the criminal event itself. An example would be one who puts poison in another person's food or who sets a timer that causes an explosion later.

A person may be criminally responsible as a principal to the commission of a crime without committing the crime directly if he aids, abets, commands, counsels, or encourages another to commit the crime. A principal under these circumstances is known as a principal in the second degree in many states, as distinguished from a principal in the first degree, described previously. The mastermind of a robbery, for example, may be a principal in the second degree even though he does not directly take anything from the victim. Similarly, one who stands watch to ensure that no intruder interrupts a crime as it is taking place may be a principal of this sort.

Normally, a principal in the second degree must be physically present at the scene of a crime as it is taking place, or at least be sufficiently nearby to render immediate assistance to the principal(s) in the first degree. However, it is not necessary that a principal in the second degree be capable of committing the crime alone. For example, although a female cannot commit rape alone in most states, a female who aids and abets a male companion as he commits a rape may be criminally responsible for this crime as a principal in the second degree.

Accessories

Accessories are of two kinds: accessories before the fact and accessories after the fact.

Accessories Before the Fact. In simple terms, an accessory before the fact is a person who would have been a principal in the second degree if only he had been present at the scene of a crime at the moment it took place. An accessory before the fact may be the originator of a crime, although this is not necessary. Such an accessory may have been enlisted only to give assistance to the principal offender(s). In most states, accessories before the fact are now prosecuted as principals in the second degree, and the distinction has ceased to exist.

Accessories After the Fact. An accessory after the fact is any person who (1) has knowledge that a felony (in some jurisdictions, even a misdemeanor) has been committed, (2) has knowledge that a particular person (the principal) has committed, been charged with, or been convicted of the felony (or other crime), and (3) thereafter conceals or otherwise gives aid to such a person intending that the person may avoid or escape arrest, trial, conviction, or punishment.

In most jurisdictions, a person does not become an accessory after the fact unless a felony has actually been completed. Thus, a person giving aid is not an accessory after the fact if he merely *thought* a felony had been committed when in fact it had not been. Similarly, a person giving aid must actually know and not just suspect that he is giving aid to a felon. Nor is it sufficient in most states that aid alone was given, unless the person giving the aid intended to hinder or impede the enforcement of the law. Thus, a physician who treats a principal offender for a gunshot wound does not become an accessory after the fact to the principal crime as long as he reports the occurrence to proper authorities at the first possible opportunity.

Many states have merged this offense with such offenses as "hindering prosecution" or "obstructing justice" (see Chapter 17). To the extent that new statutes have replaced the common-law crime of being an accessory after the fact, particular kinds of assistance and a specific criminal intent may be clearly specified in the law.

Accomplices

A person who commits either criminal solicitation or criminal facilitation becomes an accomplice if in fact the solicited or facilitated crime does take place in its foreseeable form. Principals, as well as accessories before the fact, may bear criminal responsibility as accomplices *without* concern for whether they were present at the scene of a crime when it took place. Whenever two or more persons commit the elements of a substantive crime together, a criminal *complicity* results. This is true whether the actors are two or more principals or principal(s) and accomplice(s).

An accomplice is a person who intentionally induces or assists another in conduct that foreseeably results in a crime. Thus while soliciting, facilitating, aiding, and abetting conduct may make one an accomplice, so also may other forms of assistance such as giving advice, encouragement, finances, supplies, or transportation. At least a general criminal intent is required to make a person criminally responsible as an accomplice. However, one may bear criminal responsibility as an accomplice by possessing only a general criminal intent and assisting in the perpetration of a crime for which a specific criminal intent would be required for conviction as a principal.

In most states, the felony-murder and misdemeanor-manslaughter rules apply to accomplices as well as to principals. In these states, an accomplice may bear criminal responsibility for murder if death results during the course of a felony (or for manslaughter if death results during the course of a misdemeanor), even if the accomplice did not intend any death to result from the planned crime. Except under those particular circumstances, however, the accomplice's own state of mind, and not that of the principal(s), will generally determine the degree of the accomplice's criminal responsibility. It is possible, therefore, for an accomplice to be criminally responsible for first-degree murder while the principal may be criminally responsible only for second-degree murder (or even a lesser offense), if for example the accomplice intends the victim to be killed, but the principal intends only that the victim be hurt. Although as a rule an accomplice cannot bear criminal responsibility while a principal bears no criminal responsibility for the same crime, exceptions to this rule do exist. For example, a principal may successfully raise one or more defenses that do not extend to an accomplice, such as the defense of insanity, coercion, or justification.

As a rule, one does not become an accomplice merely by failing or refusing to intervene to prevent a crime from being started or completed. An exception is when a person fails or refuses to intervene when he has a duty to intervene. For example, a sworn police officer may become an accomplice to a crime by failing to make a proper effort to prevent the completion of a crime in progress within his view.

A person cannot be criminally responsible for complicity in a crime in which he or she is the only victim. For example, a girl who has not reached the age of consent does not bear criminal responsibility as an accomplice to her own statutory rape. In most jurisdictions, also, a person cannot be criminally responsible for complicity in a crime in which he is one of the victims, unless he has arranged the events to hurt another victim. For example, a person who pays a ransom demand because one of his relatives has been kidnapped is not usually held criminally responsible as an accomplice.

Once a person has become an accomplice, he may avoid criminal responsibility by withdrawing his aid or encouragement at a reasonable time before the crime. However, such a withdrawal must consist of *both* (1) a communication to the principal(s) that the accomplice desires to withdraw his earlier assistance and (2) an effort by the accomplice to do everything possible to prevent his assistance from being useful at the time of the crime. It is not always necessary for an accomplice to warn the police or the victim, however.

Conspirators

Conspirators are persons involved in a *conspiracy.* A person bears criminal responsibility for conspiracy to commit a crime when (1) he agrees with one or more other persons to commit a crime, (2) with intent that the crime be committed, and (3) later one or more of the agreeing parties commits an overt act that helps carry out the agreement. In most jurisdictions, conspiracy is itself a substantive crime that is separate from all other crimes, including the crime or crimes the conspirators agree to commit. As such, conspiracy may be punished separately from and often in addition to the underlying substantive crime that was the subject of the agreement.

By definition, a person cannot commit a conspiracy by himself. Some agreement must be made between two or more persons. An agreement is an understanding, commonly referred to as a "meeting of the minds." Thus, an agreement involves a communication by which each agreeing party becomes aware of a common plan. This communication does not have to be spoken or written, however, as long as it is understood. A person is not considered a conspirator to the extent that all other agreeing parties harbor secret intentions which are unknown to him. Quite obviously, however, three or more persons may agree to commit one crime while two of the three agree to commit a second crime. In this situation, the two who agree to both crimes may be conspirators to both, while the one who agrees to just one crime may be a conspirator only to that one.

A person may agree with another to engage in criminal conduct without committing the crime of conspiracy if there is no criminal intent. However, it is quite possible if two persons agree on criminal conduct, for one of them to possess a criminal intent while the other does not. In this situation, only the person who has a criminal intent at the time of the agreement bears criminal responsibility for the conspiracy.

Once an agreement has been made by two or more persons, each of whom possesses a criminal intent, it is *not* necessary that all conspirators actually commit the agreed substantive crime. Indeed, the agreed crime does not have to be committed at all. Only one conspirator need commit some overt act to help carry out the conspiracy in order to make all the conspirators guilty. Such an overt act in furtherance of a conspiracy is also known as a *substantial step*. A "substantial" step is one that is meaningful to the conspiracy, but it does not have to be unlawful in itself. This substantial step or overt act must be taken by one of the conspirators or by someone acting at his direction or on his behalf. It must be designed to have some effect toward the accomplishment of the desired result of the conspiracy. An act such as the procurement of illegal or questionable substances (explosives, burglar's tools, counterfeiting equipment) may be interpreted as being designed to further a conspiracy. So also may writing a letter, making a telephone call, or taking a ride in an automobile or other vehicle, for example.

Like an accomplice, a conspirator may sometimes free himself of criminal responsibility for the conspiracy before (but never after) the time when the conspiracy terminates. A conspiracy terminates when the final purpose of the agreement has been fulfilled. Generally, a conspiracy is considered to have been abandoned if no party to it commits any overt act in furtherance of the conspiracy. Once such an overt act has taken place, however, several actions on the part of any individual conspirator are required in order for him to withdraw from the conspiracy. At the very least, a withdrawing conspirator must give notice of his intent to withdraw to each and every co-conspirator, and this must be done far enough in advance of termination of the conspiracy to enable all co-conspirators to join in the withdrawal, if they wish. In addition, some states require the withdrawing conspirator to attempt to persuade the co-conspirators to abandon the conspiracy. The Model Penal Code would require a withdrawing conspirator actually to "thwart" the conspiracy.

Although no person may commit the crime of conspiracy alone, it is possible for one person to be convicted of conspiracy while his co-conspirators never are. For example, other conspirators may have died or may not have been apprehended. An exception to this possibility is known as the "plurality requirement," which applies in most states. Under the plurality requirement, a person cannot be convicted of conspiracy if his only alleged co-conspirator has been acquitted of the conspiracy. This exception exists as a matter of fundamental fairness, since the concept of conspiracy requires at least two persons equally at fault in making an agreement to participate in criminal behavior.

In addition, it is possible for two or more persons to agree intentionally to commit a crime and to commit not only an overt act but the crime itself without being criminally responsible for a conspiracy, but only under very limited circumstances. These circumstances usually involve conduct that by its nature requires agreement between two or more persons; such as adultery, bigamy, and incest. The legal principle that the commission of these offenses and a few others cannot result in criminal responsibility for conspiracy is known as the Wharton Rule and is expressed more particularly as follows:

> ***(W)hen to the idea of an offense plurality of agents is logically necessary, conspiracy, which assumes the voluntary accession of a person to a crime of such a nature that it is aggravated by a plurality of agents, cannot be maintained.[1]

The Wharton Rule states the commonly accepted purpose of most conspiracy statutes. Ordinarily conspiracy statutes are intended to provide added punishment for persons who join with others to commit crimes that could be committed by a single person acting alone. For such crimes, an agreement between two or more persons is thought to pose a greater threat to the public safety than would exist if one person committed a similar crime by himself. No greater threat occurs when the underlying substantive crime itself requires two or more actors for its commission, and when the conduct is criminalized primarily on account of some characteristic of at least one participant—the fact that he is married, for example. Therefore, punishing such actors by making them criminally responsible for conspiracy would serve no added purpose that cannot be accomplished by punishing them for the substantive crime itself, since they had to act together to commit the substantive crime.

Whenever multiple parties to a crime are considered, a distinction needs to be drawn between two terms: *conspiracy* and *complicity*. In both situations, two or more criminal actors exist. Whenever there is a conspiracy, there is also a complicity. However, the reverse is not always true in many states.

In *Pinkerton* v. *United States* (1946),[2] the U.S. Supreme Court held that one who is proven to have participated in a conspiracy may be convicted of the underlying substantive crime(s), at least if the underlying substantive crime(s) may be considered to be reasonably foreseeable as a natural consequence of the conspiracy itself. In the *Pinkerton* case, for example, the appellant Pinkerton was indicted for conspiring with his brother to evade taxes and also for the substantive tax evasions committed by his brother while the appellant was in prison for other reasons. The Supreme Court affirmed the trial court's instruction to the jury that it could convict Pinkerton of his brother's substantive tax evasions if it found (as it did) that these were committed by the brother in furtherance of the conspiracy in which Pinkerton participated. Following the *Pinkerton* decision, it is possible for a conspiracy to involve its participants in criminal complicity, meaning that the conspirators may become criminally responsible for the underlying substantive crime(s).

On the other hand, most states have not applied the *Pinkerton* rule to state prosecutions. Instead, most states require something more than mere conspiracy to make one culpable for complicity. In one leading case, the Supreme Judicial Court of Massachusetts rejected the *Pinkerton* reasoning as follows:

> Defendant accepted another's offer to participate in a liquor store robbery. He traveled with his conspirators to the neighborhood where the store was located, but left the area prior to the robbery since, as a former resident of the area, he feared recognition. He did not agree to, and did not in fact, give aid or assistance in furtherance of the robbery or of the conspirators' escape afterwards. He was convicted of assault with the intent to rob.

The appellate court reversed, holding as follows:

> If the defendant agreed with the other persons to commit the crimes of robbery and assault and did nothing more, he is guilty of criminal conspiracy; but he was not charged with that crime. That alone does not make him an accessory before the fact or a principal to the substantive crime which was the objective of the conspiracy.[3]

This defendant, although a conspirator, was not made criminally responsible for complicity in the underlying substantive crimes.

part 4

Offenses Against the Public Welfare

Offenses against the public welfare are substantive crimes as are offenses against the person and against property. Unlike offenses against the person or against property, however, public welfare offenses do not result always in direct harm to an individual victim. For this reason, some persons have concluded that public welfare offenses are "victimless crimes," the implication being that some of them should be decriminalized. Whether or not some of the conduct that is prohibited now in public welfare offenses should be legalized, it is important to remember that even when conduct cannot be shown to have affected an individual victim it may be shown to cause a general injury to society as a whole and therefore to damage the public welfare.

In this book, public welfare offenses are divided into six chapters due to their large volume. These chapters will consist of offenses against the national defense, government processes, public health and safety, the family unit, the public peace and repose, and public morals.

CHAPTER 16

National Defense Offenses

Every sovereign state must maintain security in order to survive. Under our federal system of government, national defense is preempted by the United States government. However, each state has authority and responsibility to enforce federal laws pertaining to national defense and to prohibit conduct within its boundaries that may be detrimental to the security of the nation.

There are three major groups of national defense offenses. These include treason, sabotage, and espionage, together with other offenses relating to each. In addition to these three groups of national defense offenses, other criminal laws prohibit American citizens or anyone who is present within the jurisdiction of the United States from launching an invasion of a foreign territory or planning a rebellion against a foreign government in time of peace. These offenses, sometimes known as crimes against international relations, will be omitted in this book since recent efforts to revise federal criminal laws did not succeed in clarifying them.

Treason and Related Offenses

Offenses related to treason include armed rebellion or insurrection, instigating overthrow or destruction of the government, also known as sedition.

Treason

The Federal Constitution itself defines the offense of treason, lays down procedural requirements, and permits Congress to do nothing more than specify the penalty within certain limits. Section 3 of Article III of the Constitution provides:

> Treason against the United States shall consist only in levying war against them, or in adhering to their enemies, giving them aid and comfort. No person shall be convicted of treason unless on the testimony of two witnesses to the same overt act, or on confession in open court.
>
> The Congress shall have power to declare the punishment of treason, but no attainder of treason shall work corruption of blood or forfeiture except during the life of the person attainted.

The constitutional definition prohibits Congress from declaring conduct that does not fall clearly within its terms as treason. The requirement of two witnesses to the overt act also prevents Congress from calling an offense containing all the elements of treason by some other name.

The constitutional definition has been interpreted by the courts as recognizing two forms of the offense: (1) giving assistance to foreign enemies waging war against the United States and (2) engaging in domestic rebellion. Despite the limitations on its power, Congress is entitled to assign different penalties to the different forms the offense can take. In the following paragraphs, Form 1 treason includes the offense of assisting foreign enemies and Form 2 treason includes the offense of rebellion.

Form 1 Treason. A person is guilty of Form 1 treason if, "while owing allegiance to the United States . . . he adheres to the foreign enemies of the United States and intentionally gives them aid and comfort." The elements of the offense are that (1) the defendant owe allegiance to the United States, (2) there exist foreign enemies of the United States, (3) the defendant knowingly "adhere" to the enemies and, (4) the defendant intentionally give them aid and comfort. The basic language of the Constitution is retained.

Treason is a breach of allegiance and may be committed only by one who owed allegiance, whether perpetual or temporary. Allegiance is the obligation of faithfulness and obedience owed to the sovereign in return for protection of the law. The obligation is owed to the political entity of the United States, not to the person of the president nor to the party in power for the time being.

Allegiance may be either (1) the absolute, permanent allegiance owed by a citizen, which remains in effect at all times and in all places, even in enemy territory beyond the actual protection of the laws, until he has given up his citizenship in accordance with law, or (2) the qualified temporary local allegiance owed by an alien, unless relieved by treaty, so long as he invokes the law's protection by his presence.

The second element of Form 1 treason is that there exist foreign enemies, which have always been understood to mean a foreign sovereign and his subjects engaged with this country in open hostilities or war. The third element, adherence, is a mental state in which the offender feels or harbors disloyal sentiments. The fourth element, giving aid and comfort, requires overt conduct. A person may favor the enemy or be unsympathetic to this nation's cause, but he is not guilty of treason unless he has given aid and comfort to the enemy. Conversely, he may give aid and comfort but be innocent of treason if there was no adherence. For example, in time of war, engaging in an illegal strike for higher wages, making a speech critical of the government, or assisting an enemy agent not suspected of being such may result in giving aid and comfort to an enemy. Without "adherence," however, such conduct is not treason.

"Aid and comfort" includes any act that strengthens or attempts to strengthen the enemy in its conduct of war or in its resolve to prosecute a war, or that weakens this nation's power or resolve to resist or defeat an enemy. Examples of aid and comfort are communicating military secrets, sheltering saboteurs, assisting escaped prisoners of war, furnishing provisions, making propaganda broadcasts, and abusing American prisoners of war forced to work in an enemy war plant. The act may be of minimal significance as a contribution to the enemy's war effort. The act may be unnecessary, be frustrated, or fail. It is sufficient that the defendant did the best he could to make it succeed.

To constitute treason, assistance to foreign enemies must be given *intentionally.* The required intent in treason is not wholly clear but has been held by the Supreme Court to involve an intent to betray the United States.[1] Thus, if a person knowingly and voluntarily performs acts of aid and comfort to an enemy, he may be considered to have acted with the required intent to betray. It is no defense that he believed an enemy victory would be best for the United States in the long run, or that he gave aid and comfort for profit rather than ideological considerations. His motives do not negate the required adherence or intent to betray. If the enemy aided is a close family member, however, it appears that some degree of aid and comfort (food and shelter) can be permitted, even with the knowledge of the recipient's hostile purposes. In *Haupt* v. *United States* (1947)[2] the Supreme Court held that the jury was "correctly instructed" that "if they found the defendant's intention was not to injure the United States but merely to aid his son 'as an individual, as distinguished from assisting him in his purposes, if such existed, of aiding the German Reich, or of injuring the United States, the defendant must be found not guilty.' "

The element that the person owes allegiance to the United States is an existing circumstance. An offender who was aware of but disregarded the risk that he owed allegiance to the United States may bear criminal responsibility for treason on account of his recklessness. Resident aliens are capable of treason even though they might not know that our Constitution imposes an obligation of limited allegiance. Mere honest belief will not excuse a person who was aware of the risk that he still owed allegiance to this country, and the risk was such that disregarding it was a serious deviation from the standard of care that a reasonable person would have exercised in the circumstances.

Similarly, it must be proved that the offender was aware that he was adhering to the foreign enemies of the United States. In order to be aware that he was dealing with an enemy, an individual must know that open hostilities were in progress. Thus a person who was unaware that war had broken out but provided assistance to the enemy would not be guilty of treason. On the other hand, the person need not know that war had legally been declared provided he knew that hostilities had begun. If such a person gave assistance, he would take the risk that a court might later hold that war had begun.

Form 2 Treason. A person is guilty of Form 2 treason if, while owing allegiance to the United States, he levies war against the United States by engaging in armed rebellion or armed insurrection against the authority of the United States or a state with intent to: (1) overthrow, destroy, supplant, or change the form of government of the United States; or (2) sever a state's relationship with the United States.

It can be seen that the offense is subdivided into (1) rebellion directly against the United States, and (2) rebellion aimed ultimately against the authority of the United States but directly against a state. Activities directed exclusively against a state are not punishable under federal law, in accord with the traditional interpretation of the Constitution that such conduct is not treason unless the ultimate objective is to sever the state from the Union. To illustrate, an armed attempt to change the form of the federal government by abolishing the Congress would constitute treason. However, a similar attempt against a state government would not be a federal offense, unless the revolutionaries further intended to take the state out of the Union or if they resisted federal armed forces sent into the state to fulfill the federal government's constitutional obligation under Article IV of guaranteeing every state a republican form of government.

War is *levied* at some point before the actual shooting begins, but not before men are assembled in military order ready to move. Normally, such assembled men must be armed. The assembling of unarmed men for a treasonable purpose, if the necessity of arming is considered but the arms are not immediately available, does not amount to levying war under the prevailing view. The size of the group is not the important factor, either, since the subjective intent of the rebels, rather than the probability of their success, is at issue. Events leading up to overt levying of war, such as plotting, traveling to a rendezvous, collecting arms, and recruiting men, do not constitute treason in the constitutional sense. However, such acts may be punishable as criminal attempt, criminal conspiracy, or criminal solicitation.

Form 2 treason may be perpetrated if the purpose of armed insurrection is to deprive the government of its sovereignty over a portion of its territory (a state, a possession, or even a lesser area, such as a fort) or even to prevent the execution of a general law, such as a revenue measure. However, mere riots, or armed violation of statutes, do not constitute levying war; there must be an attempt to nullify the government generally. The force must be exercised directly against the government's officers, not merely against those entitled to the law's protection or against persons producing materiel supplies under government contract. Treason may include less than total revolution, but it must include more than mere armed violations of law.

Armed Rebellion or Insurrection

The principal and perhaps only substantive difference between armed rebellion or insurrection and treason is intent. Whereas treason requires an intent to overthrow the form of government of the United States or to sever a state's relationship with the United States, this offense requires only that the conduct be done with intent to oppose the execution of any law of the United States.

Armed rebellion or insurrection does not mean a mere riot or simple violation of law perpetrated with weapons. It is aimed at armed resistance to the enforcement of a particular law or laws of the United States, such as a federal tax or a civil rights enactment. The term "law of the United States" in this context is meant to include judicial decisions, so that, for example, a person could not successfully defend a prosecution on the ground that he did not intend to oppose a statute itself, but only the interpretation placed upon it by a court.

Instigating Overthrow or Destruction of the Government

The offense of instigating overthrow or destruction of the government is designed to cover certain kinds of conduct that, if not stopped, would result in treason. In *Dennis* v. *United States* (1951),[3] the Supreme Court, in affirming the conviction of leaders of the Communist Party, held that seditious offenses (those involving conduct intended to undermine the government) require a specific intent to overthrow the government. The court also held that it was the intent of Congress to punish only "advocacy," by which was meant incitement rather than philosophical discussion or preaching. However, the Court determined that the planned overthrow need not be immediate but could take place as "speedily as circumstances would permit" and still constitute a clear and present danger to the nation as required for prosecution in light of the First Amendment. The Court, in considering the clear and present danger test, observed:

> Obviously, the words cannot mean that before the Government may act, it must wait until the *putsch* is about to be executed, the plans have been laid and the signal is awaited. If Government is aware that a group aiming at its overthrow is attempting to indoctrinate its members and to commit them to a course whereby they will strike when the leaders feel the circumstances permit, action by the Government is required. The argument that there is no need for Government to concern itself, for Government is strong, it possesses ample powers to put down a rebellion, it may defeat the revolution with ease needs no answer. For that is not the question. Certainly an attempt to overthrow the Government by force, even though doomed from the outset because of inadequate numbers or power of the revolutionists, is a sufficient evil for Congress to prevent. The damage which such attempts create both physically and politically to a nation makes it impossible to measure the validity in terms of the probability of success, or the immediacy of a successful attempt.[4]

In *Yates* v. *United States* (1957),[5] the concept of "advocacy" was further defined as incitement to perform acts rather than merely to believe. This was reaffirmed in *Noto* v. *United States* (1961),[6] in which the court stated: "There must be some substantial direct or circumstantial evidence of a call to violence now or in the future." These interpretations of legislative intent were given constitutional status in *Brandenburg* v. *Ohio* (1969),[7] in which a state statute was invalidated because its language was not so restricted by the Ohio courts. The Court in *Brandenburg* summarized its previous decisions as having "fashioned the principle that the constitutional guarantees of free speech and free press do not permit a State to forbid or proscribe advocacy of the use of force or of law violation except where such advocacy is directed to inciting or producing imminent lawless action and is likely to incite or produce such action."

In *Scales* v. *United States* (1961),[8] the Court upheld a conviction under the so-called membership clause of the Smith Act for joining the Communist Party. It held that the defendant had joined knowing that the party advocated violent overthrow of the government as soon as circumstances permitted, and with a specific intent to bring about the forcible overthrow of the government as speedily as possible. Significantly, the Court in *Scales* reaffirmed the prior holdings in *Dennis* and *Yates* that the advocacy of future action as well as advocacy of immediate action was included in the offense.

With respect to the nature of membership, the Court in *Scales* further held that the Smith Act requires that the person's membership in an organization advocating forcible overthrow be "active," not merely passive or nominal to be criminal, since a person who merely becomes a member of an illegal organization "need be doing nothing more than signifying his assent to its purposes and activities on one hand, and providing, on the other, only the sort of moral encouragement which comes from the knowledge that others believe in what the organization is doing."

A person may be guilty of instigating the overthrow or destruction of the government if, "with intent to bring about the forcible overthrow or destruction of the government of the United States or of any state," he: (1) incites other persons to engage in immediate lawless conduct that would facilitate the forcible overthrow or destruction of that government; (2) organizes, leads, or recruits members for a group that he knows wishes to incite persons in this way; or (3) participates as an active member in a group that he knows has a purpose to incite persons in this way.

The prohibited conduct is *incitement*. As required by *Brandenburg, Yates, Noto,* and *Scales,* the incitement must be to *do* something rather than merely to believe. The "something" is to engage in imminent lawless conduct facilitating a forcible change in the government.

A person is also forbidden to organize, lead, or recruit members for a group that the actor knows has as a purpose the kind of incitement proscribed. Again, the prohibited activity must be done with the specific intent of bringing about the forcible overthrow of the government as speedily as circumstances allow. The concept of organizing includes the forming of new units, and the regrouping or expansion of existing units. The term *group* (which includes an organization) is defined to include both legal and illegal entities.

Third, a person may not participate as an active member in a group that he knows has as a purpose the proscribed incitement. The requirement of active participation is a constitutional limitation derived from the *Scales* case.

To support a conviction for instigating overthrow or destruction of the government, it must be proved that the defendant was aware of the nature of his actions. The elements that "other persons" are incited and that the entity is a "group" are existing circumstances, for which at least a reckless state of mind must be established. Thus, it must be shown that the defendant was aware of but disregarded a risk that the circumstance existed and his disregard was a serious deviation from the standard of care that a reasonable person would have exercised in such a situation. The element that the conduct would facilitate the forcible overthrow or destruction of the government of the United States or any state is also an existing circumstance subject to the same "reckless" state of mind. Finally, a defendant must be shown to have engaged in the conduct with a specific intent or purpose to "bring about the forcible overthrow or destruction of the United States or of any state."

Sabotage and Related Offenses

These are certain offenses short of treason and subversion that affect the security of the United States. They relate to physical obstruction of national defense, preparation for war, or the conduct of war. Espionage and classified information offenses are dealt with in the following section. Here, wartime sabotage perpetrated with the intent of interfering with national defense is included together with similar regulations against causing panic in war, evading military service, and obstructing recruitment and induction.

Wartime Sabotage

A person may be criminally responsible for wartime sabotage if, with intent to impair, interfere with, or obstruct the ability of the United States or an associate nation to prepare for or to engage in war or defense activities, he damages, tampers with, contaminates, defectively makes, or defectively repairs three categories of property (discussed below).

This offense is designed to punish sabotage perpetrated with a specific intent to injure the war or war preparation efforts of the United States or an associate nation. An "associate nation" is a nation at war with a foreign power with which the United States is at war. Hence, an associate nation is an ally.

The types of property protected under sabotage statutes are: (1) any property used in, or particularly suited for use in, the national defense, owned by or under the care, custody, or control of the United States or an associate nation, or which is being produced, manufactured, constructed, repaired, transported, or stored for the United States or an associate nation; (2) any facility that is engaged in whole or in part, for the United States or an associate nation, in (a) furnishing defense materials or services or (b) producing the raw material necessary to the support of a national defense production or mobilization program; or (3) any public facility that is used in, or particularly suited for use in, the national defense.

In addition, one may be criminally responsible for wartime sabotage if he *delivers* any property just described that has been damaged, tampered with, contaminated, defectively made, or defectively repaired with intent to obstruct the war or defense effort.

Finally, one may bear criminal responsibility for wartime sabotage if, with the same intent, he "delays or obstructs" (1) the production, manufacture, construction, repair, or delivery of any property described above or (2) a service or public facility used in, or particularly suited for use in, the national defense. The logic of the wartime sabotage concept thus extends to any means whereby the flow of war materiel is deliberately delayed or obstructed.

To be criminally responsible for any wartime sabotage conduct, an offender must act with a specific intent to impair, interfere with, or obstruct the ability of the United States or an associate nation to prepare for or engage in war or defense activities. The specific intent required is designed to counterbalance the necessarily broad classes of property protected. In addition, the specific intent requirement distinguishes wartime sabotage from general property destruction offenses. The saboteur's offense is intended to weaken the nation in relation to a foreign power and thus carries an added dimension beyond the fact of property destruction, contamination, or injury.

Impairing Military Effectiveness

The offense of impairing military effectiveness involves conduct nearly identical to that involved in wartime sabotage. However, in place of the specific intent to interfere with the war or national defense effort required for wartime sabotage, this offense requires only a reckless disregard for the impact the conduct would have on the war or defense effort.

A person may bear criminal responsibility for impairing military effectiveness if he engages in conduct described in regard to wartime sabotage with reckless disregard of the fact that his conduct could impair, interfere with, or obstruct the ability of the United States or an associate nation to prepare for or engage in war or defense activities. However, this offense is not committed by conduct occurring in the usual course of lawful labor strike activity or other lawful concerted activity intended for the purpose of collective bargaining or other mutual aid and protection.

Evading Military or Alternative Civilian Service

The principal offenses involved in evading military or alternative civilian service are failure to register for, report for, or submit to induction; failure to report for a physical examination; failure to keep one's local Selective Service board advised of a change of address; and failure to carry one's Selective Service card on his person. Such offenses can be committed by persons subject to the law (for example failure to register), officials of the Selective Service System and other agencies (filing false examination reports), and "outsiders" (making false statements in behalf of a registrant or printing counterfeit Selective Service cards). Since the purpose of these laws is primarily to encourage men to serve in the armed forces (or alternative civilian work programs) rather than to put them in jail, the policy of the Selective Service System and the Department of Justice with respect to registrants has been to punish persistent refusals to serve. Most prosecutions have therefore been for disobeying orders of a Selective Service board to report for induction or civilian work. An exception has been the making of false statements, which is generally considered to deserve prosecution.

A person may bear criminal responsibility for a service evasion offense if, knowing that he has a legal duty to register for military service, to report for and submit to examination, to report for and submit to induction into military service, or to report for and perform alternative civilian services, he fails, neglects, or refuses to do so.

The offenses of failing to report for and submit to induction and to report for and perform alternative civilian service are "ultimate" offenses. They involve a refusal to fulfill the final objective of the Selective Service System to select persons fairly to serve in the armed forces or, if they are conscientious objectors, to perform alternative civilian work. Similarly, failing to register is among the most serious offenses since it involves a kind of fraud on the system, and, like the "ultimate" offenses, requires that another individual be made to serve in the offender's place.

In addition, a person may be criminally liable for a service evasion offense if he makes a false statement to authorities with intent (1) to avoid or delay the performance of the military or alternative civilian service obligation of himself or another person or (2) to obstruct the proper determination of the existence or nature of such an obligation. This offense may be committed not only by one liable to service under the Selective Service laws, but by officials (such as local Selective Service board or induction personnel) or by outsiders who volunteer or furnish information (family members, friends, medical practitioners). One requirement is that the false statement be one "regarding or bearing upon" a classification. It has been held that the statement must thus be shown to be *material*. (See Chapter 10, "False Pretenses" and Chapter 17, "Perjury.")

Obstructing Military Recruitment or Induction

A person may become criminally responsible for obstructing military recruitment or induction if in time of war, with intent to hinder, interfere with, or obstruct the recruitment, conscription, or induction of a person into the armed forces of the United States, he

(1) creates a physical interference or obstacle to the recruitment, conscription, or induction; (2) uses force, threat, intimidation or deception against a public servant of a government agency engaged in the recruitment, conscription, or induction; or (3) incites others to evade military or alternative civilian service.

The conduct in this offense is creating a physical interference or obstacle; using force, threat, intimidation, or deception; or inciting others to engage in obstructive conduct. A general criminal intent is required. Therefore, it must be proved that the offender was aware of what he was doing. The remaining elements—that the conduct took place in time of war and that the use of force was against a public servant of a government agency engaged in recruitment, conscription, or induction—are existing circumstances. It must be shown that the offender was conscious of but disregarded the risk that the circumstances existed and that his disregard was a serious deviation from the standard of care a reasonable person would have exercised in the situation. Thus, it must be shown that the offender behaved recklessly in regard to the existing circumstances.

Espionage and Related Offenses

Espionage and related offenses are covered primarily by laws designed to deter the unauthorized collection and disclosure of the nation's military secrets—information concerning our national preparedness that would render this country vulnerable to attack and defeat or powerless to achieve victory—and particularly to deter such disclosure to foreign powers. The offenses discussed here are espionage, disclosing national defense information, mishandling classified or other national defense information, and failing to register as a person trained in a foreign espionage system or acting as a foreign agent.

In *Gorin* v. *United States* (1941),[9] the Supreme Court held that although intent to injure the United States and intent to give an advantage to a foreign nation might sometimes differ, each was intended by Congress as an independent alternative, so that proof of intent to benefit a foreign country would support a conviction without proof of injury to the United States or intent to cause such an injury.[10]

The court in *Gorin* approved the term "information relating to the national defense" as sufficiently precise and described the phrase as "a generic concept of broad connotations, referring to the military and naval establishments and the related activities of national preparedness."[11] The Court stated that the relationship of the information to the national defense must be direct and rational and must be determined by the jury from examination of the material and expert testimony as to its significance.[12] In *Gorin*, the Supreme Court stated further that the Espionage Act was designed to protect only "secrets," and not matter made public by the defense establishment.

Espionage

There are three major types of espionage activities: (1) entering a restricted area for the purpose of spying for a foreign power, (2) collecting information for a foreign power, and (3) communicating information to a foreign power. The subject of the criminal activity must be "national defense information."

A person may bear criminal responsibility for an espionage offense if, knowing that national defense information could be used to endanger the safety or interest of the United States or to give an advantage to a foreign power, he (1) communicates such information to a foreign power, (2) obtains or collects such information, knowing that it may be communicated to a foreign power, or (3) enters a restricted area with intent to obtain or collect such information knowing that it may be communicated to a foreign power.

The term "national defense information" includes information that relates to (1) the military capability of the United States or of an associate nation, (2) military planning or operations of the United States, (3) military communications of the United States, (4) military installations of the United States, (5) military weaponry, weapons development, or weapons research of the United States, (6) intelligence operations, activities, plans, estimates, analyses, sources, or methods of the United States, (7) intelligence concerning a foreign power, (8) communications intelligence information or cryptographic information, and (9) restricted data. The government must have made an affirmative effort to prevent dissemination of the information to the public. The precise extent of the efforts necessary to remove the information from the public domain and render it "secret" is a matter of judicial interpretation. Information that has been lawfully disclosed to the public is not within the scope of the espionage offense.

The specific knowledge that is required to support a conviction for espionage is indicated by the element that the offender acts knowing that national defense information could be used to endanger the safety or interest of the United States or to give an advantage to a foreign power. The element of knowing that information may be communicated to a foreign power is a further specific requirement that must be shown to have accompanied the conduct. This element is necessary to cover situations in which the defendant does not communicate the information to a foreign power himself but makes it available so that others can communicate it to a foreign power. Furthermore, the scope of the offense is limited by the requirement that the government must prove that the defendant obtained or collected the information or entered a restricted area in order to obtain or collect it *knowing* that the information could be used for the purposes specified.

Disclosing National Defense Information

One may bear criminal responsibility for disclosing national defense information if, knowing that the national defense information could be used to endanger the safety or interest of the United States or give an advantage to a foreign power, he communicates such information to a person who he knows is not legally authorized to receive it. The element that the person to whom the information is communicated is not legally authorized to receive it is an existing circumstance. However, the culpability requirement is that the offender "knows," thereby requiring proof that he was aware or believed that the circumstance existed.

Mishandling Classified or Other National Defense Information

The statutes forbidding mishandling of classified or other national defense information refer to persons of two kinds: those *authorized* to possess or control such information and those *unau-*

thorized to do so. A person who is *authorized* to possess or control such information commits an offense if he (1) engages in conduct that causes its loss, destruction, or theft, or its communication to a person who is not authorized to receive it, (2) fails to report promptly, to the agency authorizing him to possess or control such information, its loss, destruction, or theft, or its communication to a person who is not authorized to receive it, or (3) intentionally fails to deliver it on demand to a federal public servant who is authorized to demand it. A person who is in *unauthorized* possession or control of national defense information, commits an offense if he: (1) engages in conduct that causes its loss, destruction, or theft, or its communication to another person who is not authorized to receive it, or (2) fails to deliver it promptly to a federal public servant who is entitled to receive it.

The conduct element in this offense is unauthorized use of national defense information. The offender must be proved to have been aware of the nature of his actions. The fact that the conduct causes the loss, destruction, or theft of classified information or its communication to an unauthorized person is a result of conduct. The culpability standard for the conduct is at least "reckless," so it must be established at least that the defendant was aware of but disregarded a risk that the result would occur and that the risk was such that its disregard was a serious deviation from the standard of care that a reasonable person would have exercised in the situation.

The element that the offender was in "authorized" or "unauthorized" possession or control of classified information is an existing circumstance. The state of mind that must be shown is at least "reckless"—that is, the offender must have been aware of but disregarded the risk that the circumstances existed.

It has been proposed that prosecution of this and related offenses be barred under the following circumstances: (1) if the information was not lawfully subject to classification at the time of the offense; (2) if at the time of the offense there did not legally exist (*a*) a government overseeing agency responsible for insuring that other government agencies classify only information that is lawfully subject to classification and (*b*) a review procedure through which the defendant could obtain review, by the responsible overseeing government agency, of the lawfulness of the classification of the information, or (3) if before the return of the indictment or the filing of the information, the head of the agency classifying the information, the head of the responsible overseeing agency, and the attorney general did not jointly certify to the court that the information was lawfully subject to classification at the time of the offense.

Failing to Register as a Foreign Espionage Agent

If a person is trained in a foreign espionage system or is a foreign agent, he must register. Failure to do so is illegal, and a person is guilty of an offense if he (1) fails to register with the attorney general as required by a law relating to registration of persons trained in foreign espionage systems[13] or (2) violates certain regulations or rules relating to registration of persons trained in foreign espionage systems.[14]

Similarly, one is guilty of an offense if he is an agent of a foreign principal (or government) and fails to register with the attorney general as required by U.S. statutes regulating such registration.[15]

The conduct in these offenses is failing to register with the attorney general. The state of mind that must be proved is at least "knowing,"—the offender must be shown to have been aware of the nature of his actions. Since the conduct involves an omission, it is necessary by implication to show that the defendant knew he had an obligation to register in order to establish that his failure to do so was "knowing." The element that the offender is "a person trained in a foreign espionage system" or is an "agent of a foreign principal" is an existing circumstance. The state of mind that must be shown is at least "reckless,"—that is, the offender must have been aware of but disregarded the risk that he was such an agent. The element that the duty to register was required by law is an existing circumstance, also. It is not necessary to show that the defendant knew the particular law that requires him to register, even though it is essential to show that he had some awareness of the legal duty to register. The duty to register extends to the situation in which a person merely fails to register within ten days after becoming an agent of a foreign principal, as well as the situation in which a person "acts" as such an agent regardless of how recently he acquired his status.

CHAPTER 17

Government Process Offenses

Any government whether state or federal must administer justice fairly, impartially, and swiftly. It has been said that justice delayed is justice denied, and that may be so. Citizens have a right to believe their public servants are competent, efficient, and honest. Persons who have been accused of committing a crime have a right to a trial at which the testimony being presented both for and against them consists of the truth, the whole truth, and nothing but the truth. The civil rights of any given individual whether he is a policeman or a prisoner must remain inviolate. Therefore, crimes that impede the processes of government cannot be condoned.

These offenses include the following: extortion, bribery, and other forms of official corruption; perjury and other false statements; general obstructions of government functions; obstructions of law enforcement; obstructions of justice; and criminal contempt.

Official Corruption and Intimidation

Official corruption and intimidation offenses include extortion and bribery, graft, trading in government assistance, and oppression offenses.

Extortion and Official Bribery

At common law, a misdemeanor known as extortion consisted of the corrupt collection of an unlawful fee by a public officer under color of his office. Common law extortion could involve taking anything of value for a service which the officer was obliged to provide free of charge; taking more than the cost allowed by law; or taking even an authorized fee before it was due and payable. This offense could be committed at common law only by a public office-holder, however, and not by a private citizen. Extortion involved the wrongful taking but not the wrongful giving of the money or other valuable item.

In addition to extortion, a similar offense known as bribery existed at common law. This offense consisted of the corrupt tender or receipt of anything of value for the purpose of improperly influencing official action. Thus, bribery could be committed by a public official or by a private citizen, or by both, since this offense occurred from either a wrongful giving or a wrongful taking of a valuable item or other benefit. Since a public official could commit either extortion or bribery, a fine distinction emerged between these two crimes. If the official initiated the transaction, the offense was extortion; otherwise it was bribery. Quite evidently, this distinction has lost meaning, if indeed it ever had any.

In recent years as efforts have been made to modernize criminal laws, the conduct which involved common law extortion and bribery has become consolidated into a single offense in many jurisdictions. The distinction between wrongful giving and wrongful taking has become unimportant in defining the common offense, labeled official bribery in most states.

It is important even today to note that the recipient of the valuable item or other benefit must be a public official in order for the offense of official bribery to occur. Some states have enacted statutes to prohibit other forms of bribery such as commercial bribery (e.g. a gift to a corporate purchasing agent to influence the sale of a commodity) and sports bribery (e.g. a gift to a sports participant, trainer, etc. to influence the loss of a game or the margin of victory). These forms of bribery are not offenses against the processes of government.

Under modern official bribery statutes, a person may be guilty of this offense if: (1) he offers, gives, or agrees to give to a public servant or (2) as a public servant, he solicits, demands, accepts, or agrees to accept from another person, anything of value in return for an agreement or understanding that the recipient's official action as a public servant will be influenced thereby, or that the recipient will violate a legal duty as a public servant. This formulation combines bribe-giving and bribe-taking. While at least one of the parties must be a public servant, both may be, also, as when one official makes an effort to influence the action of another official.

The thing of value must be offered or paid knowingly as consideration for (1) the recipient's official action as a public servant or (2) the recipient's violation of a known legal duty as a public servant.

Violation (as opposed to performance) of a "legal duty" is included as a prohibited purpose of a bribe. It covers misdeeds or omissions committed by the public servant that are outside his decision-making powers or the usual scope of his job. The bribed person cannot claim a defense on the ground that the action planned or taken was not an "official action" for which he was responsible. An official's legal duties include duties that derive from all sources—the Constitution, statutes, agency regulations, agency policy (whether written or oral), and directions from supervisors. The official action need not be an improper one. An individual can be bribed to perform an act as a public servant that would be performed in any event. The fact that nothing officially wrong took place should be no defense to a bribery prosecution.

The term "official action" means a decision, opinion, recommendation, judgment, vote, or other conduct involving an exercise of discretion by a public servant in the course of his employment. It covers conduct ranging from high decision-making to minor administrative actions within the public servant's powers. However, a purely administrative act involving no discretion, such as getting a court clerk to accept certain legal papers for filing in connection with a case, is not covered in this offense. A bribe involving a wholly administrative act, while worthy of criminal penalties, is not as serious as a bribe involving a discretionary act. Bribery as an offense is confined to discretionary acts, whereas bribery involving administrative functions will be included in the following section on graft.

The term "public servant" means an officer, employee, advisor, consultant, juror, or other person authorized to act for or on behalf of a government or serving a government, and includes a person who has been elected, nominated, or appointed to be a public servant. It includes part-time employees and persons charged with carrying out government orders, even though their compensation may not come directly from the government, such as an examining physician appointed by a local Selective Service board. It also covers persons licensed to perform certain regulatory functions, such as grain inspection and fruit and vegetable grading. Persons authorized to act for or on behalf of the government include, for example, civilian employees of the military post exchange.

"Anything of value" is defined to mean any direct or indirect gain or advantage or anything that might reasonably be regarded by the beneficiary as such a gain or advantage, including a gain or advantage to any other person. A problem that has plagued the bribery area has been the breadth of the term "anything of value," which if taken literally might even refer to legitimately earned salary or fees paid to public servants. Certain exclusions from the definition of "anything of value" eliminate the possibility of abusive prosecutions but still leave the term broad enough to cover cases that do not involve money but that should be prosecuted.

Log-rolling (an agreement between legislators whereby each promises to support a bill sponsored or endorsed by the other in exchange for the other's support) poses a problem in the enforcement of bribery statutes. Log-rolling must be viewed as a realistic and permanent feature of our government system and as an unavoidable and not undesirable technique for bringing public servants of differing opinions together on some common ground. In order to limit the definition of "anything of value" to exclude log-rolling in the context of bribery, some recent statutes contain the phrase that bribery shall "not include . . . concurrence in official action in the course of legitimate compromise between public servants." Normally, accepted bargaining among public servants in any branch of government would fall under "legitimate compromise." On the other hand, an attempt to influence the vote of a member of an administrative agency in a case pending before him by a promise of some independent political benefit would be outside the normal concept of governmental give and take and should not be within the boundaries of "legitimate compromise."

There is one more area in which the exclusion from "anything of value" should apply. That concerns the problem of campaigning candidates making political promises in return for votes or other support. It is difficult to reconcile the goal of a modern criminal code with the possibility that a candidate for political office would commit a technical act of bribery when he promises to end inflation in return for votes—ridiculous as the possibility of a prosecution on such a basis would seem to be. Accordingly, it has been proposed that support, including a vote, in any primary, general, or special election campaign solicited by a candidate solely by means of representation of his position on a public issue be excluded from the definition of "anything of value." Obviously, "support" is broader than the mere quest for votes and includes the traditional forms of raising the large sums of money that are needed to wage campaign battles. However, by limiting the support sought by the candidate to that solicited "by means of representation of his position on a public issue," the exclusion would not protect a candidate who is bought by some private interest or one who sells a public appointment in return for a campaign contribution.

Legitimately earned salary or fees are not specifically exempted from the definition of bribery because the offense requires that the payment be made to influence the recipient's official action or to cause him to violate a legal duty. Clearly, salary or fees paid routinely to a public servant for the performance of his normal duties are not made with intent to influence his official conduct; rather, they are intended as legitimate compensation for his efforts and cannot support a bribery prosecution.

The offense of bribery is separate from that of conspiracy and criminal solicitation, and a person may be convicted and sentenced for both conspiracy (or solicitation) to commit bribery and for the substantive offense of bribery.

The conduct of this offense is either (1) offering, giving, or agreeing to give something or (2) soliciting, demanding, accepting, or agreeing to accept something. The state of mind that must be proved is at least "knowing." The defendant must have been aware of the nature of his actions. The elements that what is offered or solicited is "anything of value" and that the offer was to (or the solicitation was by) a "public servant" are existing circumstances for which the state of mind that must be shown is at least "reckless." The offender must have been aware of but disregarded the risk that the circumstances existed. The common element that the offer or solicitation of anything of value was in return for an agreement or understanding is an existing circumstance for which the state of mind that must be proved is also at least "reckless." The prosecution must show the defendant's awareness and disregard of the risk that the agreement or understanding was formed.

Graft

A person may be guilty of graft if (1) he offers, gives, or agrees to give to a public servant or former public servant, or (2) as a public servant, he solicits, demands, accepts, or agrees to accept from another person, anything of pecuniary value for or because of an official action taken or to be taken, a legal duty performed or to be performed, or a legal duty violated or to be violated by the public servant or former public servant. The terms "public servant" and "official action" have been explained in detail in connection with bribery. As with bribery, payments to the public servant or to third parties (family members, political parties, corporations, and so on) may constitute graft.

This offense is limited to payments or gifts of "pecuniary" (monetary) value. The practice of taking government officials to lunch or giving them theater tickets, flowers, and the like does not constitute graft. Such matters may be regulated by statutes or administrative rules providing such sanctions as dismissal or forfeiture of pay. These kinds of gifts, even if given with the hope of influencing future official acts, do not constitute a criminal offense. The line between friendship and corruption in the context of a free dinner is hard to draw; a gift of cash, however, is another matter clearly indicating graft and corruption.

The term "anything of pecuniary value" means (1) anything of value in the form of money, a negotiable instrument, a commercial interest, or anything else the primary significance of which is economic advantage or (2) any other property or service that has a substantial value. It may be very difficult to draw a clear line between those gifts having economic advantage as their primary significance and those that do not, such as an expensive watch. Such an item would far exceed in value the cost of a meal or a box of cigars, yet it is conceivable that it would not be considered to have economic gain as its primary significance. To avoid this problem and to make the prohibitions more precise, some graft statutes include a specific (even if somewhat arbitrary) value limitation such as $100. This eliminates the candy, meal, and theater ticket cases but includes major gifts.

The conduct of this offense is either (1) offering, giving, or agreeing to give something or (2) soliciting, demanding, accepting, or agreeing to accept something. The state of mind that must be proved is at least "knowing"; the defendant must have been aware of the nature of his actions. The element that the offer is made to a public servant or former public servant or that the solicitation is by a public servant or former public servant is an existing circumstance for which the state of mind that must be shown is at least "reckless"; the offender must have been aware of but disregarded the risk that the circumstance existed. The element that what is offered or solicited is "anything of pecuniary value" is also an existing circumstance which, under the same analysis, requires proof of at least a "reckless" state of mind. The common element that the offer or solicitation was for or because of an official action taken or to be taken indicates the particular purpose for which it must be proved that the conduct was performed.

Trading in Government Assistance

A person may be guilty of an offense if (1) he offers, gives, or agrees to give to a public servant, or (2) as a public servant, he solicits, demands, accepts, or agrees to accept from another person, anything of pecuniary value intended as consideration for advice or other assistance in preparing or promoting a bill, contract, claim, or other matter that is or may become subject to official action by such public servant. The term "anything of pecuniary value" has been discussed in detail in connection with graft. The terms "official action" and "public servant" have been explained more fully in connection with bribery.

The phrase "as consideration for advice or other assistance in preparing or promoting a bill, contract, claim, or other matter" covers substantially more than merely representational services and extends to all types of services rendered by a public servant. Federal and state governments dispense huge sums of money annually under a myriad of programs. They clearly have a strong interest in protecting those funds and thus try to punish flagrant conflict of interest situations such as the hiring of a public servant by a private person to help prepare grant applications or draft contracts.

The conduct in this section is either (1) offering, giving, or agreeing to give or (2) soliciting, demanding, accepting, or agreeing to accept. The state of mind that must be proved is at least "knowing"; the offender must have been aware of the nature of his actions. The elements that what is given is "anything of pecuniary value" and that it is offered to or solicited by a "public servant" are existing circumstances for which the applicable state of mind is at least "reckless." The common element that something of pecuniary value given or accepted is "intended as consideration for advice or other assistance in preparing or promoting a bill, contract, claim, or other matter that is or may become subject to official action by such public servant" states the particular purpose that the defendant must be shown to have had in offering or soliciting the thing of value. Some statutes require no showing of evil motive but require only deliberate conduct together with an awareness (knowledge) of the nature of the payment.

Oppression Offenses

Oppression occurs whenever any public official, acting under color of law or public office, corruptly causes harm or disadvantage to another person. Oppression involves only the conduct of public officials and not that of private citizens. The official must act or fail to act under color of law or of public office, rather than as a private citizen. The official must act corruptly, as indicated by depravity or serious impropriety.

In its most bizzare forms, oppression takes place when a law enforcement officer tortures a prisoner; when a public defender deliberately provides substandard legal services to an indigent client who cannot afford to retain his own lawyer; or when a judge or magistrate sets unreasonably high bail or denies bail altogether for a prisoner who has been accused of committing a trivial offense, is not dangerous, and is unlikely to avoid prosecution by flight. Oppression may take place in more subtle ways, however, such as when an election official refuses to permit a qualified citizen to vote or to register as a voter on account of race, color, creed, national origin, or sex; or when, for a similar reason, a public official discriminates during the process of evaluating a person's application for public employment, for public welfare, or for any federal or state benefit such as medicare, medicaid, food stamps, or veterans' benefits.

Some forms of oppression are punishable under federal laws created by the Civil Rights Acts of 1957, 1960, 1964, and 1968, as amended. The United States Code provides punishment for anyone who, under color of any law, statute, ordinance, regulation, or custom willfully subjects another person to the deprivation of any rights, privileges, or immunities secured or protected by the Constitution or laws of the United States. Congress deemed federal legislation to be necessary in order that individuals who are oppressed by state or municipal officials may seek redress in federal court rather than in local courts which may be administered by persons responsible for the oppression.

Perjury, False Statements, and Related Offenses

This section deals with offenses involving the making of false statements, both under oath and otherwise, in an official proceeding or government matter, and the alteration, destruction, or concealment of government records. The offenses covered are perjury, false swearing, subornation of perjury and tampering with a government record.

Perjury

A person may be guilty of an offense if, under oath or equivalent affirmation in an official proceeding, he (1) makes a material statement that is false or (2) affirms the truth of a previously made material statement that is false.

The term "official proceeding" means a proceeding, or a portion thereof, that is or may be heard before a government branch or agency or a public servant who is authorized to take oaths, including a judge, chairman of a legislative committee or subcommittee, referee, hearing examiner, administrative law judge, and notary public.

The false statement must be "material." It is material if, regardless of the admissibility of the statement under the rules of evidence, it could have impaired, affected, impeded, or otherwise influenced the course, outcome, or disposition of the matter in which it is made, or, in the case of a record, if it could have impaired the integrity of the record in question. The issue of whether a matter is material under the circumstances is a question of law for the courts to decide. This does not mean, however, that when the issue of materiality depends on disputed facts the jury should not decide the factual issues. In such a case, ordinarily, the court leaves the factual decision to the jury with instructions on the question of materiality to be applied after the decision is made.

The term "statement" means an oral or written declaration or representation, including a declaration or representation of opinion, belief, or other state of mind. A written statement made "under oath or equivalent affirmation" includes a written statement that, with the declarer's knowledge, is said to have been made under those conditions. Under this definition, and under the condition in which the actor makes or affirms the truth of a statement "that is false," the crime of perjury requires that a statement be objectively false. In some jurisdictions, perjury may be committed when a person testifies under oath that a material fact is true when he believes his statement to be false, even though the fact turns out to be true. In some jurisdictions, also, it must be shown that the defendant made or affirmed two or more mutually inconsistent but material statements. In these jurisdictions, if one statement is material but the other is immaterial, only a conviction of the lesser included offense of false swearing (covered next) can be obtained, unless the prosecution can prove that the material statement was the one that was false.

The conduct in this offense is making a statement or affirming the truth of a statement made previously. The state of mind that must be proved is at least, "knowing." The defendant must have been aware of the nature of his actions. The element that the statement was false is an existing circumstance for which the applicable state of mind to be shown is at least "reckless." The defendant must have been aware of but disregarded the risk that the statement was false. The elements that the statement was given under oath or equivalent affirmation and that it was in an official proceeding are also existing circumstances requiring at least a "reckless" state of mind. The fact that the statement was "material" is an existing circumstance, but since materiality is a question of law, as explained earlier, no state of mind needs to be proved as to this element.

Normally, it is not a defense to a prosecution for perjury that the oath or affirmation was administered or taken in an irregular manner. Thus, a mere technical defect in administering an oath (such as a mistake in the use of a seal) will not protect a person who makes a material false statement in an official proceeding from criminal liability for perjury. On the other hand, a total failure to administer the oath or a total lack of authority by the public official to require an oath does constitute a defense in some jurisdictions. In such a case, it can be claimed that the statement was not made in an "official proceeding." Note, however, that when a person submits a written statement said to be made under oath he is bound by his statement.

Normally, also, it is not a defense to a perjury or false swearing prosecution that the declarer was not authorized to make the statement. Thus, one may bear criminal responsibility for these offenses even if he did not have proper corporate or official authority to sign the false documents in question but in fact he did sign them. One who verifies a statement as if he had authority to swear to it is liable for the falsehood it contains.

Generally, it is a defense to a prosecution for perjury that the actor clearly and expressly retracted the falsification in the course of the same official proceeding in which it was made if, in fact, he did so before it became obvious that the falsification had been or would be exposed and before the falsification substantially impaired or otherwise influenced the course or outcome of the official proceeding or of a government matter related to the proceeding. This defense thus serves as an inducement to correct a false statement voluntarily by eliminating the risk or penalty of conviction for perjury in order that the truth may be learned. The defense is not made available if the retraction is offered only when it is clear that the falsification will be exposed. Nor can the defense be invoked successfully if the falsification has already caused the official proceeding to be substantially affected. In such an instance, the crime has had its harmful effect, and, even if the actor doesn't know this, he can be held liable for the result of his deliberate falsification. Because this defense is not "affirmative," the prosecution bears the burden of disproving the applicability of the defense beyond a reasonable doubt once it is properly raised.

False Swearing

False swearing is a lesser included offense to perjury that covers instances of deliberate lying under oath in an official proceeding but without regard to the materiality of the false statement. The concept of materiality is imprecise, and in some cases prosecutions for perjury have been dismissed because the defendant, though he may have lied deliberately under oath, did not, under the circumstances of the case, lie about a material matter.

A person may be guilty of the offense of false swearing if, under oath or equivalent affirmation in an official proceeding, he (1) makes a statement that is false or (2) affirms the truth of a previously made statement that is false. This offense is identical to perjury except that the additional element of materiality, present in the perjury offense, is absent here. All the elements of this offense are contained in and have been explained in connection with perjury.

Subornation of Perjury

A person may be guilty of subornation of perjury if he induces another person to commit perjury and at the same time knows or believes: (1) that the statement to be made by the other person is untrue and (2) that the other person knows or believes that statement to be untrue. Remember that perjury consists of making a material statement under oath that is false, or affirming the truth of a previously made material statement that is false, before an official proceeding.

The conduct for subornation of perjury is inducing another person to commit perjury. Therefore, subornation of perjury cannot occur until or unless perjury takes place. One person may request another to commit perjury, but if the second person does not follow the suggestion the first person has not committed subornation of perjury. In this situation, however, the person who asks another to commit perjury may bear criminal responsibility for criminal solicitation (see Chapter 15).

The applicable state of mind that must be proved for subornation of perjury is at least "knowing." The defendant must have been aware: (1) of the nature of his actions; (2) that the statement to be made by another person is false; and (3) that the other person knew or believed that statement to be false. Thus, even if the person being induced to make a statement knows or believes the statement to be false, the one doing the inducing does not bear criminal responsibility for subornation of perjury unless *he* also believes the statement to be false. In addition, if the person being induced to make a statement knows or believes that statement to be true, the one doing the inducing is not criminally responsible for subornation of perjury even if *he* believes the statement to be false. In simple terms, both persons must at least believe the statement to be untrue.

Tampering with a Government Record

A person may be guilty of tampering with a government record if he alters, destroys, mutilates, conceals, removes, or otherwise impairs the integrity or availability of such a record. The term "government record" includes a record, document, or other object (1) belonging to, or received or kept by, a government for information or record purposes, or (2) required by law to be kept by a person.

A person may be required to keep various government records, such as a Selective Service card or a license to sell liquor, operate a bar or a lodging house. The offense applies to any act that lessens the integrity, usability, or accessibility of government records. The term "otherwise impairs" applies to all conduct of the type just described.

A private citizen who is required to keep a government record is protected if he destroys the record on official authority, since the record would no longer be a "government record." Mere acts of photocopying or photographing government records are not punishable under this offense. The basic wrongdoing involved in photocopying a government record does not relate to impairing the integrity of the record but to the unlawful capture of its contents.

The conduct of this offense is altering, destroying, mutilating, concealing, removing, or otherwise impairing the integrity or availability of a record. The state of mind that must be shown is at least "knowing." The element that the record is a governmental record is an existing circumstance for which the state of mind to be proved is at least "reckless."

General Obstructions of Government Functions

This section is concerned with two forms of obstruction of government functions. Such obstructions are made criminal if carried out by physical means or if an impersonator represents himself as exercising governmental authority. Because of the size of modern government, the prominent role it plays, and its far-reaching effects, it is vital to provide criminal sanctions to safeguard the integrity of government operations and ultimately to maintain public confidence in government.

Physical Interference

A person may be guilty of an offense if he intentionally obstructs or impairs a government function by means of physical interference or obstacle.

The forbidden conduct—obstructing or impairing a function by means of physical interference or obstacle—must be intentional if a person is to be criminally responsible for this offense. Thus, it must be proved that he had a conscious objective or desire to obstruct or impair a function and to do so by physical interference or obstacle. Mere awareness of the effect of his conduct will not suffice.

The fact that the function is a *government* function is an existing circumstance, and the offender must be shown to have been "reckless" in regard to this fact. Thus, the actor must be shown to have been aware of but disregarded a risk that the function he obstructed or impaired by physical interference or obstacle was a government function. The government involved may be federal or state. A person may be convicted of this offense if the evidence establishes, for example, that he intentionally obstructed the execution of a search warrant by physical interference.

Since the conduct must be intentional, one would not be criminally responsible for this offense as a result of such actions as pulling away from an arresting officer at his initial approach or knocking away a hand suddenly placed on the shoulder to make an arrest if this type of action amounts to a reflex response.

The offense specifies conduct that "obstructs or impairs" the government function involved. The obstruction or impairment must be by means of "physical interference or obstacle," including affirmative physical acts such as barring a door against a process server, raising barriers, destroying property, using a stench bomb, or causing persistent noise. However, mere verbal efforts to obstruct a government function and failure to take action to facilitate a government function (such as unlocking a door to permit an inspector to enter) are not included.

Threats that are intended to influence government actions are penalized as extortion or menacing (see Chapter 5). Cursing and other forms of verbal abuse that do not amount to threats and that occur without any physical acts of interference or obstacle may be punishable as a contempt of court if the verbal abuse involves the courts or as disorderly conduct (see Chapter 17).

Physical interference with public servants attempting to enforce court decrees or judgments may make one criminally responsible for this offense. However, it is not intended to cover problems that arise between persons involved in civil legal actions after a judgment is made. Depending on the facts of the case, disputes between civil litigants could result in criminal responsibility for other offenses such as tampering with a witness or informant, retaliation against a witness or informant, or statutes involving civil rights offenses and contempt of court.

There is a defense to prosecution of this offense when the government function is both (1) unlawful and (2) conducted by a public servant who was not acting in good faith. Physical resistance to an arrest, search, or some other function of government is generally not justifiable, and disputes as to the legality of such government action should ordinarily be taken to the courts. The legal safeguards in the Fourth, Fifth, and Fourteenth Amendments, as well as the development of statutory remedies, now afford the victim of an illegal arrest or search several alternatives to physical resistance. The victim should resort to such legal means except in the rare circumstance where a public servant is acting not only illegally but in evident bad faith. As a practical matter, bad faith will seldom be supported if it is shown that the officer was acting to carry out a warrant or other judicial process. However, bad faith may be shown by proof that the officer harbored a personal bias against the defendant or that he clearly exceeded the limits of his rightful authority, such as by using unreasonable force or ransacking premises in the course of a search. Once the defense is properly raised by the evidence, the prosecution bears the burden of disproving it beyond a reasonable doubt, since it is not an affirmative defense.

Impersonating an Official

Impersonation of federal or state officials is a crime because such impersonation harms the effective functioning of the federal or state governments by creating suspicion of official credentials. As stated by the Supreme Court, the purpose of an impersonation statute is "not merely to protect innocent persons from actual loss through reliance on false assumptions of Federal authority, but to maintain the general good repute and dignity of the service itself."[1]

A person may be guilty of an offense if he pretends to be a public servant or a foreign official and to exercise that person's authority. Thus, the offense has two essential elements: (1) the defendant must pretend to be a public servant or a foreign official, and (2) he must pretend to exercise the authority of the impersonated public servant or official.

Once the actor has pretended to be a public servant or foreign official, the crime becomes complete when he engages in any conduct that is an exercise of that person's authority. It is not necessary for the conduct to be successful—only for it to occur. For instance, a person who pretends to be an FBI agent and then flashes a badge to try to gain access to premises violates the statute by showing the badge after pretending to be an agent. It does not matter whether he actually succeeds in gaining entrance.

Some conduct or action besides the impersonation itself is thus required for one to be criminally responsible for this offense. The test of this independent conduct or action is whether or not it is an exercise of the authority, capacity, or duty of the person impersonated. Acts that have been held to satisfy this requirement include attempting to elicit information from one person concerning the whereabouts of another, wearing firearms, and attempting to stay an execution. The act or conduct involved must to some extent be apart from the pretense itself. For example, merely stating that one is a police officer would be insufficient. However, making that statement and then entering premises in order to search or to effect an arrest would constitute this offense.

The classes of persons covered are "public servants" and "foreign officials." The former term is intended to cover all conceivable impersonations that are injurious to the authority or credibility of official credentials. The definition is also designed to cover the situation of one public servant impersonating another. It should be noted that the definition of "public servants" includes persons who act "for or on behalf of a government." The term "government" is also specifically defined to include a government agency, which in turn is defined to include a department, commission, administration, authority, board, bureau, and so on.

The term "foreign official" is defined to mean a "foreign dignitary" or a person of foreign nationality "duly notified to the United States as an officer or employee of a foreign power," which includes a government or an "international organization" such as the United Nations or the Organization of American States.

The conduct of this offense is pretending to be a public servant or a foreign official and to exercise that person's authority. It must be proved that the offender was at least "knowing," that he was aware that he was pretending to be a public servant or a foreign official and was aware that he was pretending to exercise the authority of such a person. Thus, one would not bear criminal responsibility for this offense by pretending to be a person who happened to be a public servant or foreign official if one was not aware of that person's status. It is not a defense to prosecution for this offense that the impersonated person did not actually have the pretended authority or could not legally or otherwise have had it.

Obstructions of Law Enforcement

Obstructions of law enforcement include hindering law enforcement, bail jumping, escape, and flight to avoid prosecution or appearance as a witness. The common element in these offenses is that obstruction of law enforcement efforts results from the prohibited conduct.

Hindering Law Enforcement

Hindering law enforcement consists of conduct that helps others either to avoid apprehension or prosecution or to profit from the fruits of their crimes. Statutes defining this offense also prohibit, as a form of an accessory offense, aiding the consummation of a crime. The offense is intended to include acts that do not amount to obstruction of justice or receipt of stolen property as such, but instead involve assisting other persons in carrying out an unlawful project or otherwise profiting from a crime. Examples of the conduct prohibited by this offense are acting as a custodian for the proceeds of a theft or robbery until the culprits can meet and split them up, fencing marked ransom money, and helping a thief collect a reward for the return of stolen property. Other prohibited conduct includes activities of so-called frontmen for organized criminals who invest illegally obtained funds in legitimate businesses and thus "launder" the fruits of crime.

This offense may be divided into two parts covering different types of acts that obstruct law enforcement efforts. The first forbids conduct that hinders efforts to apprehend and punish another offender. The second punishes conduct that aids another in hiding, disguising, or converting the proceeds of a crime or otherwise profiting from a crime of another. In each case, the offense involves conduct that takes place after an offense has been committed by another person or after acts that have given rise to criminal charges.

Hindering efforts to apprehend and punish offenders.

The hindering offense goes beyond the general accessory-after-the-fact statutes (see Chapter 15) by imposing criminal responsibility regardless of whether the initially planned offense was actually committed. The offense is perpetrated by assisting another person, knowing that he has committed a crime or is charged with or being sought for a crime. Criminal liability for such obstructive efforts does not depend on whether the other person is ever found guilty. Thus, even if the other person is later acquitted or if the charges against him are dropped, the person who interferes with law enforcement efforts in order to aid him can still be prosecuted.

The offender must know that his conduct interferes with, hinders, delays, or prevents the discovery, apprehension, prosecution, conviction, or punishment of another for a crime. It is an existing circumstance that the person the offender assists has committed a crime or is charged with or being sought for a crime, but the offender must have been aware of this fact in order to bear criminal responsibility for hindering efforts to apprehend him.

Four prohibited acts reflect the types of conduct that have consistently been recognized and prosecuted as hindering law enforcement. The first such act is harboring the other person or concealing him or his identity. This conduct takes place when the offender states falsely that he does not have a person of the fugitive's name staying with him or when the offender falsely identifies the fugitive to a law enforcement officer, thus concealing the fugitive's true identity. Harboring the other person and concealing him or his identity constitute conduct, and the state of mind that must be proved is at least "knowing"; the defendant must be shown to have been aware of the nature of his actions.

A second prohibited act is providing the other person with a weapon, money, transportation, disguise, or other means of avoiding or minimizing the risk of discovery or apprehension. These are the usual methods by which one actively aids a person fleeing from the law. The list is not all-inclusive, and any assistance is covered if it consists of a means of avoiding either discovery or apprehension. Providing a fugitive with money may enable him to hide or escape. Disguise includes changing a person's physical characteristics (such as surgical alteration of facial appearance or fingerprints) to prevent apprehension. In any case, the offender must have an awareness that he is supplying something.

A third prohibited act is warning the other person that he is about to be discovered or apprehended. This, too, is a clear act of interference with law enforcement. An exception is made, however, for warnings made for the purpose of deterring unlawful conduct. Thus, it is an affirmative defense to a prosecution of this offense that the warning was made solely in an effort to make the other person comply with the law. Because the defense is an affirmative one, the defendant bears the burden of proving the elements of it. The conduct in this offense is warning of impending discovery or apprehension, and the offender must be shown to have been at least "knowing."

A fourth prohibited act is altering, destroying, mutilating, concealing, or removing a record, document, or other object. It is not a defense that the record, document, or other object would have been legally privileged or would have been inadmissible in evidence. Efforts to alter, hide, or destroy evidence are obvious ways to interfere with law enforcement efforts and to obstruct discovery or apprehension of offenders. This conduct parallels a similar offense known as "tampering with physical evidence" (to be discussed later), which deals with similar acts involving a pending or contemplated official proceeding. The conduct in this offense is altering, destroying, mutilating, concealing, or removing, and the state of mind required is "knowing." The other elements are existing circumstances and the culpability level is "reckless." A minority of states have exempted from this offense close relatives who harbor, conceal, or otherwise aid an offender—such as parents, spouses, and children. Such a defense creates problems in determining just what relatives should be covered and makes it possible for people to escape prosecution even if they may have motives not arising solely from family relationships.

Aiding Consummation of a Crime.

The second part of the offense of hindering law enforcement is aiding consummation of a crime. The acts that fall under this part are somewhat like acts that might be committed by accessories—disposing of marked ransom bills, hiding stolen money—rather than preventing enforcement of the law against another offender. "Hindering" offenses and "aiding consummation" offenses might overlap if the act of hiding the proceeds of a crime also constitutes suppression of evidence. Yet they do not always overlap. For example, concealment or conversion may occur after conviction of the other offender.

The basic culpability level for aiding consummation of a crime is "knowing." The nature of this offense, prohibiting supportive conduct, requires that the prohibited acts be done to aid another person. Accordingly, the thief who invests the fruits of his own crime in a business cannot be charged under this section. Specifically, the conduct prohibited is secreting, disguising, or converting the proceeds of a crime or otherwise profiting from a crime. Secreting, disguising, and converting can be purely accessory acts with no specific profit to the actor. The offense covers all acts by which the person assisted receives some gain from the underlying criminal conduct. There is no need for the actor to profit personally, although he generally would. *Proceeds* include any kind of gain from a crime—money, tangible property, intangible property, or any form of investment.

Bail Jumping.

The purpose of statutes regarding bail jumping is to deter those who would obstruct law enforcement by failing to appear for trial or other judicial appearances and to punish those who fail to appear. A federal bail jumping statute was first enacted in 1954 to fill the void in the criminal law highlighted by the conduct of fleeing fugitives who were leaders of the Communist Party. The only available penalties before the statute was enacted were forfeiture of money and contempt proceedings. Defendants were therefore able to buy their freedom by giving up the bonds they had posted and taking the risk that they could go unapprehended. Even if apprehended, many defendants could hide for so long that the government's case, especially for major offenses, grew weak because of the unavailability of witnesses, memory lapses, and so on. Defendants would then be subject only to the criminal contempt charge, the sentence for which was usually much less than for the original offense.

A person may be guilty of an offense if, after having been released on bail, he (1) fails to appear before a court as required by the conditions of his release or (2) fails to surrender to serve a sentence as specified by a court order. The conduct element is an omission; that is, the offender "fails to appear" or "fails to surrender." The state of mind that must be proved is at least "knowing"; the offender must be shown to have been aware of the nature of his conduct. The remaining elements are all existing circumstances for which the state of mind to be established is at least "reckless."

Often a defendant realizes that he may have to appear but simply disappears, moves and fails to leave a forwarding address, fails to keep in touch with his attorney, or does not respond to notices. When later apprehended, he defends himself on grounds that he was out of town on the designated appearance date, that he never received any notice, or the like. Under the "reckless" standard, the defendant could be convicted for bail jumping if the prosecution showed that he was aware that he might have to appear but disregarded the risk. Stated otherwise, the risk involved is that an appearance date will be set and that the defendant will fail to appear. Conduct involving a failure to keep in contact with the situation amounts to a conscious disregard that an appearance date will come and pass. A person released on bail can be charged with a serious deviation from the standard of conduct that applies to the ordinary person when he fails to keep in touch with the status of his case or places himself out of reach of the authorities and/or his attorney.

Escape

Escape is a form of obstruction of a government function. Escape is removal from custody beginning at the time of arrest (or surrender) and continuing until release on bail, personal recognizance, probation, or parole, or until full, unconditional release. As the revisers of the New York Penal Law observed, in declining to define "escape" more specifically, the word has long been used in its ordinary, accepted meaning and connotes an unauthorized voluntary departure from or substantial severance of official control.

One may commit this offense by failing to return to official detention following temporary leave granted for a specified purpose or a limited period. Therefore, temporary leaves such as furloughs, release with or without guards to testify in court, to attend a funeral, or to visit a sick family member, are covered by the wording of escape statutes.

The culpability level for escape is "knowing." The remaining elements of the offense, such as "official detention following temporary leave," are existing circumstances, and the culpability level is "reckless." Thus, a person is guilty of an offense if (1) he is reckless as to the fact that he is subject to official detention (that is, he is aware that he may be in official detention—for example, under arrest or in custody—but disregards the risk that he is in fact in official detention) and (2) knowingly leaves the detention area or breaks from custody.

"Official detention" includes: (1) detention by a public servant, or under the direction of a public servant, following arrest; following surrender in lieu of arrest; following a charge or conviction of an offense, or an allegation or findings of juvenile delinquency; following commitment as a material witness; following civil commitment in lieu of criminal proceedings or pending resumption of criminal proceedings being held in abeyance; or pending extradition, deportation, or exclusion; or (2) custody by a public servant for purposes incident to the foregoing, including transportation, medical diagnosis or treatment, court appearances, work, and recreation; "official detention" does not include supervision or other restrictions (other than custody during specified hours or days) after release pending trial or appeal; after release on probation; after release on parole; or after release following a finding of juvenile delinquency.

The definition of escape excludes restrictions imposed as conditions of release under the Federal Bail Reform Act of 1966 unless the condition requires a return to custody after specified hours of release. Thus, a person who is released on bail to work during the day and who is required to return to a detention facility at night violates the escape statute if he fails to return. On the other hand, violations of other conditions, including failure to obey a third-party custody order, do not amount to escape. Failure to appear as required after release on bail is bail jumping and not escape. Second, escape does not apply to supervision of a person on parole or probation. The concept of parole or probation is release under supervision—it is not custody even if, as an incident of either method of release, the person is required to live in a community treatment facility. Third, the definition of escape excludes restrictions imposed on a juvenile delinquent after specified hours of release from custody.

It may be an affirmative defense to escape under limited circumstances that the arrest was illegal or that the committing or detaining authority lacked jurisdiction. Lawfulness of the arrest can be challenged if the escape is from an arresting officer, but not if it is from a detention facility. Under the prevailing rule, the legality of the detention may be challenged if three factors coincide: (1) the escape is not from any facility used for official detention; (2) the escape does not involve a substantial risk of harm to the person or property of another; and (3) the official detention was not in good faith. In some states, the lawfulness of an arresting officer's acts is the only test. However, an escape that creates any substantial risk of injury to the officer or another will not be tolerated, generally, since the place to test the lawfulness of the arrest is in the courts and not the streets. It should be noted that an escape from an arresting officer and the application of this affirmative defense can occur only after the person has first been taken into custody and subsequently acts to escape. Resisting arrest is a separate offense.

Flight to Avoid Prosecution or Appearance as a Witness

Unlawful flight to avoid prosecution or appearance as a witness is an offense. This offense serves as a basis for prosecuting fugitives from justice, and for the prosecution of accessories after the fact who hinder law enforcement by harboring or concealing a fugitive from justice. Federal law authorizes the federal government to assist in the location and apprehension of fugitives from state or local law enforcement authorities who have fled across state lines. The federal government, with national law enforcement authority and resources, is uniquely able to afford fugitive apprehension assistance to the states and help remove the major threat to the safety of citizens in other states posed by fugitives in interstate flight.

A person is guilty of a federal offense if he leaves a state or local jurisdiction with intent to avoid (1) criminal prosecution, or official detention after conviction, for an attempt to commit, a conspiracy to commit, or the commission of a state or local felony in that jurisdiction; (2) appearing as a witness, giving testimony, or producing a record, document, or other object in an official proceeding in which a state or local felony in that jurisdiction is charged or being investigated; or (3) contempt proceedings, or criminal prosecution, or official detention after conviction for failure to appear as a witness, to give testimony, or to produce a record, document, or other object in an official proceeding in which a state or local felony in that jurisdiction is charged or being investigated.

The conduct element is leaving a jurisdiction, and the state of mind that must be proved is at least "knowing"; the defendant must be shown to have been aware of the nature of his actions.

The element that the jurisdiction is state or local is an existing circumstance for which the state of mind to be shown is at least "reckless"—that is, the defendant must have been aware of but disregarded the risk that the circumstance existed.

The prosecution must establish that the defendant knew he was fleeing or leaving and, in the course of doing so, had an intent to avoid circumstances such as criminal prosecution, official detention after conviction, appearing as a witness, giving testimony, producing information, or appearing in contempt proceedings.

It is not a defense to a prosecution of this offense that the testimony or the record document or other object would have been legally privileged or would have been inadmissible in evidence. Once again, as in the offense of hindering law enforcement, the place to test these issues is the courtroom.

Obstructions of Justice

Obstructions of justice include such offenses as witness bribery, corrupting a witness or informant, tampering with a witness or informant, retaliating against a witness or informant, tampering with physical evidence, improperly influencing a juror, monitoring jury deliberations, and demonstrating to influence a judicial proceeding.

Witness Bribery

It is an offense for a person knowingly to offer, give, or agree to give to another person, or to solicit, demand, accept, or agree to accept from another person, anything of value in return for an agreement or understanding that the testimony of the recipient will be influenced in an official proceeding. Common terms such as "anything of value," "in return for an agreement or understanding," and "will be influenced" have been explained in conjunction with bribery and should be reviewed again now.

The emphasis in bribing or corrupting a witness is not on the fact that an official proceeding is pending. Rather, the focus is on the defendant's conduct in influencing or seeking to influence another's testimony in an official proceeding even if it is not yet instituted. It is not necessary to show that the person being influenced actually intended to testify, but only that the defendant believed he intended to testify.

The conduct of this offense is offering, giving, or agreeing to give something to another person, or soliciting, demanding, accepting, or agreeing to accept something from another person. The applicable culpability is "knowing," requiring proof that the defendant was aware that he was offering or soliciting something.

The elements that what is offered or solicited is "anything of value," and that the offer or solicitation is "in return for an agreement or understanding that the testimony of the recipient will be influenced in an official proceeding" are existing circumstances. The applicable state of mind that must be proved is "reckless"; the defendant must have been aware of but must have disregarded the risk that the circumstances existed, and his disregard must have constituted a gross deviation from the standard of care a reasonable person would exercise in such a situation.

The term "anything of value" does not include legitimate payments to witnesses for travel and subsistence expenses or a reasonable fee for the preparation of an expert's opinion.

It is not a defense to a prosecution that (1) an official proceeding was not pending or about to be instituted or (2) the defendant also committed or attempted to commit by the same conduct extortion, blackmail, or theft. Most courts have held that bribery and extortion are mutually exclusive crimes.

Corrupting a Witness or Informant

A person may be guilty of an offense if he offers, gives, or agrees to give to another person, or solicits, demands, accepts, or agrees to accept from another person, anything of value so as to accomplish any of the prohibited acts discussed in conjunction with witness or informant tampering.

The conduct is offering, giving, or agreeing to give anything to another person, or soliciting, demanding, accepting, or agreeing to accept anything from another person. The applicable state of mind that must be proved is "knowing." The elements that what is offered, given, demanded, and so on is "anything of value" and that the proceeding involved is an "official proceeding" are existing circumstances, the applicable state of mind for which is "reckless."

As with the offense of bribing a witness, the term "anything of value" does not extend to legitimate payments to witnesses for travel and subsistence expenses or to a reasonable fee for the preparation of an expert's opinion; nor does it extend to the situation where two co-defendants agree between themselves to assert their respective privilege against self-incrimination and not take the stand. Although it could be argued that they are exchanging something of value for or because of withholding testimony, a criminal statute should not interfere in this decision, and that is not an intended result of this statute.

Tampering with a Witness or Informant

A person may be guilty of an offense if he knowingly uses "force, threat, intimidation, or deception" with intent to accomplish any of the following prohibited purposes: (1) to influence the testimony of another person in an official proceeding; (2) to cause or induce another person to (a) withhold testimony or a record, document, or any other object from an official proceeding, whether or not the person would be legally privileged to do so, and regardless of its admissibility in evidence, (b) tamper with physical evidence, (c) evade legal process summoning him to appear as a witness, or to produce an object, in an official proceeding, or (d) be absent from an official proceeding to which he has been summoned by legal process; or (3) to hinder, delay, or prevent the communication of information relating to an offense or possible offense to a law enforcement officer.

This offense covers conduct that is the product of the inventive criminal mind and that also obstructs justice, such as: (1) a conspirator arranging to have an unnecessary operation in order to cause a mistrial in an ongoing case in which he was a defendant; (2) persons plying the illiterate administrator of an estate with liquor and obtaining documents from him that they then use in an effort to have a civil case dismissed; (3) the defendant planting an illegal bottle of liquor on the victim's premises in order to discredit the victim, who was planning to be a witness against the defendant in a separate case.

The conduct is using force, threat, intimidation, or deception. The culpability element for the conduct is "knowing," thus requiring proof that the offender was aware of the nature of his conduct. The elements of that conduct are as follows: that the prohibited forms of conduct were intended to influence the testimony of another person; cause or induce another person to withhold testimony, tamper with physical evidence, evade legal process summoning him to testify, or be absent from a proceeding to which he has been summoned; or to hinder, delay, or prevent the communication of information relating to an offense to a law enforcement officer all state the alternative motives or purposes of the defendant that must be proved. The element that the proceeding involved is an "official proceeding" is an existing circumstance in regard to which the state of mind that must be demonstrated is at least "reckless"; the offender must have been aware of but disregarded the risk that the proceeding was an official one.

If a person is accused of using a threat to influence another's testimony in an official proceeding, he may put forth an affirmative defense that the threat was of lawful conduct and that the defendant's sole intention was to compel or induce the other person to testify truthfully. This defense is intended primarily to avoid the possibility that a prosecutor, judge, or presiding officer would violate the law by threatening to prosecute a witness for perjury or false swearing if he testified falsely. Conceivably, it could also extend to a situation in which a person threatened to institute legal action to recover a debt unless another person testified truthfully. Since the defense is affirmative, the defendant has the burden of proving his case.

Retaliating against a Witness or Informant

Federal law bars retaliation against the person or property of witnesses and informants in official proceedings and criminal investigations. A person may be guilty of an offense if he either (1) causes bodily injury to or damages the property of another person or (2) improperly subjects another person to economic loss or injury to his business or profession because of (*a*) any testimony given, or any record, document, or other object produced, by a witness in an official proceeding, or (*b*) any information relating to an offense or possible offense given by a person to a law enforcement officer.

The types of injuries covered include harm to both person and property. Forms of retaliation such as discharging a person from his job because of his testimony or otherwise damaging him in his business or profession (by blacklisting, for example) are covered. The term "improperly" is designed to exclude such lawful actions as failing to vote for a candidate because of his testimony or failing to patronize the business establishment of a person because of information he gave to a law enforcement officer.

The conduct of this offense is (1) causing bodily injury to or damaging the property of another person or (2) improperly subjecting another person to economic loss or injury. The culpability level needed to prove the offense is at least "knowing." The elements that the conduct causes bodily injury to or damages the property of another person are results of conduct, and the state of mind that must be shown is at least "reckless." The element that the economic loss or injury was to a person's business or profession is an existing circumstance with regard to which the minimum culpability standard also is "reckless." It must also be proved that the offender's conduct was motivated by a desire for retaliation.

Tampering with Physical Evidence

One may be guilty of an offense if he alters, destroys, mutilates, conceals, or removes a record, document, or other object with intent to damage it or make it unavailable for use in an official proceeding. Proof of a specific intent is required because destruction of records can often be an ambiguous act, and criminal penalties should not be imposed except on proof that the actor's purpose was to thwart a proceeding. The focus of statutes regarding this offense is the intent to impair the ultimate availability of the object for use in a proceeding. Thus, if a person destroyed records to avoid execution of a search warrant or other process, he would almost certainly be criminally responsible for tampering with physical evidence, since his intent would normally have been extended to the prevention of the records from being used in a later proceeding. Such acts might also consitute obstructing a government function by physical interference.

The conduct of this offense is altering, destroying, mutilating, concealing, or removing records, documents, or other objects. The state of mind that must be proved is at least "knowing"; it must be shown that the offender was aware that he was tampering with an object. The element that the conduct be done with an intent to damage the object or make it unavailable for use in a proceeding sets forth the particular purpose that must be shown to have accompanied the conduct. The fact that the proceeding was an "official" one is an existing circumstance for which the applicable mental state is "reckless"; the offender must have been aware of but disregarded the risk that the proceeding to which his acts related was official. It is not a defense that an official proceeding was not pending or about to be instituted, or that the record, document, or other object would have been legally privileged or inadmissible in evidence.

Improperly Influencing a Juror

It is an offense for a person to communicate in any way with a juror, or a member of the juror's immediate family, with intent to influence improperly the official action of the juror. This offense was known as embracery at common law, and consisted of any offers, promises, threats or similarly coercive conduct.

This offense contains four basic features: First, in most jurisdictions, any communication may constitute the offense, whether the communication is written or oral. In some states, however, the communication must be written. The reason for the limitation is that it is difficult to prove criminal oral communications. Nevertheless, it seems probable that a juror could be influenced by oral as well as written communications (or any other form of communication such as hand signals or gestures). Second, the bar on communication is extended to the immediate family of the juror. Members of a juror's immediate family include as a rule the juror's spouse, children, parents, and siblings, and may include uncles, aunts, nieces, nephews, grandparents and grandchildren as well. Third, the term "juror" includes both grand and petit jurors and those persons who have been "selected or summoned to attend" as prospective jurors. Fourth, the communication must be made with intent to influence the official action of a juror "improperly." Proper communications such as requests to grand juries for appearances are permissible, as are other clearly proper communications such as those involving the court, attorneys, and others who counsel the jurors as to their functions and duties. Thus, the arguments of counsel and the instructions of the court, although they are communications with intent to influence the official actions of jurors, do not constitute offenses. This exclusion from coverage because of lack of intent to influence improperly would apply normally even if the argument of counsel was overzealous and objectionable, or if the judge's instructions were erroneous or prejudicial.

The term "communicate" would probably not encompass such acts as shadowing a juror without contacting or approaching him. However, such acts might well constitute criminal contempt or an obstruction offense.

The conduct in this offense is communicating in any way, and the applicable culpability level for the conduct is "knowing." This requires proof that the offender was at least aware that he was communicating. The element of intent improperly to influence the official action of the juror states the purpose for which the conduct must be done. However, the particular motive or reason behind the defendant's intent need not be shown.

The elements that the communication was with a juror or a member of a juror's immediate family are existing circumstances for which the applicable state of mind is at least "reckless." The offender must be proven to have been aware of and disregarded the risk that the person with whom he was communicating was a juror or a member of the immediate family of a juror. Ordinarily, in view of the required intent to influence a juror's official action, the offender will know that a person is a juror when he communicates with such a person. However, this offense permits conviction, for example, if a defendant communicates with a juror's brother with the intent to influence improperly the juror's official action but does not know (although he is conscious of the risk) that the brother is a member of the juror's immediate family.

Monitoring Jury Deliberations

A person is guilty of an offense if he intentionally (1) records the proceedings of a grand or petit jury while the jury is deliberating or voting or (2) listens to or observes the proceedings of a grand or petit jury of which he is not a member while the jury is deliberating or voting. The offense of recording the proceedings may be committed even by a member of the jury itself.

The conduct of this offense is recording, listening to, or observing the proceedings of a grand or petit jury. The culpability standard is "intentional," requiring proof that it was the offender's conscious desire to engage in the conduct. The element "while the jury is deliberating or voting" is an existing circumstance, for which the state of mind that must be shown is at least "reckless." It must be shown that the offender was aware of the risk that the jury was deliberating or voting, but disregarded that risk.

It is a defense to a prosecution for recording the proceedings of a jury that the actor was a member of the jury that was deliberating or voting and that he was taking notes in connection with, and solely for the purpose of helping himself perform, his official duties. The provision is a defense rather than an affirmative defense. Therefore, on the introduction of sufficient proof to raise the issue, the prosecution must prove beyond a reasonable doubt that the elements of the defense were not established—that is, that the actor did not take notes solely to facilitate the performance of his official duties.

Demonstrating to Influence a Judicial Proceeding

Statutes making it an offense to demonstrate to influence a judicial proceeding are intended to protect judicial proceedings from the influence of demonstrations and to avoid the appearance that judicial determinations are a product of this form of intimidation. The Supreme Court in *Cox* v. *Louisiana* (1965)[2] upheld a state statute of this kind, saying that it properly furthered the state's legitimate interest in protecting its judicial system from pressures such as picketing near a courthouse. The court also held that the statute regulated *conduct* as distinguished from pure speech so that it could not be said to infringe on the First Amendment rights of free speech and assembly.

A person may be guilty of an offense if, with intent to influence another person in the discharge of his duties in a judicial proceeding, he pickets, parades, displays a sign, uses a sound-amplifying device, or otherwise engages in a demonstration either in, on the grounds of, or (after due notice to disperse has been given) within a specified distance of (1) a building housing a court or (2) a building occupied or used by such other person. The distance varies among different jurisdictions, but usually is 100-300 feet.

Conduct intended to influence any person, including attorneys and other court officers in addition to judges, jurors, or witnesses, with intent to influence their actions in official judicial proceedings may constitute this offense. The conduct is picketing, parading, displaying a sign, using a sound-amplifying device, or otherwise engaging in a demonstration. The state of mind that must be proved is at least "knowing." The actor must have been aware that he was performing the conduct described. The element "with intent to influence another person in the discharge of his duties in a judicial proceeding" states the purpose for which the conduct must be shown to have been performed. The remaining elements—that the demonstration or other conduct occurred in, or on the grounds of, or (after notice was given to disperse) within a specified distance of (1) a building housing a court or (2) a building occupied or used by such other person—are existing circumstances. The state of mind that must be proved as to those existing circumstances is at least "reckless," that the offender was aware of but disregarded the risk that the circumstances existed.

Criminal Contempt Offenses

In the law there are two types of contempts—civic and criminal. This book deals only with criminal contempt, and the availability of simultaneous or alternative civil contempt proceedings is not discussed. The distinction between the two forms of contempt has been held to depend on the character and purpose of the punishment or sanction. If the sanction is designed to produce compliance with a court's order or decree, the contempt is considered civil. If, on the other hand, the sanction is punitive and is intended to reinforce the authority of the court, the contempt is criminal. It should be noted that a fine or imprisonment may be used as sanctions for either civil or criminal contempt.

A unique feature of the criminal contempt offense is that, regardless of the punishment imposed, the Fifth Amendment right to indictment by a grand jury does not apply.[3] Although an indictment is a permissible means of instituting a criminal contempt prosecution, the history and purpose of the offense have been held to support the conclusion that the court itself may institute proceedings to punish the contempt on proper notice.

Similarly, since the contempt offense is against the authority of the court, it has been held that the double jeopardy clause of the Fifth Amendment does not prohibit prosecution for contempt *and* another substantive offense directly arising out of the same conduct.[4]

A person may be guilty of contempt if he: (1) misbehaves in the presence of a court or so nearby as to obstruct the administration of justice; (2) disobeys or resists a writ, process, order, rule, decree or command of a court; or (3) as an officer of a court, misbehaves in an official transaction.

When the conduct element is disobeying or resisting a writ, process, order, rule, decree, or command of a court, the applicable state of mind is "knowing." The offender must be aware that he is disobeying or resisting a court writ process. This standard is consistent with case law in which it has been held that, while knowledge of the order and a deliberate disobedience or resistance of it are essential elements, it need not be proved that the offender has an evil intent.

When the conduct element is misbehaving or being disobedient, the state of mind that applies is "knowing." The offender must be aware that he is misbehaving or being disobedient. The elements "in the presence of the court" or "nearby" are existing circumstances, for which the applicable culpability level is at least "reckless." It must be proven that the offender was aware of but disregarded the risk that the misbehavior was in the court's presence or near it. Both "presence" and "nearness" have been held to require an act in the "vicinity" of the court. This element of geographical proximity is designed to distinguish between contempt and obstruction of justice offenses. The element "so . . . as to obstruct the administration of justice" is a result of conduct, and the state of mind that must be proved is "reckless." The prosecution must show the offender's awareness but disregard of the risk that the conduct caused the administration of justice to be obstructed and that the risk was such that its disregard constituted a serious deviation from the care that a reasonable person would exercise in the circumstances.

One may misbehave in the presence of a court in a number of ways. These include being noisy or participating in violent or disruptive behavior in or near a courtroom, or in any other way disturbing court proceedings. Picketing, parading, or demonstrating near a courthouse or building occupied by a judge, juror, witness, or court officer with intent to obstruct the administration of justice may constitute criminal contempt. Similarly, one who blocks passage into or out of a government building knowing that he is impeding court proceedings may be responsible for criminal contempt.

Criminal contempt may be committed when a person refuses to testify as ordered by a court or refuses to produce information after having been ordered to do so by a court, by Congress, or by a state legislature. The testimony or information that is ordered must be pertinent to the subject matter under inquiry in the official proceeding before which the testimony or information is summoned. It is an affirmative defense that the person who refuses to testify or to produce information that has been ordered is legally privileged to do so. Thus, one may be legally privileged not to testify against himself if his testimony will tend to incriminate him, since this privilege against self-incrimination is guaranteed under the Fifth Amendment to the Constitution. Similarly, the President of the United States and certain of his subordinates may be legally privileged to refuse to disclose information that relates to the formulation of official government policy, particularly foreign policy, under the doctrine of executive privilege. In addition, an attorney may sometimes invoke the attorney-client privilege and refuse to testify or to produce information that would breach a confidence that has been communicated to him by a client.

Evasive answers, such as "I don't know" or "I don't remember," when the witness is capable of concrete answers, are not viewed as a refusal to answer. Such conduct can be punished as perjury or as a false swearing, depending on whether the evasive answer was material and whether or not it was given under oath. In order to insure the possibility of prosecution for perjury or false swearing, an official or agency may always take the precaution of having the witness placed under oath.

Criminal contempt may be committed away from the presence of a court or a judge. This conduct may consist of a person's failure to appear as a witness in court after having been properly served with a court order directing him to appear and be sworn in as a witness at a specified time and place. This offense may be committed when a court order is disobeyed, resisted, or in some other way not honored. Thus, criminal contempt may occur when a temporary restraining order or a preliminary injunction has been issued by a court and served on the person or persons whose activities are to be enjoined, and the person or persons continue to engage in the prohibited activities.

In the case of a person's refusal to give verbal testimony, he cannot be made criminally responsible for contempt unless he has been advised first by the court that his refusal to respond to a question might subject him to criminal prosecution. No warning of the consequences is required, however, for a failure to produce a record, document, or other object. An order to produce physical objects or records almost always arises through the issuance of a subpoena, giving a person time for reflection, consultation with an attorney, and, often, judicial review on a motion to quash. In these circumstances, it is reasonable to require persons to act at their peril in assessing the validity of any defenses or affirmative defenses on which they later rely for failing to produce the record or object demanded. On the other hand, the situation of the witness who must suddenly make an on-the-spot decision whether to respond to a question in an official proceeding is quite different, and such persons cannot be criminally responsible for contempt for refusal to respond until ordered to do so by a judge.

Validity of the order is not an element of the offense, unless the order is transparently unlawful. Similarly, the fact that a person may have a privilege to refuse to testify or produce information will not excuse his failure to comply with an order to *appear* before the summoning body.

CHAPTER 18

Public Health and Safety Offenses

A number of public welfare offenses are designed to protect the health and safety of the public. The health and safety of human beings is dependant upon the health and safety of other living things such as animals and flora that provide man's food chain. The sum total of the public health and safety offenses within any state are far too numerous even to list, much less to discuss. However, a few examples have been selected as being representative of this class of crimes. These offenses include abortion; building, construction, and fire codes; drug offenses; environmental offenses; and explosives and firearms offenses.

Abortion

Abortion is the termination of human embryonic or fetal life. An abortion may occur spontaneously (referred to as a miscar-

315

riage), or it may be induced therapeutically or by accidental trauma. Only therapeutical abortions (those induced intentionally in order to terminate an unwanted pregnancy) have been criminalized.

At common law, it was not an offense to terminate a pregnancy prior to quickening, which signifies the first recognizable movement of the fetus in the womb and which occurs normally between the sixteenth and eighteenth week of pregnancy. It is still disputed whether abortion of a quick fetus was a felony or any crime at common law. The predominant view is that abortion of a quick fetus was at most a non-felonious offense at common law, and indeed such an abortion was not a criminal offense anywhere in the United States before 1821. During the nineteenth century, many states enacted legislation to criminalize therapeutic abortions. The 1828 New York law, which served as a model for abortion laws of other states at that time, made abortion of an unquickened fetus a misdemeanor but abortion of a quick fetus a felony punishable as second-degree manslaughter.

In this century, punishments for abortion were relaxed but therapeutic abortion remained a criminal offense in most states until very recently, except when justified to preserve the mother's life or health. A few states justified abortion to prevent the birth of a seriously deformed child. Usually, only the attending physician or lay abortionist was prosecuted for the crime of abortion, but the pregnant woman was prosecuted as a conspirator on some occasions.

In the case of *Roe v. Wade* (1973),[1] the U.S. Supreme Court held that a woman's right of personal privacy includes the privilege to terminate an unwanted pregnancy, but that this privilege is *qualified* and not absolute. As such, the abortion decision must be considered against legitimate state interests in protecting prenatal life as well as the health of the pregnant woman. The Supreme Court went on to characterize two "compelling points" that occur during pregnancy and which signify the beginning of new state interests. Following the end of the third month of pregnancy, a state if it chooses may regulate abortion procedures in ways that are reasonably related to maternal health. Following fetal viability (the point at which a fetus is presumably capable of a meaningful life outside the mother's womb, usually estimated to occur after the end of the sixth month of pregnancy), a state if it chooses may regulate and even prohibit abortion except where necessary to preserve the mother's life or health, in order to promote the "potentiality of human life." However, prior to approximately the end of the third month of pregnancy, the abortion decision is the woman's own and its execution must be left to the medical judgment of the pregnant woman's attending physician.

Following the *Roe* decision, many states revised their abortion statutes and now prohibit therapeutical abortions following fetal viability except when necessary to preserve the mother's life or health. It is important to note that in all states an abortion may be performed legally only by a duly licensed physician. While illegal abortion may be punished as a felony today, this offense is separate from and less serious than the criminal homicide offenses. In some states it is still possible for a person to bear criminal responsibility for murder under the felony-murder rule (see Chapter 8) if he performs an illegal abortion feloniously and the *mother* dies. In practice, the felony-murder rule is likely to be implemented only when the abortionist is not a duly licensed physician.

A separate issue exists as to the fate of an aborted fetus which survives the abortion procedures. In a recent Massachusetts case the physician, prosecuted for murder after destroying a fetus which the evidence suggested had been born alive but left to die, argued that a legal abortion presumes the death of the fetus. His conviction was reversed on other grounds. While the Supreme Court has stated that an unborn fetus is not a person, that Court has not yet informed the American public whether an aborted fetus which remains alive is a person. Logic would dictate that by remaining alive an aborted fetus proves its viability, becomes a person, and cannot legally be killed or be abandoned to die from neglect.

The conduct required for abortion consists of the termination of a human pregnancy by any artificial means, in violation of applicable state laws. The state of mind that must be proved is at least "knowing." The defendant must have been aware of the nature of his actions. Thus, a physician who induces an abortion accidentally while conducting tests on a pregnant woman would not bear criminal responsibility for abortion.

Building, Construction, and Fire Codes

Every state and, in addition, most counties and municipalities have statutes or ordinances which regulate the construction and maintenance of buildings. These laws are more rigid for multiple dwelling units (apartment houses), office structures, and public buildings than for single-family dwellings. The language of these laws varies from one jurisdiction to the next. However, criminal penalties may be imposed against anyone who willfully (and, in some situations, even recklessly) violates these regulations.

In most states, any building into which numerous members of the public are likely to be invited must be inspected by a licensed (certified) public engineer following completion of the construction but prior to occupancy. These buildings, which include as a rule most structures with more than ten rental units, cannot be occupied until a "certificate of occupancy" has been issued by an authorized agency of government, following inspection. Even single-family dwellings must be inspected following construction in many jurisdictions by licensed electricians and plumbers. Similarly, in many states, even when a home-owner performs his own repairs on the plumbing or electrical wiring of his house he must have the work inspected by a licensed electrician or plumber as soon as possible. Failure of an individual or business to comply with these and many other building construction regulations may make the wrongdoers bear criminal responsibility. If no actual harm results, the penalty for a violation of these laws may be slight. However, if an uninspected building burns down and, for example, the fire was started by faulty wiring which could have been detected during a proper inspection which never took place, the owners or builders of the structure may bear criminal responsibility for a felony. If death results on account of such a felony, such as when an inhabitant of the building burns to death or suffocates from smoke inhalation, the felony-murder rule may apply (see Chapter 8). In some states the felony-murder rule applies only to felonies involving violence, however.

Equipment which is used in buildings to which a large segment of the public is likely to be invited must be inspected at periodic intervals in most states to check durability of the equipment, particularly if the equipment is potentially dangerous or is necessary to avert danger. For instance, elevators and escalators are examples of potentially dangerous equipment. Fire alarms, extinguishers, and sprinklers are examples of equipment that is necessary to avert danger but which cannot do that job unless maintained in proper working order. The owners or managers of such a building may bear criminal responsibility for harm which does occur but which might have been avoided had equipment been inspected or otherwise maintained as required by law.

The fire laws of most jurisdictions require that all multiple-dwelling or multiple-office buildings over two stories high be equipped with two separate stairways or one stairway and one fire escape ladder. Areas of these buildings which are inhabited routinely by occupants and guests are required to be marked clearly with signs reciting the word "EXIT" and designating the proper doorways and windows to be used for escape in case of fire. Usually these signs must be illuminated after dark.

In addition, fire laws generally prohibit anyone from smoking in locations where crowds are gathered such as auditoriums, gymnasiums, and theaters. In order both to prevent fire and to minimize the health hazard caused by tobacco smoke, federal regulations require that all passengers on vehicles such as airplanes, buses, and trains that are used in interstate commerce be seated in a non-smoking section upon request. Smoking on these vehicles is permitted only in smoking sections, and then only at certain times. For instance, smoking is not permitted anywhere aboard a commercial airplane during take-off or landing. As with building and construction codes, the penalty imposed for violation of a fire law may be determined by the severity of the actual harm, if any, that results directly from the violation.

The conduct required for violations of building, construction, and fire codes is likely to consist of a person's failure to do an act that a legal duty requires of him, such as to obtain an inspection certificate, install fire-prevention or fire-warning apparatus, or extinguish an object he is smoking when entering an area where smoking is prohibited. In most instances, the state of mind that must be proven is at least "reckless." The offender must have been aware of but consciously disregarded the duty imposed upon him by law. In some jurisdictions, however, certain duties relating particularly to the safe maintenance of buildings or vehicles occupied by numerous persons may be accompanied by strict liability (see Chapter 3). Failure of anyone who is required to perform a duty that is accompanied by strict liability may result in that person's bearing criminal responsibility without regard for the person's state of mind.

Drug Offenses

In most states, amphetamines, barbiturates, cocaine, LSD, marijuana, opium and its derivatives such as heroin and morphine, together with numerous other drugs that are believed to be dangerous are prohibited or at least regulated. Drugs such as heroin that have no medicinal use or value are prohibited altogether. No one may possess heroin legally, except a law enforcement officer who is privileged to confiscate and destroy this drug. Many other drugs are regulated, which means that they are prohibited from being possessed by unauthorized persons. The federal Drug Abuse Prevention and Control Act of 1970 consolidated the provisions of the U.S. Code pertaining to dangerous drugs. Prior to 1970, many of these provisions were contained in unlikely places such as the Internal Revenue Code where enforcement was haphazard. The Bureau of Narcotics and Dangerous Drugs (BNDD) issues licenses to qualified physicians, pharmacists, registered nurses, and legitimate pharmaceutical manufacturers who are permitted to possess controlled substances.

A variety of different drug laws are still in effect in different states. Three types of statutes are significant for discussion. These include: unauthorized possession of a controlled substance; trafficking in a controlled substance; and violation of a controlled substance regulation.

Unauthorized Possession of a
Controlled Substance

A person may be guilty of an offense if, without being authorized to do so, he knowingly possesses a controlled substance. Substances that are controlled vary slightly from state to state. These substances routinely include amphetamines, barbiturates, cocaine, LSD, marijuana, opium and its derivatives such as heroin and morphine. A few states have begun the process of decriminalizing simple possession of marijuana. Controlled substances do not include distilled spirits (gin, vodka, whiskey), malt beverages (beer and ale), or tobacco.

The conduct in this offense is possessing a substance. The possession may be either actual or constructive. A person is in *actual* possession of an object such as a substance when he exercises immediate dominion and control over the property. Thus, one actually possesses a substance when he carries it in his pocket or elsewhere on his person, or when he permits the substance to remain in his automobile or dwelling. A person is in *constructive* possession of an object such as a substance when he exercises indirect dominion or control over the property. Thus, one constructively possesses a substance which he has purchased, found, or stolen even though he may store the substance apart from his person. Thus, if one person buys some marijuana and then asks another to hold onto it for him and return it later, both the owner and caretaker possess the substance: the caretaker, actually; the owner, constructively.

As to possession of a substance, the state of mind that must be proven ordinarily is at least "knowing." The defendant must have been aware of the nature of his actions. The fact that a possessed substance is *controlled* by law is an existing circumstance for which "recklessness" is a sufficient state of mind. The defendant must have been aware of but consciously disregarded the risk that the substance in his possession was controlled by law.

A person may defend himself from prosecution for this offense if the controlled substance was obtained directly by a valid prescription or on order of a licensed medical practitioner acting in the course of his professional practice. A physician would not be "acting in the course of his professional practice" by selling a controlled substance to a (criminal) dealer in narcotics or to an addict, or by distributing a controlled substance to an addict merely to satisfy the addict's appetite for drugs. Addiction is not a defense to a charge of unauthorized possession of a controlled substance in most jurisdictions.

Under many drug possession statutes, the penalty imposed as a result of criminal responsibility will increase in direct relation to the amount of the substance that was possessed. Thus, it usually becomes a more serious offense for one to possess ten ounces of an opiate than to possess four ounces of the same substance. In most jurisdictions, also, some controlled substances are regarded as being more dangerous than others. Possession of heroin may be punished more severely than possession of marijuana, for example.

Trafficking in a Controlled Substance

A person may be guilty of an offense if, without being authorized to do so, he knowingly traffics in a controlled substance. Under some statutes, trafficking occurs whenever a controlled substance is transported from one location to another for the purpose of changing the possessor of the substances. Thus, a person who transports some marijuana in his automobile for no reason other than to smoke it in a secluded place would not be trafficking in the drug. However, one who receives the substance from one person and then gives it to another would be trafficking, whether or not he is paid for his services.

Instead of or in addition to a trafficking statute, some states specifically prohibit the *sale* of a controlled substance. Drug sale statutes generally impose more severe penalties upon those who accept payment for the exchange of a drug than upon those who give away drugs. Prosecutions under some drug sale statutes have been hampered on account of a technical "defense" that has become known as the "purchasing agent" doctrine. A principal buyer of a controlled substance who wishes to avoid the risk of being apprehended during the purchase transaction may arrange for someone to act as his agent by delivering money and receiving drugs. The intermediary, the "purchasing agent," may argue later, if caught, that he did not resell the substance to his principal since he used the principal's money and not his own to acquire possession, and only transported the drugs gratuitously.

To avoid the fine line distinction between selling and dispensing, distributing, or otherwise disposing of possession of a controlled substance, some jurisdictions have substituted the word "traffic" to include all types of drug transfers. Under a trafficking statute, the forbidden conduct consists of delivering a controlled substance to another person or receiving a controlled substance from another person, regardless of the reason.

As to trafficking in the substance, the state of mind that must be proven ordinarily is at least "knowing." The defendant must have been aware of the nature of his actions. The fact that the substance being trafficked is controlled by law is an existing circumstance for which "recklessness" is a sufficient state of mind. The trafficking defendant must have disregarded a substantial risk, of which he was aware, that the substance in which he trafficked was controlled by law. A reasonable law-abiding person would be expected to check or inquire into the contents of a package before agreeing to carry it through customs, for instance. His failure to do so would constitute a serious deviation from the degree of care that a reasonable and prudent person would exercise under similar circumstances.

Under some drug trafficking statutes, possession of four ounces or more of an opiate may give rise to a legal presumption that the possessor intends to traffic in the drug. Moreover, usually it becomes a more serious offense for one to traffic in or to possess with intent to traffic in an opiate, for example, than a less dangerous drug such as marijuana.

Violation of a Controlled Substance Regulation

A person may be guilty of an offense if, being registered to handle controlled substances under federal or state laws such as the Controlled Substance Act or the Controlled Substance Import and Export Act, he (1) distributes or dispenses a controlled substance in violation of the laws that apply to his registered status; (2) tampers with any identifying mark such as a label or symbol required to be preserved in the handling of a controlled substance; or (3) fails to keep or to provide law enforcement authorities with records, invoices, or other information about a controlled substance as required by law.

Conduct that violates a controlled substance regulation may consist of any willful noncompliance with required procedures. A violation of some drug regulatory statutes may lead to the offender's criminal responsibility without proof of his knowledge of his recklessness. Persons who are registered to handle dangerous substances such as controlled drugs may be held to be strictly liable for any or all noncompliances with applicable regulations.

Environmental Offenses

The modern age has been accompanied by a concern for the maintenance of an environment that is both healthy and safe for mankind. Numerous laws have been enacted in most jurisdictions to minimize or prevent the disruption of the environment through thoughtless deeds. These regulations pertain to burial of the dead; pollution of the air, land, and waters; the marketing of food; and the preservation of animals and flora.

Burial of the Dead

It was an offense at common law for anyone to dispose of a dead human body other than by decent burial. A dead body was required to be placed in the ground or in a tomb so that it would not become offensive to the health of the community. A body could not be cast into a running stream or left to rot in the street. In addition, it was an indictable offense at common law for anyone to disturb a human body following burial. A body could not be exhumed and dissected, for instance, without permission of public health authorities as well as relatives of the decedent.

Nowadays, many states require that dead human bodies either be cremated or be enclosed within a stone vault prior to burial. In this way, the land within which bodies are buried will not become contaminated during the process of decomposition. Many jurisdictions prohibit the burial of human bodies except in cemeteries or other areas that have been set aside and designated for burials.

Pollution of the Air, Land, and Waters

Some of the oldest American statutes relating to the proper care and maintenance of the environment prohibit anyone from causing the unauthorized pollution of navigable waterways. More recently, these statutes have been expanded to prevent pollution of the air and the land as well as the waters. Antipollution statutes provide for punishments that are commensurate with the harm or potential harm that may result from the forbidden conduct. For instance, an industrial plant may be fined a thousand dollars or more per day that it emits noxious fumes into the air or caustic chemicals into a stream or river. An individual who litters a public roadway by discarding trash out the window of a motor vehicle may be fined a hundred dollars or more per item of rubbish disposed of unlawfully. In each instance, the conduct consists of the unauthorized disposition of waste materials. Normally, the state of mind that must be proven is at least "knowing." The offender must have been aware of the nature of his actions. The element that fumes are noxious or that chemicals are caustic is an existing circumstance for which recklessness may be a sufficient state of mind. The offender must have been aware of but consciously disregarded the risk that the fumes were noxious or the chemicals were caustic.

Federal environmental protection laws require all motor vehicles that have been manufactured in recent years to be equipped with properly maintained emission controls. A person may be guilty of an offense if he tampers with the emission control system of an automobile or if he operates an automobile that is not equipped with emission controls as required by law. Again, the conduct consists of the tampering or the unlawful operation. The state of mind that must be proved is at least "knowing." The offender must have been aware of the nature of his actions. The proper emission controls required for any given vehicle constitute existing circumstances for which recklessness may result in criminal responsibility due to inadequate installation or maintenance.

Marketing of Food

Our society relies heavily upon a division of labor in the growth, packaging, transportation, and retailing of food supplies. To avoid widespread catastrophe, basic standards must be maintained particularly as organic foods are prepared for human consumption. A person may be guilty of a federal offense if, with intent to defraud, he violates specific provisions of (1) the Poultry Products Inspection Act relating to the marketing, labeling and packaging of poultry and poultry products; (2) the Federal Meat Inspection Act relating to the marketing, labeling, and packaging of beef, pork and other meat or meat products; (3) the Egg Products Inspection Act; or (4) the Federal Food, Drug, and Cosmetic Act. Applicable sections of these laws deal with the proper inspection, preparation, packaging, labeling, sale, storage, and transportation of food products, drugs and cosmetics. Food, drugs and cosmetics must not be adulterated or misbranded to be fit for human consumption or safe for human use. Proper records must be maintained by persons involved in the business of slaughtering animals; buying, selling, importing, preparing or packaging food products; or storing or transporting food products intended for human consumption.

The conduct in these offenses consists of any noncompliance with applicable regulations. When an intent to defraud is required, the offender must be shown to have planned to deceive a subsequent consumer or wholesale purchaser of a commodity. While an intent to defraud is required for one to bear criminal responsibility for some federal offenses relating to food, drugs, and cosmetics, other federal and state offenses relating to the preparation of these commodities are accompanied by strict liability (see Chapter 3). When a statute is accompanied by strict liability, criminal intent is not an issue and one may be guilty of an offense as a result of forbidden conduct that is done innocently. Thus, for example, one who mislabels a food product may be criminally responsible for an offense even if the mislabelling was done accidently.

Preservation of Animals and Flora

A well-balanced environment requires the preservation of animals and plants that have been created by nature. Humans have traditionally tended to domesticate some animals and to hunt and kill others. Similarly, humans have acquired the habit of removing attractive plants from their natural habitat and transplanting the flora to cultivated gardens. When done excessively, these practices may become harmful to the natural environment.

To prevent the extinction of many animal species, states commonly regulate the varieties of animals that may be hunted according to season. Endangered species may not be hunted at all except in violation of the criminal laws. Animals may not be hunted during their breeding season. Immature animals and fish are not supposed to be captured. Many states permit hunting and fishing only by persons who have purchased a license to do so.

In order to prevent erosion of certain land areas, persons are forbidden to remove some wild flora from their natural habitat. Laws regulating the transplanting of cactus plants have been enacted frequently in desert states, since without the presence of these flora desert areas would become even more desolate than they are anyway. Endangered plant life, such as the wild flower lady's slipper, cannot legally be transplanted in some states in order to enhance the chances that these flora will reproduce themselves and avoid extinction.

Most jurisdictions have enacted laws to prevent persons who have domesticated animals from treating them cruelly. An animal that is kept in captivity must be fed and watered properly. To prevent communicable diseases from injuring the health of both animals and humans, laws require that some domesticated animals be administered inoculations. Similarly, federal customs regulations require that both animals and plants be held in quarantine for up to several months after being imported from a foreign country. Some fruits and vegetables that are known to harbor serious diseases may not be imported into the United States legally at any time.

The conduct in these offenses is noncompliance with an applicable regulation. As a rule, the state of mind that must be proved is at least "knowing." The offender must have been aware of the nature of his actions. The fact that a given animal or plant is an endangered species, for example, is an existing circumstance. One who voluntarily jeopardizes the life or health of such an animal or plant may bear criminal responsibility on account of recklessness. He must have been aware of but consciously disregarded the risk that the animal or plant was one of an endangered species.

Explosives and Firearms Offenses

A person may be guilty of an offense if he possesses or transports an explosive, a firearm or ammunition with intent that it be used or with knowledge that it may be used to commit a crime. In some jurisdictions, possession or transportation of such an item is an offense only if the crime to be committed is a felony. In other jurisdictions, a lesser offense may be committed by possession or transportation of such an item if the crime to be committed is a misdemeanor.

An explosive includes any destructive device such as gunpowder, blasting material, a fuze or a detonator. It may consist of a chemical compound, a mechanical mixture, or any combination of materials such that ignition by fire, friction, concussion, percussion or detonation may cause an explosion. It may include a bomb, grenade, mine, rocket, missile or even poison gas. A firearm includes any weapon, loaded or unloaded, that can expel or readily be converted to expel a projectile by the action of an explosive. Examples of a firearm include a pistol, revolver, rifle, or shotgun in addition to a bazooka, cannon, or machine gun. Under some statutes a firearm includes a frame or receiver of a firearm as well as a firearm silencer or noise muffler.

The conduct of this offense is possessing or transporting something. The applicable state of mind that must be proved is at least "knowing." The offender must have been aware of the nature of his actions. The element that the item that was possessed or transported was an explosive or a firearm is an existing circumstance for which at least the offender's recklessness must be shown. Thus, the offender must have been aware of but disregarded the risk that the circumstance existed.

In addition, some municipal jurisdictions forbid anyone to possess an explosive or a firearm for any reason whatsoever without being duly licensed to do so. Most states prohibit anyone from possessing a *concealed* weapon without being licensed specifically to carry a concealed weapon. A weapon is considered to be concealed when it is carried by a person in a public place without being displayed visibly. Thus, a weapon that is carried under a person's coat, in his pocket, or in the glove compartment of his automobile, for example, may be considered to be concealed.

Under the Gun Control Act of 1968 as amended by the Criminal Justice Reform Act of 1975, federal regulations prohibit anyone from selling, offering for sale, or otherwise distributing an explosive, a firearm, or ammunition unless he is a licensed firearms' dealer. In addition, it is unlawful even for a licensed firearms' dealer to distribute an explosive, a firearm, or ammunition to any person who (1) is under twenty-one years of age; (2) has been convicted in any court of a crime punishable by imprisonment exceeding one year (a felony, in most states); (3) is under indictment for a crime punishable by imprisonment exceeding one year; (4) is a fugitive from justice; or (5) is a narcotics user or a mental defective.

CHAPTER 19

Family Unit Offenses

The purpose of some public welfare offenses is to preserve and protect the family unit. Traditionally, our society has centered around the nuclear family consisting of a father, a mother, and their children. This nuclear family is flanked by extended relatives. Marriage is the cohesive force that binds the nuclear family together generation after generation. While our society recognizes divorce, the criminal law does not tolerate other conduct that may undermine family relationships. Family unit offenses are believed to be detrimental to conventional kin relationships.

Family unit offenses include: adultery and bigamy, criminal bastardy, criminal neglect and non-support, fornication and illegal cohabitation, and incest.

Adultery and Bigamy

Adultery and bigamy are offenses that involve two persons of the opposite sex, and neither offense can occur unless at least one of the persons is legally married to a third person. It does not matter whether both persons who are parties to the offense are married, as long as one is. Nor does it matter whether the male or the female is the married party. In either adultery or bigamy, however, even if one of the two participating persons is unmarried, he or she may still bear criminal responsibility for the offense. (But this is not *always* the case, as will be shown.)

Adultery and bigamy are two separate criminal offenses. Adultery can be (and generally is) committed without the occurrence of bigamy. As a rule, bigamy involves adultery, but in most jurisdictions the offense of adultery is considered to be a part of the more serious offense of bigamy when the same participants are involved in both. These offenses will be discussed separately.

Adultery

A married person commits adultery when he or she engages in voluntary sexual intercourse with anyone other than his or her spouse during the course of their marriage. An unmarried person commits adultery when he or she engages in voluntary sexual intercourse with anyone who the unmarried person knows or has reason to believe is married and who in fact is married to a third person.

The most important criterion for adultery is the occurrence of sexual intercourse, and a person must engage in it voluntarily in order to bear criminal responsibility for this offense. If a married woman is forcibly raped, for example, she does not become criminally responsible for adultery. The rapist may become responsible for adultery in addition to rape (although adultery is rarely prosecuted in a rape situation) if he knew or had reason to believe that his victim was married at the time of the rape. It is important to note that adultery occurs only as a result of "normal" sexual intercourse and not from "deviate" sexual intercourse (see Chapter 7). Therefore, neither oral nor anal sexual contact will support a prosecution for adultery. This is true whether the married person engages in "deviate" sexual relations with a person of the opposite sex or of the same sex. Thus, a homosexual relationship cannot be the foundation for adultery.

Generally, a married person will be presumed to have possessed a sufficient general criminal intent to bear criminal responsibility for adultery when it can be shown that he or she had voluntary sexual relations with anyone other than his or her lawful spouse at any time from the marriage ceremony to the dissolution of the marriage by a final decree of divorce or annulment. Adultery may be committed by a person who is separated from his or her spouse, even during a "legal separation." Similarly, one spouse does not have a right to "consent" to the extramarital sexual behavior of the other, and the fact that a spouse "consented" is not a defense to adultery.

Difficulty sometimes arises concerning the legality of a divorce, particularly when one or both spouses have attempted to obtain a "quickie" divorce in a jurisdiction other than the one in which they reside as man and wife. As a result, the jurisdiction in which they do reside (and perhaps other jurisdictions as well) may not recognize the "divorce" and may not consider the marriage legally dissolved. Under these circumstances, each of the married persons assumes a risk by engaging in a sexual relationship with other persons. If either spouse has sexual intercourse with a third person in a jurisdiction that does not recognize the divorce as being valid, then that spouse may bear criminal responsibility for adultery.

An even greater (and more common) difficulty arises when a person who is legally married engages in sexual intercourse with a person who is not married. The question is whether the unmarried person bears responsibility for adultery. The unmarried person *is* criminally responsible for adultery if he or she is aware of the fact that the sexual partner is married. Similarly, an unmarried person may bear criminal responsibility for adultery if he or she suspects or has reason to suspect that the partner is married but fails to find out for sure. However, the unmarried person may not be aware of the partner's marriage or have any reason to suspect the partner of being married. The married person may have lied and pretended to be unmarried. The law does not require each person who meets and dates another to conduct an investigation of the prospective sexual partner's marital status before engaging in a relationship. Similarly, the unmarried person may have heard about the "divorce" of the partner and may believe it is valid when in fact it is not recognized by the jurisdiction where the sexual activity takes place. Normally, a good faith (bona fide) belief by an unmarried person that his or her sexual partner has never been married or has been legally divorced is a defense to adultery. In some jurisdictions, the good faith defense is harder for the married than for the unmarried sexual partner to raise successfully. Courts may hold that a person has a greater responsibility to investigate the validity of his or her own divorce, for example, than to verify another's divorce. The married partner may bear criminal responsibility for adultery even when the unmarried partner does not.

Movies often show detectives taking pictures of a couple arriving at or leaving a hotel, an act that may hint at adultery. In most jurisdictions, however, more evidence than this is needed before a couple or either one of them bears criminal responsibility for adultery. It is difficult to prove that persons have had sexual intercourse unless they are caught in the act, and this is unlikely if they are discreet. For this reason, adultery is hard to prove and has become decriminalized in some jurisdictions. It remains an offense in most states, but it is seldom prosecuted as a crime. Instead, adultery is used more often as grounds for a divorce.

Bigamy

The elements of bigamy are quite similar to the elements of adultery. One important criterion is added for bigamy, and this is the occurrence of an illegal marriage. A married person commits the offense of bigamy when he or she "marries" a second "spouse" prior to final dissolution of the preexisting marriage. An unmarried person commits bigamy when he or she "marries" one who he or she knows or has reason to believe is already married to someone else.

In our society, a person can be married legally to only one person at a time. Once a person is legally married, he or she cannot become legally married to another person until a valid divorce becomes final. Thus, if a person takes a spouse in legal wedlock and then purports to "marry" another, the subsequent "marriage" is unlawful and invalid, and the person who has tried to become married twice bears criminal responsibility for bigamy. Naturally, if two persons who are both legally married to others try to "marry" each other, both bear criminal responsibility for bigamy. However, if an unmarried person of either sex completes a marriage ceremony with another who in fact is already married to a third person, the unmarried person may raise as a defense his or her bona fide belief that the partner was unmarried at the time of the illegal wedding. The second "spouse," who in reality is not a spouse at all, may be criminally responsible for bigamy if he or she had reason to believe that the partner was already married to someone else but ignored the suspicions. As in adultery, this good-faith defense will excuse the "innocent" party as a rule only if he or she was lied to by the other party or if the divorce of the other party appeared to be valid but in fact was invalid on some technicality of which the "innocent" person was unaware.

Sexual intercourse is not an element of bigamy. The marriage ceremony is sufficient, whether the ceremony is religious or civil. If the illegal "marriage" is consummated sexually, one or both of the partners may bear criminal responsibility for adultery as well as bigamy. As a practical matter, however, adultery is seldom prosecuted along with bigamy, since bigamy is considered a much more serious crime than adultery. In some jurisdictions, a bigamous couple cannot be prosecuted for both adultery and bigamy as a result of their behavior together, because in these jurisdictions one cannot bear criminal responsibility for two offenses arising out of the same facts. The prevailing view is to regard these offenses as constituting separate facts, since adultery involves sexual conduct and bigamy involves the ceremony of marriage.

Sometimes in order to avoid criminal responsibility for bigamy, a couple or one party may raise doubts about the validity of the marriage that is or may be preexisting. This is likely when the first marriage was created not by a formal ceremony but simply by the conduct of the parties at the time. Such marriages are known as "common-law" marriages, since they were valid at common law and are still recognized as valid in a number of states. These "marriages" are not recognized in many states, however. Under the Full Faith and Credit clause of the federal Constitution, a common-law marriage is recognized as valid in all states if it was valid in the state where it is supposed to have been created. A common-law marriage is created when a man and a woman live together continuously for a given period of time and create the impression that they want to be considered married. The length of time for which they must live together varies in different jurisdictions, but usually it is at least one year. Once a common-law marriage has become valid in any state, it must be dissolved formally by divorce in order for either party to remarry legally. However, a "common-law" marriage in a state that does not recognize the validity of such a union does not prevent the subsequent marriage of one or both of the parties. Either or both may marry without being criminally responsible for bigamy, and either or both may engage in sexual intercourse with others (prior to a lawful marriage) without committing adultery.

Criminal Bastardy

A male commits the offense of criminal bastardy by fathering a child but not marrying its mother before the child's live birth. Traditionally this offense pertained only to males; the female was not considered to have committed a crime. Bastardy has been decriminalized in most jurisdictions, but it remains a crime in a few states.

Criminal bastardy is not commited merely when conception occurs outside of marriage. The offense is not complete until the child is born alive. If the fetus is stillborn or if the person who is presumed to be the father marries the mother before the child is born, this offense is never completed. At common law a child who was born outside of wedlock but whose parents later married was known as a "special bastard," and in most American states such a child is considered legitimate after the marriage. Marriage between the child's mother and presumed (called putative) father after the child's birth is not necessarily a defense to criminal bastardy. In practice, marriage is the objective of prosecution for this crime, and upon marriage the prosecution will be stopped. In legal history, many difficulties have arisen when a pregnant woman has married someone other than the presumed father before the child's birth.

Criminal Neglect and Criminal Nonsupport

Criminal neglect and criminal nonsupport are committed by parents when they fail to perform their duty—particularly their duty to their children. In addition, criminal nonsupport may be committed by one spouse (traditionally the husband) in disobedience of a court order requiring this spouse to provide necessary financial support to the other spouse (traditionally the wife), or in some states requiring children to provide necessary financial support to needy parents or other relatives. Criminal neglect may be committed by a person other than a parent when he or she has assumed the responsibilities of guardianship of a minor child, a mentally incompetent person, or a person who is physically infirm (weak or frail) because of age or illness. Usually these offenses are committed by one family member against another. To the extent that they are committed outside an actual family unit, these offenses usually occur in a relationship in which someone other than a parent has become the guardian of another person. The guardian is then said to be acting *in loco parentis*. Criminal neglect and criminal nonsupport are separate offenses and will be discussed as such.

Criminal Neglect

Criminal neglect is a good example of an offense that results from omission of a legal duty rather than from the commission of an act. A person may bear responsibility for criminal neglect when, having assumed a legal duty to guard another against foreseeable harm, he or she fails in this duty and foreseeable harm occurs to the person who was not guarded properly. Once again, as in most of the offenses against the family unit, a general criminal intent is implied by the conduct that constitutes this offense.

It is more important to note that neither a parent nor a guardian is charged with guaranteeing the safety of the child or infirm person (sometimes known as a *ward*) who is to be guarded. The duty is simply to use ordinary prudence to prevent foreseeable harm. A parent who drives a child to school should not be responsible for criminal neglect if another motorist collides with the car in which the parent and child are riding, as long as the parent was not at fault. Even if the parent were at fault through simple negligence, the accident should not make the parent responsible for criminal neglect. Criminal neglect is a substantive crime and requires a degree of culpability at least as great as criminal negligence. As explained in Chapter 3, criminal negligence involves a greater lack of care than does ordinary (simple) negligence.

On the contrary, a parent who leaves a young child alone in a room beside a burning fireplace may bear responsibility for criminal neglect if the child's clothing catches fire and the child is injured, since the possibility of this harm should have been foreseen and could have been prevented by properly supervising the child. Similarly, a parent who is an alcoholic, goes on a binge, and fails to feed a small child for several days or longer may be responsible for criminal neglect. A baby sitter who has assumed parental duties and responsibilities may bear responsibility for criminal neglect by abandoning the child after having agreed to watch it until the return of the parents.

Children are the usual victims of criminal neglect, but any person, child, or adult, may be neglected if he or she is incapable of caring for himself or herself. The superintendent of a mental hospital may be held responsible for criminal neglect if a patient is not fed, clothed, washed, or sheltered properly. A patient who requires continuous medication but does not receive it may be the victim of criminal neglect on the part of the physician or nurse charged with administering the medication. The warden of a prison or the keeper of a jail may be responsible for criminal neglect if he does not take reasonable steps to be sure that a prisoner's cell is warm enough in winter and cool enough in summer and contains sufficient fresh air. The manager of a nursing home for the aged is ordinarily considered to have assumed similar duties and responsibilities and may bear responsibility for criminal neglect if he fails to perform those duties and responsibilities properly.

Normally, criminal neglect does not result from an emergency rescue situation. An ordinary citizen is not under any legal duty to rescue an unrelated victim from danger. Even if a passer-by decides to attempt a rescue of a stranger but fails due to negligence, the prevailing view is that he should not bear criminal responsibility for his well-intentioned efforts. A parent or a person who is acting as a parent is under a legal duty to intervene during an emergency to try to rescue the child or the ward. This does not mean that a parent must risk his own life by rushing into a burning building, however. It does mean that a parent who sees his child about to drown must at least try to save the child by throwing a life preserver or a rope. If the parent can swim, normally he would be expected to attempt a rescue in the water and, if successful, to administer artificial respiration if needed. A parent who stands idly by in such a situation and does not attempt to save his child may bear responsibility for criminal neglect.

Criminal Nonsupport

In every jurisdiction, parents have a legal duty to support their children by providing food, shelter, and clothing to the extent possible in view of their own economic position. In most states, a husband has a similar duty to provide support for his wife if he is able; and if the husband is unable to do this and unable to support himself, his wife has a duty to support her husband if she is able. This duty of each spouse to the other begins at marriage, just as the duty of parents to their children begins at birth. Normally, the parental duty of support ends when the child reaches eighteen years of age, unless the child is a mental or physical invalid. A few states have required affluent parents to continue to provide financial support for their children's education even after the children have reached eighteen years of age.

The duty of parents to support their children continues even after the parents have become separated or divorced. The duty of one spouse to support the other usually continues beyond separation and may continue beyond divorce, depending on the details of the separation agreement or the divorce decree entered by the court.

A person who fails or refuses to provide reasonable support to his or her dependent may bear responsibility for the offense of criminal nonsupport. In this offense, as in criminal neglect, the general criminal intent is implied by the conduct. However, one may raise as a defense his or her inability to provide the required support or to provide any support at all. Inability is not the same thing as unwillingness, however. Parents and spouses who are required by law to provide support for their dependents must try to earn or otherwise acquire legally enough money to care for the dependents. Otherwise, failure on their part to provide support is a basis for the charge of criminal nonsupport.

Fornication and Illegal Cohabitation

Fornication and illegal cohabitation are offenses that can be committed by any man and woman who are not married to each other. The offending persons may both be unmarried, or each be married to another person, or one may be unmarried while the other is married to another person. Like most crimes that require only a general criminal intent, these offenses consist of conduct that implies a criminal intent. Any person is presumed to know whether or not he is married, and if so, to whom. As in adultery and bigamy, one or both of the parties accused of fornication or illegal cohabitation may have believed they were legally married to each other at the time but may have been mistaken. A good-faith belief is a defense to these as well as most other crimes that cannot be committed by couples who are married. Fornication and illegal cohabitation are distinct offenses, to be discussed separately. Both are crimes in most states, but a few states have decriminalized one or both.

Fornication

A person of either sex commits the offense of fornication when he or she engages in voluntary sexual intercourse with any person of the opposite sex outside of marriage. Like adultery, fornication applies only to "normal" sexual intercourse and not "deviate" sexual intercourse. Thus, a homosexual relationship cannot be the foundation for this offense, nor does fornication take place when a heterosexual couple engages in oral or anal sexual activity. Fornication does, however, depend on voluntary sexual conduct. Hence, a woman who is raped does not bear criminal responsibility for fornication, although the rapist commits fornication as a lesser offense that is included in rape. Unless a couple is caught in the act, it is difficult to prove that fornication has taken place. For this reason, illegal cohabitation is a more common criminal charge.

Illegal Cohabitation

A person of either sex commits the offense of illegal cohabitation when he or she sleeps with or continuously lives with any person of the opposite sex outside of marriage. Cohabitation is defined differently from one jurisdiction to the next. While either "normal" sexual intercourse or "deviate" sexual behavior would be evidence of cohabitation, the offense of illegal cohabitation may be committed in many jurisdictions without the occurrence of any sexual activity whatsoever. An unmarried couple may bear criminal responsibility for illegal cohabitation if it is shown that they shared the same hotel room for one night or longer. In some states, illegal cohabitation may be charged when persons who are not married and not related are discovered to be sharing the same apartment or house, except in a state-approved college dormitory or military setting. Illegal cohabitation as an offense is intended to deter communal living outside of the traditional family relationship. In every state it is permissible and legal for persons of the opposite sex to live together without being married if they are related by blood, and in some jurisdictions if they are related by marriage. Adoption is considered to create a blood relationship for purposes of cohabitation. Requirements regarding the closeness of relatedness vary among the states, but most states allow cohabitation of parent and child, brother and sister, and usually aunt or uncle and nephew or niece. Sometimes first cousins are included. In practice, illegal cohabitation statutes are enforced only when the cohabitants become unruly or appear to be more like "kissing cousins" than family.

A charge of illegal cohabitation may confront couples who were once married to each other but who have been divorced. It also confronts senior citizens who feel unable to marry because of social security formulas that discriminate against married persons in the payment of benefits. Illegal cohabitation may be considered to be as "victimless" as any crime can be.

Incest

Incest is sexual intercourse between persons who are closely related, particularly by blood. In some jurisdictions incest also occurs when sexual intercourse takes place between persons who are closely related by marriage. For the purpose of determining whether incest has taken place, persons who are related by adoption are as a general rule considered to be related by blood.

With incest, as with most offenses against the family unit, the intent is ordinarily implied by the conduct. The conduct is sexual intercourse, and once again "deviate" sexual intercourse will not support a charge of the crime. In all jurisdictions that forbid incest, this offense takes place as a result of sexual intercourse between father and daughter, mother and son, or brother and sister. In most jurisdictions, incest occurs as the result of sexual intercourse between uncle and niece or aunt and nephew or between any ancestor and any descendant. Many states prohibit sexual intercourse between first cousins under incest laws.

Persons accused of incest may defend themselves successfully if they can prove that they did not know of the close relationship between them at the time of the conduct. As in adultery or bigamy, one of the two parties to incest may avoid criminal responsibility by showing lack of knowledge about the relationship even though the other party knew of the relationship and is criminally responsible for the crime.

CHAPTER 20

Public Peace and Repose Offenses

Some public welfare offenses are oriented toward maintaining public peace and repose. These offenses have been called public order crimes. However, their purpose is not so much to preserve conformity as to prevent disruption. Hence, the public order which consists of traditional customs and norms may be changed legally from time to time, but peaceably and quietly. Conduct that causes or threatens turbulence is not tolerated and may be prosecuted as constituting an offense against the public peace and repose.

These crimes include loitering and vagrancy, disorderly conduct, harassment and criminal nuisance, unlawful assembly and riot, and "blue laws" offenses.

Loitering and Vagrancy

Loitering and vagrancy are similar but distinct criminal offenses that are intended to protect the peace and repose of the public. In some states, these two offenses have been combined into a single offense under various names. However, these offenses have separate historical roots. Loitering may occur in a public place or on private property, while vagrancy usually occurs only in a public place. In addition, only persons who have no apparent means of support generally bear criminal responsibility for vagrancy. On the contrary, anyone may be criminally responsible for loitering regardless of his income or apparent income. Persons who are found loitering or who are perceived by authorities as being vagrants may be charged with being disorderly, but a person does not have to be drunk, bawdy, or otherwise unruly in order to be charged with loitering or vagrancy.

Loitering

A person may commit the offense of loitering by remaining on property that he does not own or control after having been warned to leave by someone who does own or control that property. No individual owns or controls public property, so one may bear criminal responsibility for loitering by remaining in a public place as well as on private property after being told by a person of authority to leave. The warning may be given verbally or in writing by means of a "No Loitering" sign. This warning must be authorized by the owner or lawful occupier of private property, or by the authorized government official(s) who are responsible for the public property. However, the warning does not have to be given by the owner of private property himself or by a high official such as the mayor of a city. It may be given by an agent of the owner or official, such as a watchman or a police officer.

Sometimes people think of loitering as an offense that takes place in alleyways at night. It can, but loitering may take place under other circumstances as well. The operator of a bar (or his bouncer) may ask a person to leave the premises because, for example, the person stops buying drinks or begins to solicit customers. A hotel manager or an innkeeper may notify a guest that check-out time is noon. If the guest does not check out at the appointed time or register for another night, he may bear criminal responsibility for loitering. So also may the occupant of an airplane, bus, taxicab, or train who fails or refuses to leave the vehicle after being asked to do so by its driver or crew member.

Under many loitering statutes, a police officer may arrest a person and charge him with loitering after such a person has been observed lingering or prowling around public or even private property without having any apparently legitimate reason to do so. Under some of these statutes, the police officer does not need to warn the suspicious person to move on before making an arrest. One who has been charged with loitering under these circumstances may give whatever legitimate reason, if any, he had for his conduct. If his reason is shown to be both true and valid, it may provide the person with a successful defense against criminal responsibility for loitering. Loitering statutes allow law enforcement personnel to detain and demand identification from a person who appears for one reason or another to be out of place. Such a person may be harmless, or he may be in the process of making advance preparations ("casing") for a future crime such as burglary or robbery, or he may be waiting to peddle narcotics.

It is important to stress, however, that a legitimate reason for remaining on private property (or government property that is not open to the public) is not a defense to loitering when the intruder has been properly ordered to depart by someone with authority to give such an order. This defense is available only to those who have been arrested for loitering based on suspicious behavior but without specific accusations of illegal conduct. It is unavailable to one who has been accused of remaining in a place where he has no right to be after being told to leave.

Vagrancy

A person may be criminally responsible for the offense of vagrancy by appearing in public without having any apparent means of support. Under some vagrancy statutes, one cannot be proven to be a vagrant unless he does not possess any significant amount of money at the time. Indeed, in some jurisdictions someone who possesses as little as one dollar cannot be prosecuted successfully for vagrancy.

The true vagrant not only carries little or no money on his person, but does not have a steady job or access to anyone else's funds.

Many wives, children, and aged persons who earn no money of their own are supported by spouses, parents, or other relatives. These persons are not vagrants. In addition, the vagrant usually cannot document a residence address other than that of a charitable organization that offers free accommodations to vagrants.

The charge of vagrancy is based on a person's lack of apparent means of support. Many vagrants may have relatives who might provide support in the future upon request, but such remote access to financial resources is not sufficient to defend a prosecution for vagrancy under most statutes. These statutes are intended to prevent persons from begging or "panhandling" in public places, since this kind of activity embarrasses the public and deprives the public of its peace and repose. In other words, vagrancy statutes are designed to discourage insolvent persons (those with no money) from displaying their insolvency in public areas.

Disorderly Conduct

Disorderly conduct and related offenses originated from the common-law crime known as *affray*. Affray consisted of fighting between two or more persons in a public place resulting in the disturbance of others. Traditionally, the definition of a public place has included any public street or highway, beach, park, or building. However, other places may be considered public as well, such as places of amusement, bars, lobbies and foyers of private buildings that are open to portions of the public, hotels and motels, and public transportation facilities.

In many jurisdictions, merely being intoxicated in public may constitute disorderly conduct or a similar offense such as public drunkenness or public intoxication. This is usually true whether the intoxication has been brought about by alcohol or narcotic drugs. However, a sober person may be criminally responsible for disorderly conduct, also. Whether sober or drunk, one may commit disorderly conduct by voluntarily engaging in physical violence with another person or by threatening to do so. Or one may bear criminal responsibility for this offense under many statutes by using abusive or obscene language or by making an obscene gesture in public. Physical violence leading to disorderly conduct may not constitute assault or battery (see Chapter 5) because both (or all) fighting parties may have consented to the violence. Onlookers may not have consented, however, and if the violence occurs in a public place the participants in a fight may all bear criminal responsibility for disorderly conduct. However, a person who is forced to defend himself may raise this fact as a defense to prosecution for disorderly conduct. In this situation, the offensive party or parties may still be criminally responsible for disorderly conduct as well as one or more offenses against the person of the intended victim.

Under some disorderly conduct statutes, this offense may occur when a person intentionally obstructs vehicular traffic, makes an unreasonably loud noise such as by means of a firecracker, or in some other way causes public inconvenience, annoyance, or alarm. Under a few disorderly conduct statutes, a person can be criminally responsible for this offense if he acts *recklessly.* Many statutes, however, require the offender's state of mind to be more purposeful. Since no specific criminal intent (such as intent to kill, steal, or destroy property) is required for this offense, voluntary intoxication (see Chapter 4) is not a defense, even though (as is often the case) the offender was acting irrationally at the time solely because he was intoxicated.

Harassment and Criminal Nuisance

The offenses of harassment and criminal nuisance disturb the public's peace and repose primarily because the conduct required for these offenses is annoying. Normally, harassment is inflicted by one person on another particular individual, while criminal nuisance may involve conduct that is annoying to a larger portion of the public, including persons the offender may not even know to exist.

Harassment

Under statutes in many jurisdictions, a person may commit harassment by engaging in conduct that continuously alarms or seriously annoys another and that serves no legitimate purpose. Conduct that serves no useful purpose may be termed *superfluous* conduct. Thus, to constitute harassment, conduct must be both continuous and superfluous. Any person may become alarmed or annoyed by random events that take place at one time or another but that do not continue to occur. Similarly, anyone may be alarmed and annoyed at planned events that are ongoing but that do serve legitimate purposes. Ordinarily, such events will not support a prosecution for harassment.

Different harassment statutes specify the kinds of conduct that are considered as being continuous and superfluous and that may cause alarm or annoyance. The most obvious kind of harassment occurs when one person interferes with another's peace and quiet either on several occasions or on one occasion for a lengthy period of time. Such interference may consist of abusive or obscene words or gestures; repeated telephone calls, particularly at odd hours of the night, intended only to wake up the party being called; or inexplicable messages sent by mail, telegram, or messenger. Harassment may be conducted more subtly, however. One may harass another simply by following him without having any right to do so. In some states, college "hazing" is considered to constitute harassment; some initiations into fraternal or social organizations outside a college campus also may be.

In many jurisdictions, harassment requires a specific criminal intent—intent to harass. At the very least, the offense requires a general criminal intent. The reason some statutes require a specific criminal intent is that it may be difficult to infer a general criminal intent from harassing conduct itself. Is a person who constantly turns up in another's "shadow" intending to follow that person, or is his appearance coincidental? A specific intent to harass may be shown by evidence that the offending party dislikes the victim, although mere dislike is not sufficient evidence that annoying conduct is intended to harass. For these reasons, harassment is difficult to prove unless the offender has been specifically told by the victim that particular conduct is offensive to him. Once notified that someone regards particular conduct as being offensive, a person risks criminal responsibility for harassment if he continues the conduct.

Criminal Nuisance

A nuisance is, very simply, an annoyance. A person may be a

nuisance, or an inanimate object or an animal may be a nuisance. As with harassment, events that are both continuous and superfluous are likely to be viewed as constituting nuisances. However, not every nuisance is a *criminal* nuisance. Unlike harassment, a criminal nuisance may consist of events that are neither continuous nor superfluous if these events create a condition that is dangerous to the safety or health of humans or other forms of life, particularly if very many are endangered.

In many jurisdictions, noises and odors are likely to support a charge of criminal nuisance when they are offensive for a period of time without sufficient justification. The time period is not always very long, either. A matter of hours or days, rather than weeks, months, or years, is likely to be enough. Similarly, the purpose for the nuisance may be legitimate in general but not under the circumstances. For instance, a private home in a residential neighborhood may become the setting for events that are prosecuted as a criminal nuisance if the house is converted into a music studio that transmits noise off the premises or into a bakery that transmits smells off the premises. These are illegitimate uses for a private home, even though there is nothing inherently illegal in operating a music studio or a bakery. The owner of such a residence may become responsible for the offense of criminal nuisance, particularly if he does not abate or stop the nuisance after complaints by persons who are offended.

One may bear responsibility for criminal nuisance if he creates a dangerous condition, even if that condition serves a useful purpose. For example, laws in many states require owners of swimming pools to put up a fence, either around the pool itself or around the property on which the pool is situated, to protect young children from accidental drowning. A person who builds such a pool without building a fence around it may become responsible for a criminal nuisance. Indeed, this criminal responsibility may arise when the hole for the pool is dug in the ground and before any water is poured in, since a hole the size of a pool may pose grave danger even without water.

Unlawful Assembly and Riot

An assembly is a gathering of persons for any purpose. Naturally, people gather together daily for legitimate purposes such as work, religious worship, sports, or other events. An assembly of persons becomes unlawful only when the assembled persons become violent or unruly and therefore cause or create a grave risk of causing public alarm.

Riot is a specific kind of unlawful assembly, as is a less-known common-law offense called *rout*. These offenses can be discussed together, since they are variations of the same conduct.

A person who assembles with one or more other persons for the purpose of engaging in disruptive or violent behavior or for the purpose of preparing the others to engage in such behavior may bear criminal responsibility for unlawful assembly if the conduct is likely to cause or does cause public alarm. Under some unlawful assembly statutes, this offense is committed only when three or more (in New York five or more) persons alarm the public by assembling violently or disruptively.

Some events begin innocently and develop into violence. Under many unlawful assembly statutes, a person who attends an event that begins peaceably may bear criminal responsibility for unlawful assembly once the event begins to cause or threaten public alarm if he remains assembled with an intent to promote or advance that public alarm. Some unlawful assembly offenses require that persons be shown to have acted intentionally or purposefully in order to become criminally responsible for this offense. It is possible, however, for the leader or leaders of a crowd to provoke followers to lose their self-control. For this reason, many unlawful assembly statutes provide that one may bear criminal responsibility for this offense by acting recklessly even without any evidence that his own purpose was to create public alarm. A prudent person should know when an event has become so raucous that he should leave.

A riot is an unlawful assembly, but not every unlawful assembly constitutes a riot. The distinction between these two offenses varies a good deal among statutes in different jurisdictions. Certainly the more unruly a crowd becomes when unlawfully assembled, the more likely it is that a riot may occur. Under some riot statutes, this offense takes place when persons who have become unlawfully assembled begin to assist each other in resisting opposition, particularly when this opposition comes from law enforcement personnel. Sometimes police try to disperse a group of persons who have assembled unlawfully to prevent or minimize public alarm. Often, however, a riot as distinguished from other unlawful assemblies may begin for the purpose of accomplishing an act other than the unlawful assembly itself. The intended act may be illegal, such as a lynching or the takeover of a public building by demonstrators. Or the intended act might be legal in itself if done without creating public alarm or risk of public alarm. For instance, following victory at a football game, spectators may rush onto the field to congratulate the winning players. The congratulations may be legal, but rushing onto the field may cause alarm, particularly in the minds of other spectators or players who fear being crushed. Under some statutes, in addition or instead, an unlawful assembly becomes riotous at the moment when anyone other than a participant becomes physically injured or when substantial property damage occurs.

At common law, unlawfully assembled persons who intended to assist each other in fulfilling an objective but who caused public alarm in the process could be criminally responsible only for the offense known as "rout" instead of for riot. They would bear criminal responsibility for riot if they had immediate means of accomplishing their objective; if not, they would be criminally responsible only for rout. At common law, for example, the fans at a sporting event might have committed the offense of riot by invading an arena to congratulate winning players if public alarm was created in that process. However, they might have committed only rout if prevented from actually reaching the players by a tall fence or other obstacle.

In most states, the offense of rout has become a part of unlawful assembly or riot. It is important to understand that the size of a crowd seldom makes the distinction between mere unlawful assembly and riot. However, in a number of states the degree of criminal responsibility and therefore the severity of punishment may be increased when an unlawful assembly and particularly a riot involves a large number of persons. In New York, for instance, one becomes criminally responsible for riot in the first degree by engaging in unruly or violent conduct at the same time as ten other persons and thereby creating public alarm or a risk of such alarm.

"Blue Laws" Violations

In many states and in a great many communities across America, long-standing statutes and ordinances known collectively as "blue laws" continue to exist and to be enforced to greater or lesser extents. "Blue laws" prohibit commercial transactions or at least certain kinds of commercial transactions on Sundays and sometimes on other days of religious significance. These laws are vestiges of the past, when most work activities stopped and people enjoyed a day of rest on the Sabbath. The difficulty is that Sunday has come to be more a day of enjoyment than of rest for many if not most persons. Indeed, persons of several religions do not celebrate their Sabbath on Sunday at all, but perhaps on Friday and/or Saturday.

"Blue laws" may restrict all commercial activities on Sunday, or at least before noon on Sunday, presumably so that persons attending church services may enjoy peace and quiet without interruption. "Blue laws" very often prohibit the sale of alcoholic beverages on Sunday. In most areas, however, alcohol may now be served in bars and restaurants on Sunday, but it may not be sold by the bottle in stores. Thus, there is some indication that many "blue laws" that are enforced today are regulating the morals (traditionally acceptable social behavior) rather than guaranteeing the peace and repose of the community. A person may become just as unpeaceable (or more so) in a bar than in his home.

"Blue laws" have inspired numerous constitutional challenges in courts of law without much success. Mostly, these challenges have come from proprietors of department or hardware stores who feel discriminated against because they are forbidden to stay open on Sundays while food stores are permitted to transact business. The current view is that lawmakers may distinguish between types of commercial transactions that may be conducted on Sundays, so long as any person who wishes is permitted to engage in a business that is not forced to close on Sundays. It would be discriminatory and unconstitutional for one department store to be forced to close on Sunday while its competitor was allowed to remain open.

A major problem with "blue laws" is that they apply not only to the owners or proprietors of businesses but also to clerks. Hence, the employee who rings up a cash register on a Sunday may bear criminal responsibility for a "blue law" violation along with the store manager and the store owners or its board of directors. "Blue laws" have died out in some parts of the United States, particularly in the West, but they remain in full force and effect throughout many Eastern states, especially Massachusetts and Pennsylvania.

CHAPTER 21

Public Morals Offenses

A few public welfare offenses can be committed without disrupting the peace and repose of the community and without actually endangering the national defense, government processes, public health or safety, or the family unit. These offenses prohibit conduct solely because legislators, who at least pretend to represent the views of the silent majority of citizens, consider the underlying conduct to be immoral. Public morals offenses are the most difficult of all criminal laws to justify, because they do not directly cause tangible harm to individual adult victims or to the community in general as long as the forbidden conduct is not performed in front of children.

These crimes include gambling offenses, indecent exposure, obscenity and pornography, and prostitution offenses.

Gambling Offenses

A person engages in gambling when he stakes or risks something of value on the outcome of a contest of chance or on a future contingent event not under his own control or influence. A contest of chance has been widely interpreted to include any game or scheme that involves either an agreement or an understanding that a person will receive or "win" something of value in the event of a certain outcome. Some illegal contests involve no skill at all. However, even contests that do involve some skill on the part of the player may be prohibited by laws against gambling.

Laws prohibiting or limiting gambling vary from one jurisdiction to the next. Most forms of gambling are legal in most counties of Nevada and in Atlantic City, New Jersey. Even in those areas, however, gambling is legal only in licensed establishments. In most jurisdictions, the only forms of gambling that are lawful are state-operated lotteries and racing together with bingo and other contests sponsored on a nonprofit basis by social organizations.

Illegal gambling takes many forms. The two most prevalent are "bookmaking" and "policy" (the "numbers" game). Bookmaking involves the acceptance of bets based on the outcomes of future contingent events. These events are likely to be horse races or dog races, but may include other sporting events such as baseball, basketball, or football games (particularly playoffs), car races, or boxing events. The numbers game (policy) is a form of lottery in which the winning chances (plays) are determined not by a drawing but by future events, which may be sequences of horse races or other sporting events or sequences of trading on a commodities or stock exchange. Future events may stem from formations of playing cards, dice, or roulette wheels, and therefore in most jurisdictions it is unlawful to play poker, craps, or blackjack on the chance of winning anything of value, such as money.

Gambling itself is the least serious of gambling offenses, however. Statutes regarding gambling are intended to punish persons who promote illegal gambling rather than those who participate in the activities as players. Three offenses are important to discuss: promoting gambling, possession of a gambling device, and possession of gambling records.

Promoting Gambling

A person promotes gambling when he knowingly encourages or profits from unlawful gambling activity. In most jurisdictions, a person cannot bear criminal responsibility for the promotion of gambling unless it can be shown that he knows what he is doing. Knowledge may be inferred from the conduct, however. In New York, for example, a person is presumed to know that he is advancing or profiting from an unlawful gambling activity when he engages in bookmaking by taking more than five bets totaling more than five thousand dollars in one day, or when he receives in connection with a lottery or policy scheme more than five hundred dollars in one day.

Possession of a Gambling Device

Possession of a gambling device is an offense that is usually enforced to punish persons who are planning to operate the machine in the promotion of gambling by others. Thus, the offense does not consist of the possession of playing cards or dice. It may consist of the possession of a slot machine, particularly one that accepts currency rather than slugs. It may consist of possession of a roulette wheel or bingo or cribbage equipment under circumstances indicating that these devices are to be used other than for nonprofit social events. This kind of statute is designed to criminalize the manufacture, sale, and transportation of gambling devices and therefore affect the ownership, custody, or use of them under unlawful circumstances. Generally, knowledge is required for one to bear criminal responsibility for this offense. He must be shown to have been aware that he possessed a device. The fact that such a device is prohibited as a gambling tool is an existing circumstance, requiring proof of at least a "reckless" state of mind. The offender must have been aware, but disregarded the risk that the device is prohibited as a gambling tool.

Possession of Gambling Records

Some forms of gambling require no devices. Bookmaking and policy, for instance, involve little more than the recording of bets on paper, often in a ledger. In New York, as with the offense of promoting gambling, knowledge is required in order for a person to be criminally responsible for possession of gambling records. In that state, however, a person is presumed to have knowledge that such records are unlawful when the records can be shown to represent more than five hundred plays or chances. In New York and elsewhere, it is a defense to this offense that the writing, paper, instrument, or article possessed was neither used nor intended to be used in the operation or the promotion of a bookmaking or policy-making scheme or enterprise.

Indecent Exposure

Indecent exposure and similar offenses involve the unlawful exposure of the human body, particularly a person's genital areas or a female's breasts (known as erogenous zones). In some jurisdictions, this offense may be committed when one displays an inappropriate picture of the human body. However, pictures that illustrate the body unlawfully are more likely to support the offense of pornography, which will be discussed later in this chapter.

Indecent exposure is usually committed by displaying the human body publicly without proper attire. The purpose of indecent exposure statutes is to protect the public sensibilities and to prevent public lewdness. Public exposure may occur if one exposes his body in a public place such as a street, a public building, or a beach. It may occur even within private premises if the exposure can be observed by persons from a public place or from another private place. Thus, a person who stands nude in front of a window where he or she can be viewed by passers-by may bear criminal responsibility for the offense of indecent exposure, even if the window is situated in his own bedroom or bathroom. A general criminal intent usually is required in order to make a person criminally responsible for this offense. However, the intent may be inferred from the circumstances. A person who undresses on the street or on a public beach will be presumed to have intended the public exposure of the body. Similarly, one who undresses in front of a window without bothering to close the shade may be presumed to have acted at least recklessly, which is sufficient to support a prosecution for this offense in many jurisdictions.

There is little doubt that nudity constitutes exposure. The more important question, however, is what constitutes indecency. Our society does not require female persons to shield their faces from public view, as do some Arab cultures, for example. Under most conditions, we do expect persons of either sex to cover their genitals in public, and we expect females to keep their breasts covered in public. Many state laws contain provisions that permit, as exceptions to indecent exposure statutes, partial or even total nudity during entertainment to which only adults are invited. Usually each local community may define for itself the conditions, if any, under which female breasts or the genitals of either sex may be exposed legally to public view. Thus, one community may permit only "topless" burlesque shows, while another may permit "bottomless" striptease shows as well.

As with gambling offenses, many states make it a separate offense for one person to promote the exposure of another, particularly of a female. Such a statute or ordinance is directed at the proprietors of burlesque theaters and others who may cause persons other than themselves to make indecent public exhibitions, particularly for profit.

In addition to nudity, other factors may cause or contribute to the indecency or the offensiveness of public exposure. Some jurisdictions forbid persons to compete in "marathon" dances, bicycle races, or other contests involving physical endurance. Jurisdictions have enacted legislation to prohibit anyone from being held up to ridicule in public. One may be ridiculed within the meaning of such a law by being made to stand against a wall, for example, while knives, arrows, darts, or balls are thrown at him. The consent of the person being ridiculed is not a defense to prosecution under such a statute. The purpose of these laws is not only to protect the individual being endangered, but to prevent the public from being a party to this sadism and masochism.

Obscenity and Pornography

Probably no criminal offenses are more difficult to define with precision than those that are based on definitions of the words *obscenity* and *pornography*. Obscenity statutes relate to a wide variety of behavior that involves more than mere nudity itself. Obscenity statutes seem to prohibit the display of a human body in a purposefully provocative manner. A person's body is considered to be displayed provocatively under many obscenity statutes when it is shown or otherwise depicted to be engaging in an activity that may intensify another person's sexual desire. These activities include but are not limited to masturbation, sexual intercourse, "deviate" sexual conduct, sexual contact between two persons of the opposite or the same sex, sexual contact between a human being and an animal, and sado-masochistic behavior such as bondage (immobilizing a person's limbs with chains or ropes) and flagellation (whipping). Obscenity seems to include this conduct whether it is performed in person before a live audience or portrayed in film, pictures, sculpture, or sometimes prose. Pornography as a rule is limited to film, still pictures, and prose. Most courts have included pornography as a form of obscenity and have directed their rulings toward the more general classification (obscenity) rather than the more specific (pornography). The distinction between the two terms is artificial for purposes of understanding the nature of these offenses.

What is the meaning of obscenity? What one person calls obscene another may swear to be artistic. Even the U.S. Supreme Court has encountered repeated confusion in its efforts to delineate a standard for obscenity. Three Supreme Court decisions are important to note—not for their clarity, but for their confusion. These cases are *Roth* v. *United States* (1957),[1] *Stanley* v. *Georgia* (1969),[2] and *Miller* v. *California* (1973).[3]

In the *Roth* case, the Supreme Court set forth what has become known as the "tripartite" definition or test for obscenity. Under this definition or test, material may be proscribed by law as obscene only if: (1) the dominant appeal of the material, taken as a whole, appeals to a prurient (lustful) interest in sex, *and* (2) the material is clearly offensive in light of contemporary community standards, *and* (3) the material involved is completely without redeeming social value. In *Roth,* the Court said that "prurience" is characteristic of material that has a "tendency to excite lustful thoughts" and the appeal of which is to "a shameful or morbid interest in" sex.

The Supreme Court held in *Roth* that obscene material is not protected by the First Amendment, which protects normal freedom of speech and freedom of the press. The Court backtracked in *Stanley,* however, by holding that obscenity may be protected by the First Amendment. Indeed, in *Stanley,* the Court said that federal and state governments may not prohibit the private possession of obscene materials. It is interesting that even in *Roth* the Supreme Court prohibited obscenity primarily because it observed that historically obscenity had not been tolerated by our society. In both *Roth* and *Stanley,* the Supreme Court refused to find independently that obscene materials are harmful to those who come into contact with them. Therefore, the Court has ignored the social effects of obscenity, if indeed obscenity has any social effects at all.

Social effects are different from social value. Some law enforcement personnel believe, for example, that obscenity may contribute to violent sexual crimes, since many violent sexual offenders are apprehended with obscene materials in their possession. If it is true that obscene materials incite some persons to violence, this would be an example of a social effect. Social value is a defense to an obscenity prosecution. Presumably a film, a novel, or a play that depicts or portrays issues of historical, philosophical, or social significance may have redeeming social value and therefore not be obscene. In *Stanley,* however, the Supreme Court indicated that mere entertainment is not social value. For this reason, movies (such as *Last Tango in Paris,* for example) that show sexual and even "deviate" sexual intercourse as a means of depicting boredom, loss of identity, or the disintegration of the human personality are less likely to be considered obscene than are movies (such as *Deep Throat*) that show similar sexual episodes for amusement.

A major breakthrough in the Supreme Court's long history of obscenity litigation was reached in *Miller,* when a majority of justices concurred in the following statement of guidelines to be used in determining whether particular material is obscene:

(a) whether the "average person, applying contemporary community standards" would find that the work, taken as a whole, appeals to the prurient interest, (b) whether the work depicts or describes, in a patently offensive way, sexual conduct specifically defined by the applicable state law, and (c) whether the work, taken as a whole, lacks serious literary, artistic, political, or scientific value.

The court noted that this would allow punishment only for the sale or exposure of materials that depict or describe "hard core" sexual conduct and gave the following illustrations of what a State statute could define for regulation under part (b) of the standard announced in the *Miller* decision.

(a) Patently offensive representations or descriptions of ultimate sexual acts, normal or perverted, actual or simulated.

(b) Patently offensive representations or descriptions of masturbation, excretory functions, and lewd exhibition of the genitals.

With respect to the standard to be employed in assessing whether material appeals to the prurient interest and is "patently offensive," the Court in *Miller* further held that juries may constitutionally be instructed to make such determinations based on the standard that prevails in the state or local community; they need not utilize a national standard.

Community standards vary from one town to the next and in the same location from one year to the next. What may be offensive this year in Cleveland may not be offensive there next year, and may not be offensive this year in New York. National standards influence local standards at least to some degree. Indeed, the more movies and magazines of a questionably obscene nature become distributed, the more likely it will be that standards for obscenity will become relaxed.

Federal laws relating to obscenity are oriented almost exclusively toward the *distribution* of such materials, especially through the mails. An effort is made by the federal government to limit the unsolicited mailing of potentially offensive materials, particularly when these materials are mailed to unconsenting persons whose names have been obtained from "rented" mailing lists. Under recent anti-pandering provisions, a person who has received undesired material containing sexual advertisements may have his name deleted from the mailing list of the sender. It becomes an offense for the same mailer to send similar material to the complaining person again.

In *Miller* and its companion cases, the Court was dealing with material directed to the average person. However, where obscene material is aimed at a deviant sexual group, the court has made it clear that the community standard to be used in gauging prurient interest is that of the deviant group (such as homosexuals or pedophiles). Likewise, that in determining whether borderline materials are obscene because they appeal to prurient interest, the method of advertising them may be considered.

Knowledge (scienter) is a constitutional prerequisite to any statute regulating the dissemination of obscene matter. However, the Supreme Court has held that it is not necessary to require proof that the offender knew the material was obscene, but only that he had knowledge of the contents of the materials and knew their character and nature.

Prostitution Offenses

Prostitution is committed when one person agrees to engage in sexual or "deviate" sexual intercourse in return for something of value, usually money. Note that this offense does *not* consist of the sexual act itself, but of the agreement to engage in sex for pay. Perhaps this is one reason why many persons are charged daily with prostitution, but few are ever charged with fornication (sexual intercourse outside of marriage; see Chapter 16). An undercover police officer does not have to copulate or cohabit with an offender in order to support a charge of prostitution. Evidence that an agreement has been made is sufficient, and the actual exchange of currency is added support. In practice, the agreement is usually recorded by means of a hidden tape recorder.

Males as well as females may bear criminal responsibility for prostitution. This is true whether the male or female agrees to have a heterosexual or a homosexual relationship for pay. However, only the recipient of the pay is criminally responsible for prostitution. In some states, the "john" or the person who agrees to purchase the sexual favors commits no crime at all. In other states, this person may bear criminal responsibility for the separate offense known as patronizing a prostitute. A female "jill" may patronize a male prostitute (gigolo) or a lesbian prostitute, just as a male "john" may patronize either a female or a male homosexual prostitute.

Two additional offenses exist in relation to prostitution. These are promoting prostitution and permitting prostitution. A person, such as a "pimp" or a "pander," *promotes* prostitution when he or she procures or solicits a patron for a prostitute other than himself or herself, or when he or she operates a house of prostitution or otherwise profits from prostitution. A person such as a hotel clerk or innkeeper *permits* prostitution when he or she has possession or control of premises and, knowing that they are being used for prostitution, fails to make a reasonable effort to prevent or stop the premises from being used for prostitution.

In addition, some jurisdictions have an offense known as soliciting. A person, usually of either sex, commits this offense merely by offering to pay another or to receive payment from another in exchange for sexual favors. The purpose of a statute forbidding soliciting is to prevent prostitutes from standing in public places trying to entice passers-by into paying for sex. In this context, soliciting might be considered an offense against the public peace and repose, similar to loitering (see Chapter 17). Soliciting usually carries a heavier punishment than ordinary loitering, however, and the only logical reason for the greater penalty seems to be the preservation of the public morals. Moreover, in many jurisdictions a prospective patron of a prostitute may bear criminal responsibility for soliciting but not for loitering by making an offer to pay for sex. When a prospective patron "propositions" an undercover agent posing as a prostitute, he is usually charged with soliciting. Since the undercover agent cannot agree to perform the expected favors, the "john" cannot generally be charged with patronizing a prostitute. Nor can he be charged with promoting prostitution, since he is soliciting favors for himself and not for someone else. Soliciting is the catchall offense.

Similar Sexual Offenses

Prostitution is illegal because most jurisdictions consider it immoral for one person to pay another for sex. Prostitution does not ordinarily involve harm to either a victim's person or his property, at least not directly. Just as the commercial element of prostitution is regarded as corrupting the public morals, several other forms of voluntary sexual conduct are considered to be morally corrupt even though they involve no direct harm to a victim's person or property. Such offenses include consensual sodomy and sexual misconduct (both discussed in Chapter 7) and miscegenation, although miscegenation has been decriminalized by the U.S. Supreme Court.

As explained in Chapter 7, sodomy occurs whenever "deviate" sexual intercourse is engaged in by two persons—either a male and a female or two males. Consensual sodomy is in a way the counterpart to fornication, since the latter offense must consist of sexual intercourse. However, while statutes forbidding fornication may be justified as preserving the traditions of reproduction only within the family unit, consensual sodomy is hard to justify for any reason other than as a means of prescribing moral behavior.

Sexual misconduct often but not always pertains to voluntary sexual contact between an adult and a child who is under the age of consent. (Sexual misconduct is different from statutory rape, which involves sexual intercourse—or in some states "deviate" sexual intercourse as well—between an adult and a child under the age of consent.) Normally, sexual misconduct involves fondling that is intended to arouse sexual desire in the adult, the child, or both. This offense is unlikely to cause physical harm or even psychological harm as long as the child participates willingly (although without legal capacity to consent). If the child does not participate willingly, an assault, a battery, or a more serious sexual offense is committed. Thus, it is hard to justify this offense as existing for any reason other than to prescribe moral behavior.

Miscegenation statutes used to prohibit a person of one race from engaging in sexual intercourse with someone of a different race. The statutes applied to persons of either sex, both inside and outside of marriage. Indeed, most miscegenation statutes prohibited interracial marriages entirely, without regard for whether or not these marriages were consummated. In a few states, miscegenation statutes applied only if one of the parties were Caucasian. In these states, therefore, neither party bore criminal responsibility for miscegenation if, for example, a person of Oriental descent copulated with a black person. Since miscegenation causes no harm to either party, this offense could be justified only as attempting to prescribe moral behavior. In the case of *McLaughlin* v. *Florida* (1964),[4] the Supreme Court invalidated on equal protection grounds a statute that prohibited cohabitation between a black person and a white person but that did not apply to two persons of the same race. While this decision did not specifically deal with the issue of whether an interracial marriage may result in criminal responsibility of the parties, later state decisions have decriminalized miscegenation within marriage. Outside of marriage, copulation or cohabitation may be regulated by fornication and illegal cohabitation statutes, but only to the extent that all couples are regulated equally without regard to race. Thus, of the major offenses that appear to have been enacted primarily for preservation of public morals, miscegenation is the first to have been held unconstitutional in court.

Notes

CHAPTER **1** — The Elements of Crime

   1. 342 U.S. 246.

CHAPTER **3** — Criminal Responsibility

   1. 342 U.S. 246.

CHAPTER **4** — Defenses to Criminal Responsibility

   1. See Easter v. District of Columbia, 361 F.2D 50 (D.C. Cir. 1966).
   2. Regina v. Dudley & Stephens, L.R. 14 Q.B.D. 273.
   3. United States v. Holmes, 26 F.Cas. 360 (No. 15,383).
   4. Sorrels v. United States, 287 U.S. 435 (1932).
   5. Sherman v. United States, 356 U.S. 369 (1958).
   6. Ex parte Lange, 18 Wall (U.S.) 163.

CHAPTER **6** — Criminal Coercion Offenses

1. 18 U.S.C. § 1584.
2. 18 U.S.C. § 1586.
3. 18 U.S.C. § 1581.
4. 18 U.S.C. § 1201.
5. United States v. Jackson, 390 U.S. 570 (1968).
6. 18 U.S.C. § 2113.
7. 18 U.S.C. § § 1583, 1588.
8. 18 U.S.C. § 1584.
9. 18 U.S.C. § 1583.
10. 18 U.S.C. § 1585.
11. 18 U.S.C. § 1586.
12. 18 U.S.C. § 1582.

CHAPTER **9** — Theft Offenses

1. People v. Estreich, 297 N.Y. 910, 79 N.E.2D. 742 (1948); Kilbourne v. State, 84 Ohio St. 247, 95 N.E. 824 (1911).

CHAPTER **10** — Criminal Conversion Offenses

1. 18 U.S.C. § 659.
2. 18 U.S.C. § 641.
3. 18 U.S.C. § 1702–1704.
4. 18 U.S.C. § 1343.
5. 18 U.S.C. § 1017.
6. 18 U.S.C. § 1020.

CHAPTER **11** — Fraud Offenses

1. 18 U.S.C. § 1543.
2. 18 U.S.C. § 1546.
3. 18 U.S.C. § 1426.
4. 18 U.S.C. § 498.
5. 18 U.S.C. § 500.
6. 18 U.S.C. § 478.
7. 18 U.S.C. § 506.
8. 18 U.S.C. § 485.
9. 18 U.S.C. § 477.
10. 18 U.S.C. § 495.
11. 18 U.S.C. § 489.
12. Ibid.
13. 18 U.S.C. § 502.

14. 18 U.S.C. § 504.
15. 18 U.S.C. § 471.
16. 18 U.S.C. § 479.
17. 18 U.S.C. § 486.

CHAPTER **14** — Crimes Against the Person and Property

1. 18 U.S.C. § § 871–876.

CHAPTER **15** — Preparatory and Ancillary Crimes

1. 2 Wharton, Criminal Law § 1604.
2. 328 U.S. 640.
3. Commonwealth v. Perry, 357 Mass. 149, 256 N.E.2d. 745 (1970).

CHAPTER **16** — National Defense Offenses

1. 325 U.S. 1 (1945).
2. 333 U.S. 631.
3. 341 U.S. 494.
4. Id.
5. 354 U.S. 298. The Court stated (Id. at 324–325): "The essential distinction is that those to whom the advocacy is addressed must be urged to do something, now or in the future, rather than merely to believe in something." (Emphasis in original.)
6. 367 U.S. 290, 297–298.
7. 395 U.S. 444.
8. 367 U.S. 203.
9. 312 U.S. 19.
10. Id. at 29–30.
11. Id. at 28.
12. Id. at 31–33.
13. 50 U.S.C. 851.
14. 50 U.S.C. 854.
15. 22 U.S.C. 612; 22 U.S.C. 614(a), 615, 617; 22 U.S.C. 611 et seq.; 5 U.S.C. 9109.

CHAPTER **17** — Government Process Offenses

1. United States v. Barnow, 239 U.S. 74, 80 (1915).
2. 379 U.S. 559.
3. See Green v. United States, 356 U.S. 165, 183–187 (1958); United States v. Bukowski, 435 F.2d 1094, 1099–1102 (7th Cir. 1970), cert. denied, 401 U.S. 911 (1971).

4. For example, United States v. Rollerson, 449 F.2d 1000 (D.C. Cir. 1971). Defendant's hurling of a water pitcher at the prosecutor during the trial was held to establish both a criminal contempt and assault, each of which could be separately prosecuted and punished.

CHAPTER **18** — Public Health and Safety Offenses

1. 410 U.S. 113.

CHAPTER **21** — Public Morals Offenses

1. 354 U.S. 476.
2. 394 U.S. 557.
3. 413 U.S. 15.
4. 379 U.S. 184.

Index

369

About the Author

David A. Jones is a professor at the University of Pittsburgh. He has been a faculty member at The American University, Georgetown University Law Center, State University of New York, and the University of Tennessee. Dr. Jones holds a Ph.D. from the School of Criminal Justice, State University of New York at Albany; a J.D. from Union University; and an A.B. from Clark University. A practicing attorney, he is a member of the Bars of Massachusetts, New York, the District of Columbia, and the Supreme Court of the United States. Professor Jones has served as general counsel of the National Justice Committee, Inc., and as a consultant to the Massachusetts Committee on Criminal Justice, the New Hampshire Governor's Commission on Crime and Delinquency, and the New York State Office of Criminal Justice Planning. He is the author of *The Health Risks of Imprisonment* and of several journal articles. He is a member of the Association of Trial Lawyers of America, the National District Attorneys Association, and many federal, state and local bar associations.